BOLDNESS
BE MY FRIEND

Richard Pape

BOLDNESS
BE MY FRIEND

headline
review

First published in 1953 by Elek Books Ltd

This edition published in 2007
by HEADLINE REVIEW

An imprint of Headline Publishing Group

1

Cataloguing in Publication Data is available from the British Library

ISBN 978 0 7553 1625 0

Typeset in Perpetua by Palimpsest Book Production Limited,
Grangemouth, Stirlingshire

Printed and bound in Great Britain by
Mackays of Chatham plc, Chatham, Kent

Headline's policy is to use papers that are natural, renewable and recyclable
products and made from wood grown in sustainable forests. The logging
and manufacturing processes are expected to conform to the environmental
regulations of the country of origin.

HEADLINE PUBLISHING GROUP
A division of Hachette Livre UK Ltd
338 Euston Road
London NW1 3BH

www.reviewbooks.co.uk
www.hodderheadline.com

To the
Guinea Pig Club
and its great benefactor
Sir Archibald McIndoe

CONTENTS

CONTENTS

DIAGRAM AND MAPS

INTRODUCTION

Richard Pape, a tough red-headed Navigator from Yorkshire, was shot down and captured in 1941 while returning from a bomber raid over Berlin. Inspired by Douglas Bader, whom he met in his first camp, he made up his mind to escape from Germany at all costs. After incredible adventures and severe hardship he did so in 1944 exactly three years after his capture. The method he finally adopted was at least novel.

Shortly after his return to England and following a second crash, he came under my care. At that time, though anxious to fly, he still showed the mental and physical marks of his sufferings in enemy hands. Contact with his own kind, however, did much to restore his health.

Readers will congratulate him on his indomitable courage and his remarkable endurance under the most nerve-racking circumstances. They cannot fail to be impressed by this unvarnished record of his unending fight for freedom.

ARCHIBALD MCINDOE.

East Grinstead
   8 April 1953

PROLOGUE

DESTINATION BERLIN

(I)

'You're wanted in the crew room right away,' yelled Stinker Sinclair from the bottom of our barrack staircase.

Any importance in his message was mainly lost on my half-awakened senses, and my only reaction was to concern myself more with the effects of a hangover, complete with the more positive feeling that breakfast time had long since passed. I made a remorseful effort to clarify my recollections of the mess party that had been maintained at full throttle well into the early hours of the morning.

It had been a particularly 'heavy on the bottle' gathering, cele-brating a highly successful daylight raid less than twenty-four hours before. We had landed at base with nothing more than a few odd rips in the wings and had shot down a brace of Messerschmitts. By depositing a quantity of the best British explosive on the right spot we had caused the centre of an enemy iron and steel works to disappear.

'Oi, there!' yelled the irate Stinker. 'Climb out of that ruddy bed.'

'I can hear you,' I shouted back. 'What's all the commotion in aid of?' Stinker's reply was more conciliatory. 'Get along to the crew room immediately. You're holding up a briefing,' he explained. 'It's a very special one, and the rest of the fellows are already assembled.'

I was out of bed in a flash.

'It must be something pretty big,' Stinker said as I rushed down-stairs. 'A brass hat landed from Group Headquarters an hour ago

1

and called for a briefing extraordinary'. He gazed up at me with a knowing smile. 'What's more,' he continued, 'the armourers have already been ordered to work on the aircraft. They're fixing the new petrol-can type incendiary containers.'

'So soon?' I asked petulantly. 'There's never any rest in this racket! A daylight raid yesterday. A nine-hour sweat to Berlin the night before. And now something to keep our bowels working tonight.'

Stinker grinned broadly. 'I'm not down to fly,' he commented. 'The mechs. haven't got my kite patched up to their liking yet.' He licked his lips. 'A few whiskies at the Red Lion tonight, and maybe that nice blonde Waaf from the parachute section and a cosy cinema. Oh boy! You twerps'll be dodging the flak!'

'Louse!' I retorted.

Stinker paused at the door and flung back a parting crack. 'Don't forget, if you go for a Burton I'm grabbing your camera and pin-up girls,' he said, 'so write out a collect note, will you?'

It was like that: Always the same facetious patter about staking a claim for personal mementoes and possessions in the event of no return. Authorisation notes would be left behind before a raid listing certain items of private kit to go to closest friends.

As I pulled on my battle dress, the rattle of rain on the window prompted a check on the weather. Heavy black cumulus drifted low above the flat Huntingdonshire landscape. Good, I consoled myself, lousy-looking weather and every possibility that operations will be scrubbed if it thickens and clamps down.

The internal barrack loudspeaker blared. 'Will Warrant Officer Pape report at once to A flight crew room?' said the chilly voice of the unseen announcer. 'Repeat . . . Will Warrant Officer Pape report at once to A flight crew room? He is holding up a briefing.'

From the moment I poked my head round the crew room door

it was obvious that something out of the ordinary was afoot. The crews of twelve Stirling heavy night bombers – a new type of aircraft in 1941 – were standing about the Squadron Commander, intently following the tracings of his long cane over the 14-foot wall map of Western Europe. I stood just inside the doorway, feeling rather guilty about my late arrival.

'Now, crews,' the C.O. exclaimed, 'tonight is the night. We're sending over three hundred aircraft . . . a maximum effort. This squadron's been given the honour of being pioneers over Berlin with the new petrol-can type of incendiaries, plus the usual five-hundred pounders H.E. The incendiaries are not healthy things to carry, I warn you, but they merit all risk of conveyance, according to the experts, in that they create devilish fire raising. We've got to put up a first-class show and I want photographic evidence to support.' He repeated his favourite expression as he scrutinised his crews. 'Pictures speak louder and more truthfully than a thousand words of personal line-shoot. I want to see good photo-flash pictures of target destruction.'

The Wingco had barely finished emphasising his point when the brass hat came in from the chief navigator's sanctum. Tall, stern-faced, he made no preparatory preamble about 'target for tonight'.

'Other squadrons,' he said, 'will close on Berlin from the south, east and west in short relays. Don't dawdle over the target. Scram as soon as you've taken photo-flash pictures of your bombing.' He paused for a moment. 'Last week over Frankfurt, six valuable bombers and forty members of aircrew were written off, not through enemy action but because of mix-up and collisions over the target area. Don't loiter and menace the safety of oncoming aircraft. Is that clearly understood?'

A chorus of voices agreed that it was.

3

The Group Commander spoke more decisively. 'Flying conditions will be most unpleasant . . . damned sticky according to met. forecasts . . . just as bad as we want them for this particular job. But we want to catch the Germans off-guard if possible. The weather will, we hope, lull them into not expecting a full-scale onslaught on their capital. The target tonight is vital. Details about it will be given to all of you prior to take-off. Wireless operators . . . contact base as soon as you've bombed and confirm. Good luck and happy landings.'

Our own Wingco took over, and wound up with 'O.K., fellows . . . get in as much shut-eye as possible before final briefing tonight at 8 p.m.'

As I was checking the newly indicated flak positions on the wall map, a tap on my shoulder brought me face to face with the Wingco. 'I'd like to have a few words with you in the Chief Navigator's office,' he said. Half anticipating a reprimand for my late arrival at briefing, I followed him to the small office at the other end of the long crew room. Seating himself at the desk, and without looking up, he unrolled a one-inch-to-the-mile target map.

'You've done quite a number of satisfactory operations, Pape,' he said. 'Your crew is an exceptionally solid one, and together you've worked well. You can count the operation tonight as your most important, and I'm relying on you and your crew for special results.'

My reply was automatic, but I wondered what the devil all this was in aid of.

'Here is the general target,' he said, 'and north-west of it lies this lake. It's singularly easy to locate. Ten kilometres due north of that is where you are to bomb independently of the other aircraft.'

He placed his pencil point on the edge of a green wooded outline, and went on: 'Our intelligence informs us that just inside the

4

perimeter of this wood is situated Herr Goering's Berlin residence, and the brain centre of his anti-aircraft and night-fighter patrol intelligence for the defence of the capital. In turn, this centre controls defence liaison further afield. This nest has to be wiped out to facilitate the safety and success of our bombers operating on a vital target in the industrial section of the city. This disloca-tion of this brain centre before the main weight of bombers arrive will throw out of gear the German anti-aircraft box barrage system which has proved so damnably accurate and expensive to us lately and will enhance the chances of our bombers reaching and destroying the important industrial objectives. Only extreme flying skill, the most precise stick bombing, exceptional crew diligence and concen-tration can achieve what is required. You will be responsible for the bombing, and I ask you here and now, if you have the slightest doubt of your navigational ability, or inclination or enthusiasm to see it through, please be candid.'

'My crew is as good as the best,' I replied, 'and all conditions not being too humanly impossible, I can, I am sure, pinpoint the wood and straddle it.'

'Good . . . Good,' the Wing Commander exclaimed.

But I was not feeling quite as keen as that. Only a couple of nights back we had battled and sweated over Berlin, and every damned thing had been impossible and unreasonable. Bursting shells and great blue searchlights had proved phenomenally accurate and indescribably intense. From the time we arrived over Germany's capital to the moment we got away from it we had received no peace or respite.

'I've already had a talk with your skipper,' the Wingco told me. 'Both of you will report to me one hour before the general briefing for special target information.'

I stole a look out of the window, and remarked injudiciously: 'The weather is frightfully thick, sir. I shall need a cloud opening tonight. Suppose Berlin is ten-tenths cloud covered?'

'Of course the blasted weather is going to be ticklish,' the Wingco said sharply. 'We've waited weeks for a night like tonight when thick weather stretches uniformly from here to Berlin. This operation is vital. What's more, I was of the opinion that the combined efficiency of your crew was a match for any cloud and weather difficulty.'

'Yes, sir,' I said, inadequately.

'Good luck, Pape,' he added.

I saluted. Resignedly I thought: 'That's it, chum. You don't see Blondie the Waaf tonight. Better go and cancel.'

I strolled back to the mess, coldly practical, unconcerned. And then it happened. As I walked through the deserted crew room my eye caught the enormous map of Europe on the wall. A terrible feeling of panic gripped me. I stood motionless, staring at the map, my eyes hypnotised by the coloured tapes that indicated the bombing routes. My heart pounded violently; I leaned against the wall gasping and breathless.

To try and pull myself together I began to swear – my infallible cure for nerves. As I steadied, blind panic gave way to stark horror. Five words beat into my brain with maddening repetition: 'You will not come back. You will not come back.'

I knew then that I was doomed.

(2)

I headed desperately for the parachute section. I wanted my little Blondie. I craved to hold her, to kiss her hair, her hands, her lips. But when I found her I did none of those things.

She was laying out a large silken canopy before refolding and packing it. I saw its number: 88. It was the parachute allotted to me.

'Pack it with loving fingers, darling,' I said blithely. 'On Ops tonight.'

She looked up quickly. I saw fear in her eyes. Under the spell of her questioning look I told her all I knew. Foolishly, I even mentioned 'special target'.

Her face went white and her lips quivered. Somehow, because of the love between us, she knew my own fear that I would not return. She tried to persuade me to go sick – the first time she had ever attempted to transgress the flying man's code.

'I'll make it,' I said blandly. I even managed a smile. 'You know me. I'm damned lucky.'

That night we met for the last time. We lay together on my thick flying-coat on some waste land alongside the bomb dump. I stroked her small, oval face. The touch of her soft skin is alive in my senses even today. I cupped her golden hair in my hands, smothering it into my face. A faint and personal fragrance sweetened the air.

We lay there for a long time. A fighter plane droned across the sky, bringing me to my senses. It was time to part.

I took her memory into the sky. But she did not wait. The Germans would not allow it. Three months later, during a trip to London to seek information about Richard Pape, 'missing, believed killed,' a bomb destroyed her. The enemy did not even leave me a grave, for there was nothing left of her to bury.

I learned the shattering news of Blondie's death through enemy action five months after we crashed in Holland, soon after I had been taken to Stalag VIIIb. It was a bleak winter morning in February,

1942. I will never forget the day; the cold depression of it still haunts me.

Her death changed everything. With Blondie alive I would never have taken such risks with my life as I did during the coming years.

(3)

Our squadron contributed twelve aircraft towards the all-out effort by Bomber Command. The dozen four-engined Stirlings were lined up on the rim of the aerodrome, impressively grouped together, their long thick snouts poised stubbornly thirty feet above the ground. Huddled in deep shadows, they gave the impression of sinister, antediluvian monsters.

In our twelve aircraft sat ninety-six youthful aircrew adjusting their gear for an eight-hour session aloft, each man an expert at his job, as good as the Royal Air Force could make him. Forty-eight 1,800 horse-power engines roared evenly. Within their bomb-bays, lying symmetrical and compact, were 120,000 lbs. of blast, fire and destruction for the enemy's captital city.

But the opening phase of the operation of September 6, 1941, did not begin any too propitiously. German intruders nearly caught us.

The aircraft in front of us had just acknowledged the radio signal to taxi into position when bombs scattered and burst in rapid succession over an adjacent field. The German attack was a complete surprise . . . and a most uncomfortable one.

First there came a series of blinding flashes, followed by dull thuds which caused the structure of our bomber to shake and tremble. For a second or two I thought it was one of our own aircraft exploding – the volume of noise from our engines had smothered the wails and shrieks of the descending bombs. But a moment later our bombers were sharply silhouetted against the flickering greenish light from scores of gushing incendiaries. By their light the Stirlings looked stricken and helpless.

Our tail gunner, Sergeant Dobbs, always expressive, croaked over the inter-com.: 'Hell's bells! I suppose a miss is as good as a mile, but I hope we don't stand about here long enough to give Jerry time to unhook another load.'

The wireless operator laughed scornfully and a little jerkily. 'This mission was top secret!' he said. 'I'll bet those Jerries upstairs are telling Germany that we're on our way, and arranging to meet us with a nice little reception.'

The flying control officer asked by radio if everything was all right. In turn a dozen pilots confirmed that they had not been hit or damaged. Seconds seemed an eternity before instructions came from control for quick succession take-off, with a warning to watch carefully for marauders and not to circle the aerodrome for the usual radio check.

We zig-zagged our aircraft to the runway. Quicker than ever before we centred the bomber's nose between the converging pinpricks of lights. Our throttles went forward, the earth slipped back and we slid upward into the dusky night.

'Berlin or bust,' laughed the voice of the front gunner. 'Roll on return, a nice gargle of rum, and lots of eggs and bacon.'

'Shut up, you greedy food maniac,' answered the wireless operator.

The third and final voice was that of the skipper, Flt.-Lt. Wallace-Terry. 'Forget everything but watching the skies or we may not eat again,' he said.

Every mind in the crew was alert and all eyes searched every foot of sky as we climbed on course towards the Essex coast. We ascended through a layer of heavy storm cloud into a realm of pale white light . . . an interminable sea of moonlight. We felt safer now, and I was the first to break the silence with: 'Hello . . . navigator speaking to pilot. Our estimated time of arrival over Walton-on-the-Naze is 21.55½ hours.'

Wallace-Terry's laconic voice answered: 'O.K., navigator.'

At 9,000 feet tail gunner Dobbs quietly informed us that a black object was to be seen moving on the port quarter. Involuntarily our muscles tensed. I stowed away certain navigational instruments in case of rough and drastic evasive action. My ears cocked for the rattle of machine-gun fire, the opening signal of an air scrap. Our nose instantly dropped and ten Browning machine-guns swung over to port. The black shadow was picked up, followed, scrutinised, but it peacefully maintained a course parallel to our own.

'It looks like one of our Stirlings,' remarked the seasoned operational front gunner.

'Yes, yes, sir, it is,' yapped the kid of a mid-upper gunner, who was making his first trip. 'Yes, sir, I can recognise the shape,' he added in excited relief.

I stopped chewing hard, withdrew my precious instruments and took up charting again.

'I'm climbing,' crackled the skipper's voice in the earphones. 'But keep your eyes peeled, gunners. Jerry must know of this operation after what's happened. Messerschmitts will probably be mooching over the Dutch coast like birds on the wing.'

Three microphones clicked as three gunners replied: 'O.K., sir.'

I crept forward to the front of the bomber and, lying prone, searched through the observation window for a break in the clouds.

All was serene. There was nothing but fluffy cloud formations like gently rising hillocks. I spoke to the crew, and the oxygen which was now circulating in the mask seemed to inflate my lungs to twice their size.

'Hello, crew . . . look out for a patchwork of waterways on the coast. Harwich should be a few miles to starboard.'

Less than half a minute before we were due to arrive over the English coast the front gunner spotted an appreciable opening in the clouds a few degrees to port. We circled over the large cloud crater. Immediately below stretched the English coastline between Harwich and the Naze.

It was the last we saw of the earth until we were almost on top of Berlin . . .

We crossed the sea and entered over Holland . . . across Holland and into Germany proper . . . and Lady Luck smiled on us. Nothing disturbed our peace and progress except a little light coastal flak. We throbbed our way through the great dark chamber of the night . . . a vast, empty emptiness; crystal clear coldness. Deep into Germany we flew, over millions of cloud edges rippling with silver light. For thirty minutes the moon danced. It seemed just above the bomber's nose, slipping first to the left and then to the right, gently swaying, rising and falling.

Then star-gazing was suddenly forgotten. A rapid series of vicious explosions made the bomber buck and rear. Flak hemmed us in. Sickly cordite fumes filled the interior of the cabin. Thunderous bursts and crimson flames sent shell fragments pinging about the machine.

My thoughts flashed to the aircraft's bellyful of bombs. As metal rasped against metal below my feet, the suspense of waiting for a big 'whoff' contracted my gullet to the size of a straw.

It never came. The skipper gave the joy-stick and rudder-bar all

11

he knew and after about five minutes we got clear. Nobody was injured, nothing had broken off, nothing had started to burn.

As we neared Berlin a brief crew conference was held. We agreed that if no cloud clearance occurred after five minutes over the target we would dive below the cloud ceiling and risk a low-level sorting out of position and subsequent attack. All members of the aircraft were enthusiastic over the prospect of destroying the predictor/intelligence headquarters, and quite ready to risk whatever such low-level flying incurred if only it enabled us to increase our accuracy over the target.

The morale of the crew was superb. Even the nineteen-year-old mid-upper gunner, entrusted to us as new material for breaking-in purposes, was exemplary. In reply to the pilot's inquiry as we neared the target, he said: 'Thanks, skipper, I'm fine. This operational business is grand. It's exciting, isn't it, sir?'

I was ready to wager he was steaming and oozing sweat, grinding his teeth, his legs criss-crossed to prevent them jerking and trembling. I remembered my own first mission. If the kid gunner's reactions were any different to those which affected all aircrew on their first operational flights, well, he just wasn't normal.

My attention was now concentrated on locating the tiny woodlands about Berlin: rivers, roads and any other landmarks. I studied the small secret target map, burning into my mind the dispositions and guiding features. I was confident that if I got a clear and uninterrupted view of the ground, I could quickly pinpoint myself. The most dreaded worry was the possibility of the ground gunners boxing us in with flak and preventing us from making a dead-steady run over the target. Although in fifteen minutes we were due over Berlin, for some uncanny reason nothing came up at us.

'I guess the Huns don't want to give us any idea that we're near their ruddy capital,' muttered the pilot. 'Maybe they hope we'll fly straight over it with all this cloud about.'

The crew gave a final check to their equipment and braced for action.

'Swing open the bomb doors,' I told the wireless operator, 'and slip a photo-flash bomb into the tube.'

To the pilot I gave an alteration of course that should bring us over Berlin's northern sector – providing, of course, that my navigational reckonings had been accurate from the British coast – then I crawled up to the nose of the Stirling and, stretching out on my belly, carefully polished the bombing window. With great care I checked, rechecked and adjusted the half-dozen knobs and indicators.

From the strut alongside I unhooked a soldier's tin helmet and strapped it over my flying headgear. I always wore a tin hat to stop any stray flak fragments that chanced to be propelled in the direction of my skull. The idea had been borrowed from a shrewd South African navigator attached to a Wellington Bomber Squadron.

Just as important and as protective as the tin hat were my Morris motor-car steel hub-caps. I had been put wise to their use by an unfortunate Australian navigator. He had stopped a chunk of whizzing shell which had inflicted severe injuries. Now, under the webbing of my parachute harness where it passed between my legs, I always positioned the two hub caps. The poor Aussie had thought of this unique type of protection too late and nothing had halted the flak which had burst through the floor of the aircraft. Surgical treatment had made amendments to compensate for his physical loss, but his condition was permanently tragic and was affecting his mind.

When on leave from hospital he always made a point of mixing-up with active aircrew in the pubs in Cambridge. I felt sorry for him and invariably bought him the odd whisky and gave him a game of darts. 'Ginger,' he would say sadly, after a few drinks, 'for God's sake cover 'em up with something. I wouldn't wish the foulest Hun my lot. I'm a man no longer, and Heaven only knows how I wanted to be a father when I returned home to my wife.'

I peered downwards, searching every square mile of cloud flooring for an opening that would provide a view of the ground and enable me to get an accurate pinpoint. For the second time it was the eagle-eyed front gunner from his little perspex turret who was first to locate what I was so anxiously seeking.

'See it . . . See it!' he bellowed and, raising my eyes, I certainly saw it . . . a half-mile square opening of broken stringy cloud a short distance to starboard.

Identification was comparatively easy. We were only a few degrees off track and flying parallel to a main railway line. Autobahn inter-sections were exactly the same as those on my target map.

We got closer to Berlin proper, and Wallace-Terry spoke aloud the thoughts none of us cared to express at the spectacle in the sky not too far distant. A dull, reddish glow was visible, slowly breathing, pulsating, with varying intensity.

'Looks as though we've been beaten to the city,' he said. 'Our boys've unloaded their busters by the look of things. That fire glow looks pretty real to me.'

At briefing we had been specially warned not to be hood-winked by manufactured fires. The Germans were brilliant exponents at the art of cunning camouflage. They deliberately created false fires in order to encourage British bomb-aimers to unsaddle their loads in harmless vicinities. They even went so far as to erect spurious built-up areas of considerable size to misguide target location. But this time we realised all too clearly that other aircraft were over the target and fighting it out.

And then it happened. A sudden deluge of flak shells exploded everywhere over the city, simultaneously, and millions of cascading pin-points of red fell from where the brilliant flashes died away.

'Good God . . . I've never seen it so thick in all my thirty ops,' the front gunner muttered, with perhaps too much casualness.

More and more flash bursts thickened, intensifying to a closer-knit pattern for miles across the sky. It was literally a wall of an indescribable volume of gushing sparks. As we got nearer they grew bigger and brighter, myriads of fiery flecks. We knew only too well that every fleck represented a chunk of white-hot, jagged, tearing steel.

'Don't panic, blokes,' reassured the skipper, 'we've got to go through it, but it's damned amazing how widely the stuff is separated when we actually get mixed up with it.' I knew full well that this patter was especially for the consoling benefit of the kid in the mid-upper turret. 'Sure,' I answered as blithely as I could. 'When we get back to base and get stuck into those eggs and bacon, our new mid-upper gunner'll wonder if he saw anything at all.'

As if detecting that we were putting over a word act for his benefit, the young gunner broke in on the inter-com. In a high jerky voice. 'Don't worry about me. I'm not scared . . . honestly I'm not . . . isn't it a wonderful sight in front?'

Jock's jovial Scottish voice piped up. 'Good boy!' he exclaimed. 'We're certainly pleased to have you in the best crew of 15 Squadron. Just let your guns rip and blaze away if we come down low. It's a wonderful tonic to see the tracers curving away.'

Our combined attempts at reassurance appeared hollow, however, when half a minute later one of our bombers was pounced on and held in a cone of light from half a dozen searchlights. The flak gunners below encircled the plane with scores of bursting shells.

'Hell . . . some poor bastards are sweating it out!' broke in the front gunner, unable to restrain himself. 'Christ! Are they catching the heat blisters!'

'Quiet!' ordered the skipper.

At that moment, in a mighty crimson flash, superimposed on the pale white of the searchlights, the bomber exploded. A muffled scream came from the mid-upper gunner. Not a word was spoken by any other member of the crew. Flaming fragments fell slowly down, down, and before they had finally disappeared finale had also been written to a second of our bombers.

I cursed freely to prevent my thoughts straying. Forcing my gaze downwards across the floor of cloud, I was contemplating giving the skipper the O.K. for a dive through ten miles from the city when, with uncanny suddenness, the clouds broke up, not partially, but completely. We cruised over what amounted to a vertical wall of greyish padded layers of cloud encompassing Berlin's outer areas. Immediately below were houses, streets – the typical and familiar layout of a thickly populated area. For over three hours we had barely seen the ground, and no sooner had we reacquainted ourselves with it than the Germans sent up a raving hell. Shells burst with violent thuds on our left and right, in front and behind. A cordite-laden atmosphere filled the interior of the cabin with acrid fumes. The attack eclipsed all previous operational flak jams I had experienced. I had flown over this same capital three nights before, but nothing like the same quantity of metal had been pumped up at us. The din outside was infernal, the heat inside stifling, and all the time the aircraft was tugging, straining and twisting in furious evasive action.

My nose was glued to my observation bombing window in the floor of the Stirling when a fantastic gush of brilliant purple light blotted everything out. I pressed my head hard against the metal side of the machine. I could see only a shiny blackness relieved by narrow jumping streams of liquid green. 'Blind,' I told myself as flak rattled all about the Stirling like hail on a tin roof.

I gripped a metal strut, and with my free arm felt for my eyeballs. I desperately wanted to find out if they had been pulped. As I massaged them I started to see again. My temporary blindness was the result of a very near German magnesium flash shell of incredible brilliance. It had burst directly below the bombing window.

We were now in a screamer of a dive and, glued to the floor, I wondered if it was intentional or the result of a hit. I soon knew. It was intentional, for my stomach dragged itself upwards as the Stirling's nose wound round a tight half-circle and we straightened out again. The skill of our pilot had disentangled us from the foulest box barrage we had ever encountered.

Someone croaked over the inter-com.: 'When this bloody war is over . . .' Sharply, the voice of the pilot cut in: 'Get pinpointing, navigator. Quick as you can. Let's bomb the stinking place and get to hell out of this.'

The moon silvered the roofs of the buildings below. Roads stood out like vague luminous twine. Built-up areas stretched away indefinitely like a huge web. Berlin was overcast with the softest of sheens. In a flash came the reward of my navigational studies, the crowning success of my Royal Air Force pinpointing career. I located the northern edge of the lake, positively identified, as well as the surrounding pattern of ground objects and features. Everything below corresponded to the picture of the target map emblazoned on my mind. I reached for the map and checked and rechecked by the dim bulb over the bombsight.

'Got my bearings smack on,' I yelled over the inter-com. A little cheer acknowledged the news, and I gave instructions to the pilot so that the nose of the Stirling was faithfully lined up for the most crucial bombing run of our careers.

Twice as we ran up to the target I lost the silhouette of the wood below for an odd second; twice I picked it up again with a gasp of relief. The target came up clear and precise as the aircraft steadied down to a beautiful even flight, not a tremor, not a half degree waver. The pilot was holding on course magnificently. My eye was glued to the bombsight, the triangle of wood below crept closer along my drift wires, the pointer on the top of the height bar seemed a permanent part of the pupil of my eye. Target concentration was so intense that I doubt if I could have blinked.

The wooded triangle below slipped towards me, two inches to go . . . only one and a half . . . and at this vital point a stream of shells came up at us. We kept on. The shells burst wide. Goering's defence team of backroom boys were going to get it in a few seconds. Only a direct hit on us could save them now! One inch to go . . . half an inch more before the wood coincided between my bombsight's two pointers. Now!

I pressed the tit. Never before had I pressed it with such certainty or relief. Even the Stirling seemed to breathe a sigh of relief. It sprang upwards as the bombs fell away. We did a steep diving turn, and the burst of engine roar was thrillingly reassuring. It seemed to say: 'You can rely on me, now.' I still peered through my bombing window and along the extreme edge of it I watched the bombs straddle the target, bursting one after another, almost imperceptible pricks of yellow. The skipper and I had co-operated perfectly.

Switching on my inter-com., I spoke to the wireless operator, a *Daily Express* reporter before he joined up. Instantly he signalled base, telling them that the target had been successfully bombed.

We returned to the target in an easy waltzing movement, and all eyes watched reddish spurts stirring across the dark surface.

'Cheers! We've certainly started something burning in that wood!' cooed the tail gunner.

For a further three minutes we admired our handiwork and virtual freedom from anti-aircraft attack buoyed us with confidence. As we set course for home it was a gladdening sight to see our fires growing.

We had barely left the target behind when the kid upper-gunner yelled 'Look!'

'Look what?' inquired the pilot.

'Sorry, sir,' replied the excited youngster, 'to port.'

A number of British bombers had unleashed their eggs on an industrial target, and a great swirl of flame was shooting upwards from a base of deep bluish green.

'Looks like oil they've fired,' yelled the front gunner. 'When we busted up the petrol plant at Dusseldorf it burned pretty much the same colour.'

We were on our return course in the best of spirits. The outer reaches of built-up Berlin were behind us. The Stirling was throbbing peacefully on course and then, without a second's notice, the German flak gunners reached up and surrounded us with shells.

'Funny,' croaked Wallace-Terry. 'Jerry taking pot shots now!'

Hardly had he finished the sentence when an incredible array of intense blue searchlights pounced on us without wavering or warning. The Stirling was plumb in the centre of a brilliant cone of blinding light. Standing in the confined cabin I experienced the weird and phantom sensation of actually floating within the machine itself.

'Hell!' screamed the pilot. 'This must be Berlin's outer defence team operating independently of the city! . . . Hold tight for evasive action!'

The giant bomber twisted, writhed and dived. We employed every known evasive trick in our repertoire, but to no effect. We seemed to be securely attached to the end of those uncanny and intelligent searchlight beams. Nothing we attempted was a match for those long rivers of light. From one battery of searchlights to another we passed with ease, each formation taking over with deadly earnest.

'Can't do a damned thing!' screamed the skipper. 'I'm diving . . . open up with all guns straight down the beams!'

The Germans, as if thought-readers, forestalled us. A shell exploded smack in front of us, shattering the outer starboard motor. It was a mind-reeling crash, as if an explosive cracker had been plugged into my eardrums. Searchlights, stars, aircraft and sight gyrated in catastrophic confusion. The crippled engine belched into a globe of flame as petrol from the severed pipelines caught fire.

The second shell burst in the near starboard region. As the aircraft lurched I was pitched violently forward. Clutching wildly for support I unwittingly wrapped a finger about the Very light pistol screwed into the roof and released a coloured cartridge.

Two more shells exploded close to the Stirling's tail and punched large holes in the aircraft's metal skin around the photo-flash rockets suspended on the fuselage wall. We went into our second dive of the evening, the fastest I have ever travelled in a bomber. As we tore earthwards the slipstream howled through the holes and rents, creating a noise like a series of discordant and shrieking organ pipes.

The wireless operator fell on my shoulder through the opening in the armour-plated bulkhead partition. As I turned he spewed full into my face. His damp vomit was cool and refreshing.

How we came out of the dive I shall never know. We were all waiting for a smack into the ground, but with a hideous groan and a wrench the bomber pulled out of the dive into a state of chugging flight, the port wing uncomfortably low. We had lost a lot of height and the Stirling was now staggering at a perfect altitude for Luftwaffe night-fighter attack. Fortunately we were not attacked, neither did another shot come up at us from the guns. The speed and force of the dive had shipped back the flames over the trailing edge of the wing and providentially extinguished them.

The abrupt realisation that we were at least flying horizontally, even though sadly listing to the right, plus the knowledge that we had cheated a write-off, galvanised the crew into action. The engineer turned off the petrol flow at the cocks which fed the useless engine and rapidly checked his fuel readings.

'We've lost the best part of three hundred gallons,' he told the skipper. 'We can't get home tonight.'

While this calculation was taking place I ripped the fur collar from my flying suit and cleaned my face of sweat and vomit. Bursting open an orange I used the juicy pulp as an astringent.

'Too bad!' yelled Wallace-Terry. 'Navigator, work out the shortest route to the coast. We might be able to lob down in the sea.'

I set to work on my maps.

Remembering the young mid-upper turret gunner, Wallace-Terry's voice quietly inquired over the inter-com.: 'How are you making out, mid-upper gunner?'

The voice that replied seemed huskily mature. 'I'm not crying over spilt milk. I just want to go to bed right now and sleep and sleep and sleep,' was the ingenuous reply.

The Stirling was now a mass of mechanical agony. It was a battered and maimed bomber that struggled gamely over Germany at a speed that was the merest flicker above stalling. A once strong and arrogant port wing listed alarmingly. The outer starboard engine was a total write-off, and the inner starboard engine was dangerously out of alignment and synchronisation, causing the whole flying structure to shudder and tremble. Frequently a strange groan from a straining section put our hearts in our mouths. We prayed that the kite would hang together just a little longer.

The vibrations were infectious. After a spell of shuddering flying our limbs involuntarily jerked and shook in unison. The fact that the Stirling might fold up at any moment was obvious, particularly when the lone starboard engine glowed crimson hot, and kept faltering and losing revolutions. We were tracking a course which was the nearest line to the Dutch coast, but with every few miles the bomber lost height. The single starboard engine was dying rapidly and with the loss of power we were at times almost standing still in the teeth of the 50 m.p.h. head wind. The bomber would be rebuffed and then would stagger forward, palpitating and straining, literally inch by inch.

The burned-up engine finally petered out with a quick convulsive gasp. Like a monument to the corpse the propeller stood out stark and motionless. The remaining two engines were throttled forward to the limit. Feverishly the engineer and I worked out petrol reserve and distance. Even with the best of luck we could not get farther than the near edge of the Zuider Zee. We had to come down in German-occupied Europe, but if we could somehow stretch things we stood a reasonable chance of a pancake landing on the water and a better chance of preserving our necks, instead of baling out. Besides, we felt certain that our landing wheels were pretty badly shot up. Our only concern about coming down in the drink was with our dinghy in the wing stowage nacelle. If shrapnel had peppered the rubber the prospect was not too rosy.

I spoke to Wallace-Terry, and he forced a lively tone. 'Cheer up, fellows,' he said. 'Could have been a hell of a sight worse. If we dive the old Stirling into the Zuider Zee at least we don't give the Germans the satisfaction of picking up the pieces, and I guess we'll paddle to the shore somehow.' As an afterthought he added: 'Check up on your parachutes and Mae Wests in event of emergency action.'

Height was slipping away badly. Instructions were given for all loose gear to be slung overboard to lessen weight, including guns and all ammunition belts. It was a blow to the three gunners to have to unlock their babies and drop them out into the night, for it robbed us of all protection. Fortunately, no German night fighters spotted us.

The two functioning engines were being flogged to the limit and now they, too, began to lose revolutions and burn at a dangerous temperature.

I began to check on my parachute. In the air I seldom wore the pack on my body. Moving about and working over maps was easier without it. A special container was fixed to hold it on the starboard side of the aircraft and in an emergency I could quickly snatch it. When now I pulled it out, the silk fell listlessly, almost mockingly, about my feet. The rear of the pack had been badly ripped, and the rip-cord elastic binders completely severed. I examined the folds. A piece of shell had drilled itself through and through the folded silk and, looking at the side of the cabin where the chute had been attached, I saw a hole as big as my fist.

The wind blew in, agitating the loose white silk about my feet. I was seething, and rebelliously furious. But my safety-valve, cursing, did not let me down and I managed to stabilise my feelings.

I went to the tail of the bomber and then worked my way back to the fore part of the aircraft. Seven perspiring and exhausted faces managed to pucker up a grin. Each man knew full well that 'Special Target Berlin' was almost over. Each man must have speculated on just how much longer we could remain aloft, and silently conjectured on just how many of the crew would remain alive when the engines cut out.

Returning to the main cabin, I collected my damaged parachute, pressed it into a tight ball and stuffed it out of sight under the pilot's seat. What did it matter? What did anything matter any more? I was sky dreaming when the pilot spoke. I hardly noticed his voice. With astounding clarity I visualised details of familiar pubs in the vicinity of our Huntingdonshire aerodrome, and the pencil gripped between my lips was as soothing as the rim of a whisky glass. I sucked at the drippings of sweat which trickled continuously from my upper lip and let my imagination happily believe that the moisture was whisky-flavoured rather than salty.

I thought of Blondie in the parachute-packing section. She had always made the packing of my particular 'chute one of especial attention, and had kissed it good luck whenever I collected it. She would never know that all her painstaking and affectionate work had been cancelled out by a single chunk of anti-aircraft shell. When the news came through that we were missing in action she would console herself with the belief that I had baled out; she would be confident, too, that my 'chute had opened perfectly because she had methodically folded the silk so that it could not do otherwise.

'Pape . . . for Christ's sake!' Wallace-Terry yelled. 'Give me a position. What the hell's wrong with you?'

I reacted quickly, feeling ashamed that I was neglecting my duty in selfish concern over past niceties of life.

'Twenty to thirty miles from the Dutch-German border,' I replied, after a couple of minutes' work on my charts.

Wallace-Terry, as if talking to himself, slowly muttered: 'I'll get this aircraft that far if this bloody, fantastic petrol from nowhere only continues a while longer.'

The petrol gauges stood at zero. From what the needles indicated we were bone dry and flying on nothing. The inner port engine started to cough badly and kept spluttering.

'Swing back the escape hatch, somebody,' called the pilot. 'Bale out while you have the chance, you chaps.'

I crept forward and down the short ladder into the Stirling's bombing well. As I passed the pilot's seat I raked up saliva and spat on my dud 'chute in respect of my feelings for the enemy; then I paused and touched the silk with a quiet thought in respect of my admiration and affection for Blondie, the Waaf.

As I released the escape hatch in the floor, the inrush of cool air was clean and refreshing. I peered into the darkness and instinctively felt the earth's close proximity. We were only 1,500 feet above it. I could not see any sign of the dull lustre of water on which a possible pancake-landing could be made.

And then it happened. In one choking sobbing struggle, the two functioning starboard engines died with a mechanical death rattle. Stirling by name and sterling by nature our bomber had steadfastly refused to give up the scrap. From the time it had received its mortal wounds it had struggled gamely to carry us as far as the Dutch-German border. Its engines had groaned and gasped, its petrol arteries, ripped and bleeding, had seen its vital spirit drain away. With wings listing and shaking it had stubbornly kept going, refusing to give up the ghost without a fight. But now our kite had had it.

We started plunging earthwards. The wind moaned and hissed. One of the crew started to bawl: 'We'll meet again, don't know where, don't know when . . .'

The strong Scottish voice of Jock burst in: 'And I'll be in Scotland afore ye, and me and my true love . . .'

Wallace-Terry cut it short. 'You crazy idiots!' he bellowed, 'for Christ's sake bale out while you still have sufficient clearance. You've only a few hundred feet left.'

'If you're sticking to the controls, skipper,' piped up a voice which sounded like the kid gunner's, 'then I'm sticking to you and the kite.'

It was then that the inter-communication, with a short burring, went dead.

The ground was frighteningly close. I started to crawl back to the centre of the bomber, the safest place for the big dig-in. My hand was on the top ladder which led into the cabin when a body hurtled forward, boots crunching my fingers. I turned to see head and shoulders slip from sight through the opening. Before I had time to move forward again, a second body leaped forward and disappeared through the hatch, out and down into the night. As I braced against a metal stanchion and drew up my knees for the impact with the ground I wondered which members of the crew had got out.

In the short remaining time I attempted to bolster up my morale by a vicious tirade of cursing against God and the Germans. I screamed out hate and vituperation against the Almighty for my peppered parachute. I paused for breath and started to swear again, then folded up like a pricked balloon. I was dead scared. I knew it was only a matter of seconds before we smashed a hole into the earth.

A terrific shock . . . A blinding white flash . . . A realisation in the thousandth part of a second that it was the ground . . . hard, hard ground!

BOOK I

WEST THROUGH HOLLAND

CHAPTER I

LOYALISTS

We had crashed a shade west of the Dutch-German border a few kilometres from Hengelo. Only by a very narrow margin had we sneaked across the border out of Germany into Holland.

Nothing short of a miracle had saved our lives – though full credit cannot be accorded to Providence, because Wallace-Terry was an absolute virtuoso of joy-stick and rudder-bar. But Providence certainly *had* intervened, for when we were only a couple of hundred feet from the ground, and much less from the roof of a small church, the Stirling, with a strange energy, suddenly jerked upwards its huge snout. Considering we had no engine power it was most unusual. Nevertheless, it made all the difference in the world. Instead of a mighty crash straight through the roof, in which case we should all have died in church with our boots on, we passed over it by inches, streaked forward horizontally and hit the ground a short distance beyond at something like 150 m.p.h.

Another amazing thing was that the field in which our raid finished so ingloriously was fantastically small. I doubt if a single-engined aircraft could have landed safely on it. We ploughed deeply across its surface, and the belly structure of the bomber was shorn to tatters. As we struck, the thirty tons of Stirling was bounced back into the air like a rubber ball, then down again, shuddering and grinding. A few yards from the edge of the field a tree stood in exactly the right place. Gallantly it intervened as a brake. In slow motion, almost, we swung about it and came to rest.

Two minutes later – or twenty – my mind cleared. Pains stabbed

29

everywhere, and my head seemed to be opening and shutting to a steady beat. Rain was falling, soothing my cracked cranium. I struggled desperately for air, and through a floating mass of shadows and flashes I gradually brought into focus the strong face of the Scottish engineer, Jock Moir. My hand felt uncommonly numb and, raising it to my mouth, I could not grasp at first why three of my fingers flopped uselessly on my face. Where they joined the palm of the hand they had been severely gashed.

Slowly the whole gruesome situation dawned on me. I looked at Wallace-Terry and saw a ghastly white mound of bone of hellish size on his forehead. It was pouring blood. Dazed, but sufficiently conscious to realise that he had work to do, he kept muttering: 'Jerry bastards mustn't get a clue. Destroy everything, burn everything, mustn't get a clue, mustn't get a clue.'

Moir was the most mobile of the group, and without pause he assisted us as capably as his badly shaken and bruised condition would allow.

We sorted ourselves out as best we could, but it was a haggard, bloody group of men that limped about the wreckage.

Moir was everywhere, decisive, level-headed, giving aid. He located the first-aid box. Quickly and without mercy he tucked my fingers into the palm of my hand and wrapped the right hand up in a few yards of bandage. As he tied it, he slapped my face and jerked me to my feet.

'Come on, Ginger, snap out of it,' he commanded sternly. 'We've got to get into that aircraft and bust and burn everything. Jerry can't be far off.'

Together we climbed to the top of the fuselage proper. Once inside the main cabin I gathered together all maps and charts and the air log and fired them. Jock worked like a demon with the axe.

All instruments were splintered and hacked, especially the bomb sight. Before we returned to the open air we unlocked the camera magazine and set fire to the film which carried the evidence of our successful bombing operation. Everything inflammable was heaped on the fire in the cockpit, even my peppered parachute.

Coughing, sweating and spluttering, we dropped to the ground. Barely had we time to fill our lungs with clean air before the Germans warned us of their approach. Three red rockets flared into the night sky and a volley of rifle shots crackled in the fields just behind us.

'The bastards are closing in on us,' gasped Jock. 'It's now or never. I'm moving off. Can you make it? You can rely on me to help you all I can.'

'I'm coming,' I replied.

More rockets lit the sky, accompanied by a medley of yells.

'They've spotted the bloody kite burning,' hissed Jock. 'They're just behind the line of trees.'

'C'mon, chum,' was my reply. 'Let's get to hell out of here.'

For a couple of seconds we turned towards the others, huddled in a group on the ground, the flames from the burning machine flickering across their ashen faces. Not a word was said. It was a situation in which words could not come easily. The young gunner's expression was ghastly. His eyes seemed to be fixed on some object in the sky, and glowed like bright coals. He looked very old. Wallace-Terry was retching and bowing his head up and down like clockwork. He looked up and paused in his vomiting, and waved his hand in a vague effort at salutation.

Moir and I started off, picking and weaving our way in the opposite direction to the oncoming searchers. Eventually we reached a narrow earth roadway which was heaven after the obstacles of the fields. Breathing was painful, and after a few hundred yards every toe on my feet seemed to have enlarged to the size of turnips. My right hand and forearm were dead. I chuckled as I plodded up the road when I imagined what a queer business it would be learning to write with my left hand. I stooped to suck up water from a ditch and fell headlong into it. Moir heaved me out, laid me out, and lit a cigarette for me. Quietly I began hissing my choicest expletives.

'Keep it up,' Moir said, 'now I know you're getting your guts back.'

It was rapidly growing light. As we continued to drag our way up the road the flat and murky landscape was a miserable sight. But two thoughts drove us on: it was our duty to avoid capture at all costs; and we had to put more distance between ourselves and the searchers.

Six times we were compelled to roll into the oozing ditch, and six times we emerged dripping when the German patrols had clattered past. The Germans were certainly active. They must have found the Stirling because green rockets twittered about the sky immediately over its position.

'My God,' Jock muttered, 'they must be calling in half the occupation troops.'

Once, as we grovelled in the muck and slime of the ditch, a dozen or more shots rang out. Birds in the hedge alongside were startled into flight. Moir spoke, pale with fury.

'If those German bastards've pumped holes into the rest of the crew, I'll haunt 'em to hell,' he exclaimed.

Tucked away among a few scraggy trees, less than a hundred yards from the roadside, we found a dismal stone cottage. It looked forbidding and the roof was noticeably sunken in the centre. Moir advanced to reconnoitre with the parting instruction to keep out of sight but to continue to move slowly up the ditch to a point a hundred yards beyond the cottage.

I wriggled up the filthy gully and wallowed in the appointed spot for about five minutes before I saw Moir sneaking back behind the screen of sparse trees.

'This is a queer joint we've struck,' he panted, helping me to my feet.

It started me guessing too, as slowly we advanced towards it. The front area was a junk heap of old cans and rusty ironmongery. As we neared the place a dog's bark indicated that the place was inhabited. The animal was at the rear of the cottage, and a metallic rattle and clatter made it plain that it was bounding about at the length of a chain. The knowledge that the dog must have an owner brought us down on all fours.

We reached the door and the partly boarded windows, and for fully five minutes remained absolutely motionless, but the dog, although more subdued, continued to let out intermittent growls and barks.

'Hell!' whispered Moir. 'That lunatic animal will warn the Jerries for sure. Wait here . . . I'm going to do it in.'

He picked up a formidable piece of rusty iron tubing and was about to move around to the rear of the cottage when, with a motion of my arm, I stopped him. From inside the cottage there came a noise. Someone was stirring. I pressed hard against the wall, and picked up the nearest weapon: a piece of old iron grating.

Moir made towards me, but I waved him back and motioned with my lips for absolute silence. I kept my eyes fixed on the wooden door. It creaked, moved a fraction. There was a long pause, then it slowly opened outwards, inch by inch. As the angle of the opening door increased I was compelled to move backwards to avoid interrupting its progress. The occupant, I conjectured, was either going to make a dive for it, or cautiously investigate the reason for the dog's excitement.

The door was open at least two feet before any human form appeared. Then it was all very sudden. Like the dart of a snake's tongue, the wrinkled face of an old woman shot out on the end of a long scraggy neck, spotted me, and withdrew, just missing my downward plunge with the iron grating.

I cannot say why I instinctively tried to brain the old woman. I acted in the name of expediency, not pausing to question things. I pitched forward, and was just quick enough to insert my injured hand in the last few inches of aperture to stop it fully closing. The old woman was screaming, and her strength was extraordinary as she tugged at the door. I experienced the most excruciating pain, but with Moir's aid I quickly forced open the door.

Inside, the place stank. In the half light the old woman was cringing against the opposite wall. She clasped her hands above her head and swayed as she whimpered. She was bedraggled and dirty. Then she started to scream and the dog joined in.

Sweeping her junk of crockery from a small table on to the floor, I advanced towards her with both hands in the position for a stranglehold. I jostled, and got my pad of bandage round her gnarled throat. She writhed, strained and twisted. I kicked her shins.

Then suddenly I moved away and cursed myself.

Jock was rapidly carrying out a search for food in the adjacent room and knew nothing of my attempt to silence the old woman. Gazing at her, I could see her bulging eyes full of a mixture of hate and pity. I dropped my eyes to her thin scraggy neck, and saw the beads of a black rosary dropping away inside her dress. Involuntarily,

I forced my hand underneath the dress and withdrew a white crucifix. I felt a revulsion of disgust at what I had tried to do. I realised that a fugitive could never achieve much freedom by killing an old and defenceless woman.

The rumble of vehicles on the roadway outside prompted the old girl to make a spurt for the door. I moved after her, and fortunately she thought better of indulging in a screaming campaign.

Moir stood tense beside me until the clatter of the patrol had died away in the distance.

'Got to soothe the old girl somehow,' he remarked. 'She's dynamite.'

We tried gentler tactics. Moir patted her head and quietly spoke to her. 'Take it easy, Grandma, take it easy,' he said.

Trying to reassure her, I mustered sufficient German to say: '*Vom England, Frau, Fliegers vom England, und der Engländer ist gut Mensch.*'

She watched me closely. I knew she understood.

'Flak, flak,' I continued. '*Mein Flugzeug krachen, kaputt.*' I pushed out my damaged hand and slowly encircled my face. '*Verwundet, mir und Kamerad verwundet.*'

This seemed to work, as it soothed and silenced her.

We started to work out a plan of campaign. Food was the first essential. The total bag was a loaf of black bread, a dozen fat sausages, margarine, some apples and a tin of coffee. In a small chest of drawers we found some old petticoats which we ripped into serviceable bandages. While water was heating over the oilstove Jock had fixed, we ate ravenously. The food was incredibly revitalising both physically and morally. We scalded the coffee and chewed and gulped in silence. Our previous meal had been taken in Britain at 8 p.m. the day before.

The old woman watched us devour her entire larder. I handed her a pot of hot coffee, but so great was the twitching of her hand that she spilled the lot over her lap. Twice German transport was heard near by, and twice we silenced the old woman with severe looks.

The task of washing and cleaning my wounds was effected quickly and skilfully. As Jock fastened the last piece of bandage I stood up a new man, and more in the mood to face what lay ahead. Jock disappeared outside on reconnaissance and, in my halting German, I instructed the old woman to keep her mouth shut after we had departed. With a fixed expression on her face, she followed my words and gestures, croaking out '*Ja, ja,*' and '*Gott sei Dank.*' She was certainly fervently thankful that we were departing. I dared not leave anything to chance however and, uncharitable of me though it was – but by this time not genuinely meaning to kill her – I brought her to a full understanding of my instructions by putting my hands together again in the strangle-hold grasp of pointing to her neck.

Jock returned sweating. 'Quick,' he panted. 'They're pretty close, searching down the road.' He led the way through the backyard. 'Guess this is the only way we have left,' he muttered.

The long meadow in which we found ourselves had a low hedge stretching diagonally for some distance across it. We followed it, keeping well down and moving as fast as our doubled-up positions would allow. The hedge finished at a boundary of widely spaced props strung with double strands of wire.

'Down,' rapped Jock, and we fell prone.

As we had crossed the meadow in the lee of the hedge, the ground had risen slightly. From this semi-elevated point we commanded a reasonable view of the flat landscape which, here and there, was dotted with a few small clusters of trees and shrubs.

On the horizon, at intervals, figures could be plainly seen. We clearly could not retreat, while in front of us there was only open country with no cover whatsoever. It was essential that we should reach one of the small woods in the distance, but this seemed virtually impossible without the German watchers spotting us.

'Think of something, for God's sake!' Jock requested ruefully.

In front of us, about 400 yards away, half a dozen cows stood motionless except for an occasional turning of a head. I scrutinised them closely, and it suddenly occurred to me that they were standing in either water or long grass.

'Belly-crawl to those cows,' I exclaimed.

We wriggled close to the ground. After every hundred yards or so we stopped, lying absolutely still for a few minutes. Luck was with us, no yells or shots heralded detection from the nearby Germans, and finally we wriggled right in among the cows. They made no sign of panic or retreat.

Close to the beasts we found a long straight dyke, slightly sunken, stretched across the fields. It was about six feet across and shallow. Nevertheless it was a God-sent avenue for movement out of the danger zone. We slipped into the water and, as near horizontal as was humanly possible, we pulled and slithered our way along the bank. Progress was strenuous, and made big inroads on our strength. At intervals we were forced to submerge, and there was one long pause when we dared not move an inch owing to the nearness of the Germans.

So far the dyke had run in the right direction, towards two reasonably large clusters of trees, but half-way across the next meadow it abruptly altered course.

'C'mon,' puffed Jock, 'we've got to break partnership with this dyke and make a bolt for it straight into those trees.'

He had hardly finished speaking when the fact that we had taken refuge in the old hag's cottage was loudly proclaimed by a crisp volley of rifle shots. It meant we had to reach the coppice before the Germans topped the rise and saw us.

Dripping and aching we left the dyke and ran like mad things towards the coppice.

We had almost reached its outer edge when Jock sobbed: 'Christ!'

A boy in short trousers stood less than a couple of hundred yards away.

We entered the wood and fell flat on the ground. We sobbed and panted. Our bodies steamed. I felt that my heart would burst.

'That kid spotting us was bad luck,' Jock said, when he could at last speak. 'Let's hope and pray that he is a loyal Dutchman and doesn't blab.'

We moved farther into the trees, right into the middle of the wood, which was roughly 200 yards long by 50 yards wide. We had to find a place of concealment. I was surveying likely clumps of undergrowth when the bright idea struck me that it would be stupid to hide in the centre.

'Get on the fringe of the coppice,' I argued with Jock. 'The Jerries'll tear up the centre as a matter of course, and pay far less attention to the perimeter.'

Jock agreed. The wood was well furnished with blackberry bushes and creeper growth, and we had almost completed an inspection of the side in which we had entered before the ideal spot was discovered, a perfect growth of non-prickly bush standing at least four feet high. It was on the very edge of the wood and perhaps three feet from the pathway which bordered the outside meadow. We scrutinised it from every angle.

'It's the goods,' Moir muttered optimistically. 'Hurry . . . help me collect odds and ends of branches to fill in a couple of gaps.'

I wriggled into the middle of the tent growth so that he could do a thorough check-up from the outside.

I called out to my companion that it could not be better. Twelve inches of leaves filled a natural saucer-like formation in the ground. I dug in, and carefully scattered leaves over my body and up to my neck. Jock, from his observation on the outside, informed me that it was perfect.

Barely had I relaxed my head on the soft pillow of leaves before I was asleep, and in the forgetful folds of slumber I remained for eight hours. I would doubtless have slept much longer had I not been disturbed by the pressure of Jock's hand over my mouth. He kept it there until I was sufficiently aroused to understand his whisperings.

'The bloody Germans are standing not ten yards away,' he mouthed. 'They've been through the wood twice already, and a couple of the bastards are posted on guard with tommy guns.'

Hardly daring to breathe at this frightening news I cautiously turned over and looked through a spy hole in the wall of brush growth. The picture I saw on the outside was fantastic. Two German guards were literally on top of us! One of them was a big, obese man with an extraordinarily wide back, and from his shoulder was slung a nasty-looking sub-machine gun. His mate was shorter and thinner, the wiry, rat-like type, and leaning on his rifle he stared out over the fields.

The big German spat lustily and took a cigar from his tunic pocket. In the process of lighting it he said something to his short companion.

'*Ja, ja,*' was the only reply from his statue-like companion.

The cigar pulling satisfactorily, the big German started a short beat up and down the pathway. He passed within a foot of our screen of bush, and for the first time in my life I scrutinised a pair of jackboots at uncomfortably close range. The aroma of a strong cigar was wafted to our nostrils. Not a whisper or a flicker could be exchanged between Jock and myself, but gradually we relaxed.

For almost an hour we were compelled to remain motionless in a cramped position. Even the occasional rustle of leaves had to be avoided. Then suddenly the two guards showed a spurt of action. They adjusted their equipment and from their alertness we realised that something was afoot. Voices and the tramping of feet heralded the approach of a small body of soldiers in charge of a non-commissioned officer. Standing to attention our two wood-watchers answered a number of questions levelled at them by the fellow in charge of the detachment. Then the party was split up. Three units of four men each marched briskly off to the end of the wood.

'Hell's teeth,' Jock muttered. 'It looks as if we're in for another search.'

When the searchers started to advance in line abreast we both experienced heart quails. Not more than twenty yards away the Germans opened fire into the dense undergrowth in the centre of the wood. Jock trembled at my side. It was unbearable. I simply had to raise my head and open the screen of foliage with my arm to take a look. A short distance away two Jerries grasped rifles with fixed bayonets. They appeared to be the outside men, and as they advanced and trotted around the bushes at the edge of the woods, the rifle, with bayonet attached, would be thrust into the under-growth like a spear.

'Get under those leaves, quickly,' I told Jock. 'Tense your body . . . keep rigid.'

The men strode forward a few more yards. I was on the verge of panic. My courage ebbed to the point when I almost screamed out at the top of my voice '*Kamerad! Kamerad!*'

I resorted to whispered cursing instead, and it worked as it had always worked. I dug in quickly, rearranged the leaves and kept on cursing. The stabbers were up to the bush, they let fly and a shaft of steel disturbed the leaves near my left ankle. Then they passed on to the next clump of bushes. German thoroughness had failed by a fraction, and luck was still with us.

'God in Heaven!' panted Jock.

The searchers moved through the wood, regrouped and cleared off. We lay submerged for some time to make certain that no guards had been left behind.

'Reckon we're in the clear at last,' I remarked as I scrambled clear of our hiding-place.

Moir grinned. 'Where do we go from here?' he asked as he pulled out his precious fags. 'Have a smoke . . . we've six and only six left.'

Rashly we smoked a couple each as we mooched about near the edge of the coppice and idly surveyed the landscape. Nothing moved; not a German was in sight. Time passed and the numbness from my hand and forearm extended slowly right up to my armpit.

It grew chilly, and the first tinge of welcome eventide flushed the sky.

Suddenly, alarmingly, the noise of wood-chopping disturbed the evening stillness. We dropped flat on our faces and slowly crept back to our original hide-out, listening all the time. The chopping continued, a steady, dull, rhythmic thud, thud, thud, thud. There was no other noise. We decided after a safe pause on the ground that it was high time to carry out a tour of investigation and we parted ways.

As I turned the far end of the coppice, I saw in front of me not more than 500 yards away, a small wooden cabin, and to the left

41

of it two out-houses. In a clearing in front of the cabin a man was slowly wielding an axe and beside him there was a stack of roughly shaped pieces of timber.

After a while, Jock arrived and together in the diminishing light we watched the man go inside the hut.

'See what I see?' Jock asked jubilantly.

Then I, too, spotted the pair of trousers hanging from the door of an out-house.

'One of us could do with those,' sniffed Jock.

Those pants would certainly be a precious escape acquisition and quickly we worked out a plan of campaign and I wriggled off. All went well right until I pulled the pants from the door. I had barely hidden myself in the lee of the shed when the door of the shack opened noisily. The man came out and stood, idly puffing a cigarette. I lay very still. The cigarette finished, the man tossed the end away and returned indoors. Jock wasted little time and wriggled to me trailing the large axe.

'All's well,' he remarked. 'Certainly got a scare when he came up for a breather!'

For some moments we held a conference in whispers. Jock was keen to rap at the door and attempt his hand at intimidation. I felt that the only safe method was to kill the man and bury him, and that we certainly did not want to do. If the Jerries found out that we had committed murder, we could expect little mercy if they bagged us.

'If we bash him up and leave him alive,' I said, 'it'll be worse than doing him in. He'll squawk his head off and the Germans'll really put out an intensified man hunt.'

We agreed to quit the place peacefully and move farther into Holland during the night. Once clear of the crash zone and the border country, we would trust to the good graces of Lady Luck.

Wriggling back to the sanctuary of the wood, we returned to our own particular bush. We wouldn't have to wait much longer now before we could get moving and warm up our blood with brisk walking. It had grown fearfully cold.

I had just got into the old corduroy trousers I had purloined, when we heard someone approaching. A man coughed, frequently and intentionally, and loudly jangled a metal can. It seemed that he was deliberately announcing his approach. At least four times he cut across the wood from edge to edge before he came into range. Jock gripped his axe. From the screen of our bush we watched the figure in the shadows.

It was not yet completely dark, and we saw that it was the wood-chopper, and that he was carrying a haversack and two small tin cans. Falteringly he moved to a point a few yards away, then turned diagonally and took a few more paces which brought him even less distance away. His actions showed that he was decidedly nervous. As if suddenly imbued with a flash of courage he quickly clanked the two metal cans together.

Not a word came from either of us. In the dusk we could see that he was moving his head mechanically as he jerked it from bush to bush.

'Might be a hoax . . . wait,' Jock whispered.

This eventide visitation was certainly odd; the bloke hadn't dropped in just to rattle funny little cans. After a couple of minutes I told Jock I was going to show myself.

'This chap may be able to help us,' I said. 'We dare not miss any opportunity. You keep low and come up briskly if he starts any nonsense. If he is a stooge for the Jerries, and they suddenly appear, get under our bush again.'

The wood-chopper was looking the other way when I quietly raised myself and coughed. He started around like a trapped burglar, and even in the subdued light I could see that his face showed fear. We gazed at each other for fully thirty seconds before he found his tongue.

'*Englischer Flieger, englischer Flieger*,' he said softly. I nodded. Promptly he burst into a rapid spate of words which I could not understand. At the same time he moved towards me. I shot out my arms and exclaimed in what German I could remember, '*Halten Sie, stehen*.' He came to a standstill, and then spoke again, very slowly, but I could not understand the meaning of his words, which seemed to be Dutch.

'*Nicht verstehen*,' I replied, and in broken German said I was only capable of understanding if he spoke very slowly.

Slowly he started to give me information which was enough to make me want to call for Jock, but I decided to play the stranger a little longer. I learned from his reiterated statement that he was a loyal Dutchman, and wanted to assist the shotdown British airmen.

'Is your comrade dead?' he asked, 'I have brought you both food.' He emphasised the fact by pointing to the haversack and the two tin cans.

I did not reply to his question, but made a slow advance towards him. Separated by only a few inches I peered intently into a white face, and I saw that he was trembling. A not unnatural suspicion, coupled to no small amount of fear and a high state of personal tension made any effort at speech on my part for the moment quite impossible. Had it not been for the fellow before me dropping to his knees for no apparent reason and uttering the words 'Winston Churchill,' heaven knows how long I would have stood toe to toe in grim, distrustful silence.

'Churchill is a good man, he is our god,' the kneeling Dutchman reverently proclaimed. 'We want to help Winston Churchill's airmen.'

This was something for which I had never bargained, a few words which set my spine tingling. My immediate reaction was that the whole strength and decency of Britain was emanating from the man on his knees, kindling my morale and refreshing my patriotism. I felt giddy. I dropped to the ground beside the Dutchman and called for Jock.

In that dark wood life had suddenly taken on a new complexion, and as I painstakingly unravelled the Dutchman's sentences and translated what he had to say, our optimism soared. Haversack and tin cans were opened, and the conversation halted while we ate. We disposed of cold sausages and raw bacon between slices of black bread and strong, black, stimulating coffee. Our benefactor further added to his reputation when he produced a medicine bottle full of schnapps, and ten cigarettes apiece, as well as a couple of cigars.

He told us that after the Germans had visited the old woman and learned positively that two British airmen were on the run, this man and all other patriotic Dutch people in the area had been rounded up and temporarily jailed in the village schoolroom in Hengelo. Not until the Germans had scoured a wide area of countryside and satisfied themselves that we were not in the immediate vicinity, had the good Dutch fellow and his neighbours been released. Now they were ready to help us to safety.

The Dutchman gave us careful instructions about the route which had to be followed to get us safely to a rendezvous near Hengelo. A code word to be exchanged with the Dutch patriots who would be watching and waiting for us along the route, was arranged. They would challenge us with the word: *'Churchilldagen'* (Churchilldays).

Our wood-cutting friend bade us goodbye, and disappeared. Before we left that little Dutch wood I threw a coin into the centre of the little clump of bush which had so valiantly protected us. It was an old shilling with a hole in it given me to carry for luck in my flying clothes.

Then, with the Pole Star in line with my shoulders, we set course and started forward. Twice we waded dykes, and our wet clothes clung about us. At the third I slipped and fell headlong into the water, completely saturating my precious cigarettes. I cursed, and we rested awhile on the bank. During the pause we heard a vehicle rumbling in the distance. We listened. The noise of the engine grew louder and louder, and we spotted dimmed headlamps approaching straight towards us. It passed in front of us not more than forty yards away.

'Phew!' whispered Jock. 'Thank God that truck passed when it did. We're slap bang on top of the road!'

To our consternation we heard, a hundred yards to the left, and eighty to the right, the crunching of boots as two German sentries trod their beats.

'I only hope the bastards did not hear me fall into that dyke and start cursing,' I whispered in Jock's ear.

We both decided that this was not the perfect place to make a crossing and, retracing our way belly flat in the direction we had come, we arrived at a point well clear of the road. Turning parallel to it, and crouching, running and ducking, we covered the best part of a third of a mile. For a second time we closed with the roadway, and a second time we had to beat a hasty retreat.

'Blast the German efficiency!' I muttered. 'They certainly don't intend to let any stray airmen get in or out of that village.'

The next spot was better. We could not see anyone, although we heard definite stamping to our right; but at least the noise seemed a comfortable distance away.

I pulled off my flying boots, buckled one to the other, placed them firmly in position around my neck and got set in the ditch with Jock on my heels. Then we bolted like rabbits and did not relax our speed until we were a couple of hundred yards across the meadow on the other side. There we rested awhile, donned our boots, and felt much happier now that the major stumbling block was safely behind us.

I checked up with the North Star for a further walk of half a mile due east before we altered course in a northerly direction.

'Soon be turning in the straight for Hengelo, buddies and supper,' Jock laughed.

Stinking, sweaty, bruised and stiff, we stumbled on for what seemed an interminable period, but no landmark appeared, not even the vaguest outline of any wood with the tallish trees that we had been told to look for.

'Three and a half miles to Hengelo,' spat Jock. 'Hell, man, we seem to have covered ten already! Yet I'm certain that wood-cutter bloke was all right. Some of those villagers ought to be just about on top of us by now.'

Suddenly a clear-cut sound of human movement came to our ears, the noise of shuffling and scraping boots. We lay very still, and with time to concentrate in the slight luminous glow of that particular night's darkness, we adjusted our vision to three shapes not far away to the right.

'May be haystacks,' I whispered in Jock's ear. 'All else I can see are two small patches that look like bushes about thirty yards in front.'

A dog, not far away, barked spasmodically, otherwise all was very quiet. Then, as startling in its suddenness as any anti-aircraft shell, there was the sound of human throat-clearing, and it came from what I had presumed were bushes. We waited through another long pause of dead silence. Our suspense was given a quick jolt when a figure, coughing slightly, moved forward out of the deep shadows. The silhouette wavered and advanced and then it stopped dead, twenty feet from where we lay pressed to the earth.

My stomach jumped with a mixture of fear and hope. One way or the other this was the beginning or the end. Jock was feeling the tension too. He moved slightly and created a slight rustle. It was now or never. I called out 'Churchilldagen'.

A man's voice replied at once, and there was a comforting eagerness in his voice. 'Churchilldagen,' he said.

We leaped to our feet. He was between us, a strong Dutch arm around our shoulders. We moved forward. From the dark patches which were reasonably sized bushes two other men appeared. They spoke excitedly in whispers. All I could do was stupidly repeat, 'Zwei englische Flieger.'

The four of us, linked together like long lost brothers, and with the odd man leading the way, moved slowly along a pathway to the farmstead near by.

It was superbly refreshing by the light of the living-room lamp to see the kind faces of the Dutch family and it was indescribably reassuring to listen to the low hum of their voices. Their name was Besselink they told us.

Mevrouw Besselink was pale and nervous when she saw us for the first time. Filthy and bedraggled, we must have presented a frightening spectacle, but she quickly rallied into a person of calm efficiency. Buckets of hot water were made ready, bandages and disinfectant laid out, food prepared.

Tactfully we were not plied with questions until we had eaten. It was almost unreal, blissfully wonderful, sitting there watched by strong country faces. Each countenance showed solemnity at our condition, each face reflected pride at our being in their protection.

Four Besselinks were present – apart from the Mevrouw – the master and his three brothers, men whose lives had been devoted to honest work in Dutch soil, men of a family respected in and about the village of Hengelo for over a century.

The master was about fifty, his wife much younger, a comely woman. In her house clogs, with a pretty floral design on the front, she moved about with attractive ease, issuing instructions to the male members of her household. One brother was sent off to find the priest and the doctor; another brother was told to hasten to the men waiting to intercept us, to tell them that we were in safe keeping, and the third brother sent to watch the precincts of the farm, and to give warning of any danger.

On reaching the door this man bowed in gentlemanly manner towards us and surprised us by remarking: 'English friends . . . all well will be. My family is good Churchill Dutch.'

The elder Besselink, a man of quiet strength, tenderly undressed me, and took off the dirty bandages covering my wounds.

Jock was already nodding in the rocking chair. His face revealed lines which I had never seen before. I watched him with immense gratitude in my heart. What immeasurable comradeship and true Scottish courage he had shown!

My wounds had been cleansed and disinfected by the time the doctor and priest arrived and I was in a half-conscious state of drowsiness. The heat from the fire played soothingly on my almost naked body.

The doctor made sure that I went to sleep, and with soft Dutch voices hovering around my ears I left all pain and worry behind me for many hours.

Jock was not so lucky. For a couple of hours he was questioned in perfect English by a local journalist, John Agterkamp. The story of our Berlin sky adventure, and our subsequent trials was told. Later I learned from Jock that they were all aglow with pride to be so closely associated with men of Churchill's air force, the men for whom they prayed night after night as British aircraft throbbed directly overhead *en route* for German targets.

Shortly after Jock had finished our story a breathless loyalist broke up the gathering. The Germans had suddenly sprung a house-to-house search in the village, and it was bound to widen to the farmsteads outside. Less than an hour had passed since the Germans had posted up notices offering a reward for information about two British 'murder fliers' still concealed in the district.

A hideout was prepared for us at the top of a haystack. At all costs we must not remain in the Besselink home, for the penalty for harbouring enemy escapees was death. The haystacks in Holland are put up under corrugated umbrella-like roofs, poised on four steel legs. Between the ground and this roof the hay is tightly packed. The Besselinks made a hollow in the centre of the hay just below the roof. When we were safely in place the hay was recompressed about us to show no sign of disturbance, and the long ladder removed. When I eventually awakened the next day, snug and comfortable in the haystack, I found that the Besselinks had thought of everything in case we were compelled to remain there a few days: blankets, food and flasks of water, a necessary bucket, even a pile of picture magazines had been provided.

Our Dutch friends had been in bed for at least an hour following our entry into the haystack when the Germans surrounded the farmstead and carried out a quick search of the property and adjacent out-buildings. In reply to questioning, the elder Besselink informed the searchers that no hateful Englander had been around his place, and eventually the Germans clattered off.

CHAPTER 2

UNDERGROUND
MOVEMENT

For ten days we lived in the Besselinks' haystack, snug and well cared for, gradually recovering our strength. The good Besselinks looked after us unstintingly, dressing our wounds, bringing us B.B.C. news and arranging long talks around their fireside in the evening.

But as we grew fitter so our confinement became more and more wearisome. Jock fell into long silences and I could see from his face the nature of his thoughts. His wife in the Kyles of Bute was well advanced in pregnancy. Not unnaturally he was worried about her, and the effect which the fateful Air Ministry telegram might have produced. Only once did he speak of his anxiety.

'I don't want the lousy news of my being missing to affect the child,' he said. 'I pray that the kid will be sound in mind and limb.'

I, too, was itching to get on the quest for freedom.

Then, one rainy afternoon, John the journalist came to us. We were drowsing when he poked his head through the trapdoor and happily remarked: 'O.K., boys . . . I think all your troubles will soon be over.'

After many setbacks, John had gained access to the inner sanctum of the resistance movement, and had given them all our details. He was assured that a special agent would soon visit us.

Three days later the promised agent arrived. He was a man of fine build, fully six feet four in height, and with a pronounced military bearing. In flawless and cultured English he introduced himself as Peter, and courteously, but with an uncompromising air of stiffness, asked us to tell our story from the time we left our base. He listened with a slight suggestion of disinterested benevolence. When we had finished, he casually made a number of notes, and fired questions at us rapidly. Our private lives, the schools at which we had been educated, details concerning our parents, features of our birthplaces. More notes and still more questions. I was canny when the interrogation demanded information of a secret nature about Bomber Command policy and activities. I politely refused to answer certain questions on the pretext that they contravened R.A.F. rules and regulations. In the circumstances, however, we provided enough information for him to be able to check up on our flying careers and training.

'A successful escape back to Britain will entail lots of trouble and risk by many persons,' Peter told us. 'It is necessary to check conclusively every detail concerning yourselves. If we decide to help you, as Britishers your national honour and loyalty must keep you from ever divulging anything you may see, hear or learn about the Dutch underground movement. If you get hurt, as true Britishers you must never squeal. In all matters from now on I shall be known to you as "Tiny Peter". Obey all instructions implicitly. If there is delay, there is no need to get alarmed or upset.'

As the agent was talking he observed on my wrist an R.A.F. navigational watch.

'That, of course, is Government property,' he said. 'May I take it along with me?' Unwillingly, but without saying a word, I handed it over.

The interview with Tiny Peter brought results quicker than we had hoped for. Two days after his visit a smartly dressed woman, aged about twenty-six, came to see us.

'I am from Tiny Peter,' she told us with emphasis, and in perfect

English. She explained that it was wished that we should write about a thousand words each on what we believed would be the future course of the war. The essays would be collected that same evening when she returned.

'Oh . . . and Ginger,' she remarked lightly, 'you must have a short haircut this afternoon. Tiny Peter wants Mr Besselink to trim those golden locks.'

By the time she returned the essays had been completed, and my hair close-cropped. When we entered the farm parlour that evening, Tiny Peter's emissary was seated at the table with various small bottles in front of her. I was accorded a sweet smile, and informed that Tiny Peter wanted my hair dyed.

'Hell's teeth,' I murmured to Jock. 'Hair cropped in the afternoon, hair dyed after supper. Probably get a face massage before breakfast tomorrow.'

Using a small brush and some dark liquid she skilfully changed my red hair to dirty brownish black. Even my fairish eyebrows and lashes were similarly titivated. Jock, tickled pink at my colour alteration, laughed aloud.

Following the woman's visit, things really started to move. Instructions were given that we should leave the Besselink farm on the evening of the next day.

Before we stepped away from the Besselinks into the darkness of the night the whole family gathered together in the parlour to wish us God speed. It was a memorable farewell. Mevrouw Besselink had cooked a magnificent meal and John Agterkamp played his part nobly with a gift of two bottles of very good Moselle wine. The good Mevrouw cried unashamedly when we prepared to leave.

'I shall pray for you both every hour of every day,' she sobbed, 'until I know you have reached safety.'

We said goodbye and followed the journalist in the lee of a hedge until we reached the dirt road leading into the village. Once again we were venturing into the obscurity of a veiled future, but with a difference. Now we were strong and well, wounds were healed, and even if the future appeared a little frightening after the hospitality of the farm, it was inexpressibly satisfying to know that we were not adventuring alone, that solid Dutch friends were behind us.

Jock was experiencing a similar reaction to my own. 'Funny,' he whispered, 'when a guy is nicely laid up and everything laid on, he gets timid and reluctant to take his chances in the open again. Never imagined I'd feel shivery at hitting the trail again. How are you feeling?'

'From now on we represent Scottish and Yorkshire invincible hell let loose,' I told him. 'We'll soon get case-hardened.'

We reached our destination, a barn, without incident. Inside we found a supply of food and clothing which fitted remarkably well. Satisfied with our civilian appearance, John asked for the parcel of souvenirs, including a spoon bearing the Hengelo coat of arms – a gift to Mr Churchill – which the Besselink family had given to us. Nothing must be in our possession which might give the slightest clue as to our past whereabouts.

'Churchill will willingly wait for his spoon,' he remarked, and added: 'I will not be seeing you again.' As he prepared to leave, he said: 'It's been nice having you. The underground people are your guardians from now on. I do not know what future arrangements have been made for you both after you leave here in the morning, but rest assured you are in loyal and clever hands.'

He locked us in, and that was the last we ever saw of him or the other friends of Hengelo. But years later I learned that John

Agterkamp, the precise and slow-speaking newspaperman who had been so good to us, had been shot by the Germans.

It seemed an eternity before the rattle of a key in the lock signalled zero hour. The door opened a few inches only and we were addressed in perfect English by an unseen speaker.

'Are you both fit and ready to leave in a few minutes?'

'Yes,' I replied.

'Listen carefully to what I am about to tell you,' continued the speaker and then gave us detailed instructions, followed by a warning. 'Keep your mouths sealed if anything should go wrong. Tell the Germans that you stole your civilian clothes, also your cycles, and convince them that you have both been living from place to place. You cannot remember any names, neither have you ever been near Hengelo. When I say place to place, I mean you have travelled by your own wits and have not in any way received help from Dutch people. I am leaving now. Leave also in about two minutes.'

Slowly the seconds crawled by as I counted. Then we left. Jock led the way. Following instructions we walked straight to two bicycles, mounted nonchalantly and rode away.

We pedalled for at least ten minutes before a chiming bicycle bell behind told us that we were being overtaken. A man fitting the description given to us, cranked ahead. It was the guide all right . . . barge cap, black jacket, light blue pants and half his rear mudguard painted yellow. We kept our distance, cycling in silence. At one point we had to swerve wide of a stationary German transport. The enemy driver leaned against the bonnet of his vehicle, and surveyed us coldly as we pedalled past.

After the first dozen miles we felt a glow of adventure. It was interesting, if embarrassing, to pass quite a number of German troops. Light and heavy Wehrmacht transports passed us *en route* to and from Zutphen. Twice we were compelled to hug the kerb as screaming sirens heralded the approach of staff cars.

Maintaining a consistent ten miles an hour we cycled by neat Dutch houses and picturesquely clad Dutch folk, and it was approaching eleven o'clock when we finally approached the environs of the ancient town of Zutphen.

The stream of traffic deepened vexingly, and our guide became unavoidably engulfed in the flow of carts, trucks and an incredible volume of cyclists. Our man had just passed an important cross-road when a policeman on point-duty signalled us to stop to allow a flood of traffic to cross from the opposite side. It passed and he was on the point of beckoning us forward when a convoy of German lorries blared round a corner.

Truck followed truck, each packed with sitting Germans in their greenish uniforms, stiffly erect, rifles between their knees, and square steel helmets on their heads. Three escorting motorcyclists braked their machines a few paces in front of us and casually watched the lumbering transports sweep by. The riders looked diabolical in their padded leather suits and black knee-boots.

The convoy safely over the road intersection, we moved forward again, searching every yard of thoroughfare for our guide. It was an infuriating task dodging in and out of the crawling traffic as people bustled along the edge of the pavement and stepped aimlessly into the roadway.

Jock's keen eyes spotted him first. 'He's fifty yards ahead,' he whispered, 'near that green cart. He's smoking a pipe . . . can't possibly miss us.'

As I cycled slowly past him I tinkled my bell and was rewarded with an inscrutable gaze, but in less than a hundred yards he had resumed his position of leader.

56

From then on we disobeyed instructions by tagging on to his tail at a much closer distance: circumstances and common sense demanded it.

'We'll stick to blue pants like Spitfires on the tail of a Dornier,' I warned Jock.

Up one street and down the next we cycled to a baffling design. The congestion of people gradually thinned out, and we saw a bridge some distance in front of us. Instinctively we knew that our cycle journey was almost ended.

Blue pants dismounted, lazily propped his bike against the stone parapet, and with utter nonchalance gazed into the water twenty feet below. We also parked our cycles and peered indifferently downwards over the opposite parapet. A dozen yards from the end of the bridge four German soldiers roared with laughter in typical carefree off-duty manner.

'Let's have a cigarette,' I said to Jock in an undertone.

'Shut up and count the bloody fishes,' he hissed back.

We did not have to wait about long on the bridge before we spotted Tiny Peter approaching. His huge bulk was unmistakable. He paused alongside Jock to light a cigarette and, like a ventriloquist, softly instructed us to follow him at a distance of ten yards.

Street length after street length we trailed his tall figure, twice retracing our steps to pass the stately cathedral. Every now and again he paused to look idly into some shop window. Immediately we did the same.

After about an hour of this we found ourselves in a quiet, suburban, tree-lined avenue. In a secluded spot Tiny Peter slumped down on a bench. As we passed he smilingly remarked, 'O.K., fellows . . . come and join me.' We then received further instructions. We were to go the next stage by train – to Amsterdam.

Before we got moving I was given a soiled piece of dressing to stick over the corner of my mouth. Our caps had to be pulled well down, and we were to feign drowsiness as well as possible. If any passengers on the train happened to be Germans, and showed the slightest conversational friendliness, I was advised to pick my nose. Apparently the Germans had a very acute aversion to nose pickers. If we were arrested, we were to say that we had stolen our civilian clothes, as well as the money for our rail tickets, and that we had been wandering around Holland at random.

Again we had to give a sacred promise that on no account would we talk if arrested. We were reminded that any mention of our previous helpers would certainly spell a firing squad for them, and possible reprisals against the whole village of Hengelo.

At the station we mooched about for fifteen minutes before the train came in, carefully holding on to the tickets we had been given. And then occurred one of the nastiest shocks of the day. Two minutes before the train came in at least two hundred young Luftwaffe Germans marched on to the platform.

We lunged into the first compartment that stopped opposite us, some fifty yards to the right of the German airmen, and occupied the first two seats on the right-hand side of the carriage. Tiny Peter was happily placed four seats away on the opposite side.

The German airmen swarmed and scrambled along the corridors like a gush of troops on any British railway station. Two fine young Germans plumped into the two vacant seats opposite us. One of them reminded me strikingly of Stinker Sinclair, my old squadron buddy.

We wasted precious little time in pretending to be asleep, although in fact I paid close attention to the Germans' animated conversation as well as my understanding of the language would allow.

The two Germans – in fact the whole two hundred – had just passed out from bombing training school. They were on their way to augment squadrons based at Schiphol aerodrome.

'At last, *gegen* England,' one of them said. 'Now for a glimpse of London burning in my bombsight mirror.'

I felt the sweat rising, but attempted to console myself with the thought that it was only natural. I had dropped a tidy packet of British explosives on his bloody Berlin, and seen his beloved capital blazing in my own bombsight.

The rest of the German airmen were kicking up a hilarious din, and filling themselves on beer, bread and liver *Wurst* from their knapsacks. The man in front of me settled down after his food to read the newspaper. Every now and again he would repeat to his companion some item of news which tickled his interest. Winston Churchill had apparently been expressing himself in public speech, and his sentiments called forth the German's jeers and insults.

Suddenly I realised that I had unconsciously been staring at the German opposite. He laughed, and looked me directly, quizzically, straight in the face. I froze, and reacted to the situation by closing my eyes. Then I recalled Tiny Peter's advice and oafishly started to pick my nose.

A second later the open palm of the German caught me a resounding stinger on the side of my face. My head jerked back against the wooden rest.

'You filthy Dutch pig-dog,' he roared. 'We'll teach you barbarians manners!'

A sergeant came up to see what all the fuss was about. He laughed when the airman explained, and bestowed on me a dirty look as he moved back to his seat. I never opened my mouth, but I gleamed white inside. I wanted to lash my fist straight between his eyes.

The first leg of our journey lasted a nerve-racking eternity. Then our speed fell away as we neared a station and Tiny Peter dropped first his newspaper and then his pipe.

We entered the station, and followed our guide the length of the corridor. One young German, with a smirk on his face, intentionally stretched out his legs across the gangway. German wartime manners! We were, of course, grimy-looking civilians, and doubtless he had not forgotten his friend's slap across my face. The rest of the coach tittered. The cocky young German glowered at us with supercilious disgust. I stepped over his shiny jackboots with a hangdog expression. What did it matter, anyway? It was a means to an end.

The middle phase of the journey was less tense and dramatic. We followed Peter into a compartment filled mostly with civilians. Two happy Dutch schoolgirls chatted ingenuously on the two seats opposite but not a word was spoken in our direction. The final leg of the journey to Amsterdam was perhaps as haunting as the first.

A German *Feldwebel* sprawled on the seat opposite. His face carried a permanent look of flintlike glee. He was tough, and as hard as they make them anywhere, a born fighter, and capable of taking a tremendous hammering. He snorted to himself and fumbled in his pocket for matches to light a cigar but could not find any. Giving me a baleful look he spat, and said: '*Streichholz.*'

Without a murmur I handed him my box, and Jock and I closed our eyes and dozed.

It was late afternoon when eventually we pulled into a bustling Amsterdam railway station. We wasted no time in setting course when we left the train. For an hour and a half we followed ten yards behind Tiny Peter. He was nobody's fool, and he was making absolutely sure that we ourselves were not in turn being trailed.

It was almost dark when at last our guide slipped into a doorway standing a few yards back from the street.

'This is it,' grunted Jock.

We followed on Peter's heels into the darkness beyond the open door. Off the street I felt a thrilling sense of relief. It was like touching down safely at base after a long and hazardous flight. We stood close together for perhaps three or four minutes, in a small recess at the base of a staircase. Then Tiny Peter's voice broke the silence.

'Forewarned is forearmed, so hang on to every word,' he informed us. He lit three cigarettes before proceeding, handing one to Jock and one to me. 'You two are now British members of a Dutch subversive organisation, and every day is fraught with risk. You must accept the possibility of death or even worse . . . torture . . . but you must never squawk.' In a different tone of voice he continued: 'We Britishers have been taught to take it over the centuries. That's why there's still a Britain.' So he was British, this Tiny Peter. I had guessed as much.

'O.K., boys. That's all,' he said. 'Now come and meet Mr X and his most attractive daughter. I'm handing you over to them.'

Half-way up the stairs he paused and called out, '*Gewaltmarsch Depesche*' ['Forced march telegram'] and with a final 'Wait here and good luck,' he walked down the stairs and out into the street. It was the last we saw of him.

As the street door banged loudly, sealing us in the house, a door on the landing above opened and a pleasant English voice invited us to come in.

Mr X was a short, wiry, white-haired man. Something brilliant about his eyes conferred a distinction and trust on his countenance. Before the war Mr X was a foreign correspondent of one of the foremost national newspapers in Britain and when I told him of my own association with the British Press – I was on the *Yorkshire Post* – a bond of friendship was formed and for a time we exchanged animated newspaper gossip. Mr X had married a Dutchwoman and had lived in Holland and about the Continent for many years. Now, to all intents and purposes, he was a pukka Dutchman.

Mr X was one of the brains in the Dutch underground movement, and his twenty-two-year-old daughter, despite her sex and comparative youth, had achieved notable results against the Germans by her intelligence and daring. At University during the daytime, which she used as a guise to cloak her main activities, she was a veritable terror by night.

Her father told us of her exploits, including one episode during which she had played an exciting and important role in stealing a seaplane which had enabled a Dutch nobleman to escape to Britain from under the Germans' noses.

Miss X prepared an excellent meal and afterwards we drank a toast in a fine hock recently stolen from a German officers' mess. It was a toast to an Allied victory and Mr X, smiling, added: 'To your virtually guaranteed return to Britain within a couple of months.'

He went on: 'While you are waiting you will probably be called on to engage with certain teams in duties both distasteful and risky. But such activities are an inevitable part of the underground game.'

I listened with horror as he made himself clear. 'Getting acclimatised to organised killing is not agonising. The circumstances make it permissible. After the first death you will feel nothing but the thrill of achievement.'

I questioned his philosophy fiercely. The thought of placidly taking life was repulsive to fair play and decency. But Mr X was right.

During my three years in Europe I did kill, I had to kill or be killed. And Mr X's assurances that repulsion would vanish after the first killing of one of Hitler's uniformed thugs was true. Personal tautness – 'stab-fright' the underground men called it – disappeared as the knife vanished into the soft flesh with a velvety glide. As it was withdrawn there came a feeling of calm exhilaration.

When I had become experienced, I always preferred the knife. Strangulation was sweaty and rough-shod and shooting has no personality. By comparison the knife is clean and respectable.

Suddenly, as we talked, the telephone shrilled. Mr X answered the caller in monosyllables but I knew that the conversation related to Jock and myself. As he replaced the receiver, Mr X said: 'Sorry, but you must change stations immediately. You will follow a short distance behind me.'

We left the home and tagged along behind Mr X in the cold night air. We did not have far to walk, not more than thirty minutes at medium pace. Then Mr X entered the gates of a large and pretentious house. At the end of the drive he turned to us.

'This is your rendezvous,' he said. 'I shall leave you here. Ring six times . . . quick bursts. Goodbye.'

Pausing on the front step, I whispered to Jock, 'Variegated fate, eh . . . haystack to mansion?'

Our ring was quickly answered, and our welcome was pleasant and genuine. Mr and Mrs B. were people of good breeding, and accustomed to the better things of life.

Our new quarters were delightful. Mr B., a leading professional man in Amsterdam, was a person of prestige and social standing. He had successfully convinced the Germans that he was strongly anti-British and consequently he was off the list of local suspects.

His wife, a charming woman, about thirty-five years of age, was a perfect linguist. Apparently her genealogical tree was traceable to a once noted personality in British politics.

Their lovely home was a Jekyll and Hyde establishment, a pivot of power and intelligence in the system of underground control and administration.

At dinner one night we were introduced without warning to a Mr and Mrs Leonhardt, a delightful couple who told us that we were to leave with them after the meal.

Billy, as we called Mr Leonhardt, told us that Gestapo were down in force from Berlin to comb out the haunts of Amsterdam and maintain the strict vigil, day and night, on all the canals.

'Oddly enough,' he chuckled to me, 'they are anxious to locate a person with a face similar to yours.'

We departed in a small car, the fuel for which was supplied from a monstrous gas-filled container affixed to the roof. Zonal police stopped us on the city boundary but our papers were in perfect order and the remainder of the journey to Laren, not far from Hilversum, was without interruption or incident.

Our new home was idyllic, set in spacious grounds and completely screened by large trees. We lived royally, but my days were not spent idly. I spent considerable time transcribing, in secret code, information which would be of value to Britain. It was executed in a harmless-looking Dutch-English language book.

While we were with the Leonhardts, Jock and I were told of some of the brilliant sabotage activities of Dutch workers at the big radio factory a few miles distant and the exact location of German bomb dumps in the area. Troop and transport train movements were recorded and the best spots worked out for destroying them and dislocating transport.

All the latest information about Luftwaffe radio devices came into my hands, technical developments which were superior to our own at that stage of the war. It was even arranged that I should visit the factory, disguised as a workman, and inspect certain important work.

Just before we left Laren trouble flared up. Special investigators and Gestapo police flooded the factory and the district in search of saboteurs and their arrival hastened our departure.

At dinner that night I noticed that Billy was decidedly nervous and worried. When Jock and I were with him in the library I was told to take down from the bookshelf a medium-sized volume.

'Look inside,' Billy said.

In a small cavity hollowed out of the pages was an automatic pistol.

'If the Germans investigating at the factory find out about our activities,' Billy said, 'I shall not hesitate to shoot my wife and then myself. But if I am shot first and Mona is still alive, I rely on one of you.' He tapped the pistol significantly. 'We've known the finest men crack up under Gestapo inquisition.'

That night we attached a coiled rope to our bedroom window. If the Germans made a quick approach the dogs would give us fair warning and we would be able to jump outwards and downwards among the trees.

It was an uneasy night, and next morning we were still sweating on the top line at the prospect of a total purge at the factory, but fate decreed that we left the danger zone just before the Germans turned on the heat and made scores of arrests. Mr X, the Amsterdam underground man, unexpectedly arrived with a tall stranger.

'I bring you good tidings,' he said. 'If all goes as planned, you'll both leave for the United Kingdom tonight. A submarine is to rendezvous off the coast west of Leyden.'

We were given no time to discuss this staggering information. In fact, we were speeding away from the Leonhardts' home within fifteen minutes of Mr X's arrival.

Before I got into the waiting car I strapped my innocuous-looking language-cum-code book to the inside of my thigh, and slipped my knife into my pocket. It was a leader's knife of the Hitler Youth Movement, with an embossed swastika on its blade.

I remained outwardly calm as the car moved off and I waved farewell to Mona, but it was an effort not to allow my face to mirror my feelings. It was the last we ever saw of her. A few days later Mona and Billy were arrested and sentenced to death. The death sentences were commuted to life imprisonment and for almost four years they existed in the horrors of a concentration camp. I heard from them after the war. They were in Nova Scotia, Canada, and in spite of terrible suffering were happily making quick strides back towards health, and contemplating a new life in either Jamaica or Bermuda.

Our journey to Amsterdam was uneventful. The tall stranger drove the car, and remained uncommunicative. Mr X gave us very few details about our scheduled trip to Britain but we were reminded that decent weather was vital to the success of our night's adventure. If a heavy sea mist settled, all liaison between coast intelligence and submarine would break down. I prayed for the right proportions of mist so that all the necessary signals could be safely effected.

The knowledge that we would be back in Britain within twenty-four hours was shattering. It was tremendously wonderful news. Jock's face was pale with suppressed excitement but his only comment was: 'I guess that new baby of mine will soon get used to having his pappa fooling around with him.'

As we approached the boundaries of Amsterdam, Mr X informed us that we would not leave the city for at least a couple of hours. 'We have to call at a friend's house,' he told us, 'to pick up identity cards and various zonal papers to get us safely through to Leyden.'

Such a trip demanded a special briefing, he added, as it was a tricky journey. We must drive past the closely guarded Schiphol aerodrome *en route* to the coast, and the utmost alertness would be required. From this aerodrome German aircraft were taking off day and night to bomb Britain and the place was thick with Gestapo police, security officers and troops.

In a quiet suburb of Amsterdam we alighted from the car and entered a small, neat home, where we were introduced to a man with a remarkably agile face, a cripple tied to a bath chair.

He was the forger of all underground movement papers, and his bath chair and paralysed legs provided him with a certain freedom from German suspicion. He was a brilliant artist; his penmanship was absolute perfection. His friends, who were printers, worked with him in secret collaboration, and a block-making concern also assisted his efforts. From him we received our passports, zonal papers and factory workers' identity cards.

He asked that we should let him see everything in our possession. The coded Dutch-English language book which was to accompany me to Britain was carefully scrutinised. After a few minutes of solemn assessment, he wheeled himself over to a small cupboard and removed two or three small bottles.

'I'm going to run over some of your markings,' he informed me. 'The Germans are no fools. This solution will temporarily obliterate everything.'

He uncorked a small bottle. My face must have registered a

67

quick flash of distrust, because he added: 'There's no need for any suspicion. Here . . . I'll do a test piece for you.'

Carefully he spotted certain letters in a number of words – words which bore minute scratchings which had taken me hours to inscribe. He allowed the solution to dry before inviting me to pick out the letters I had used in my code. I could not . . . all the printed letters were exactly the same.

'Now we will counteract the solution,' he said, without looking up. He applied another liquid. All my minute and original scratchings were intact. After an hour's work he returned to me the treated code book.

Mr X looked at Jock and me with a resolute grin. 'Pocket your papers carefully,' he told us. 'We're on our way. Our next stop will be Schiphol aerodrome, and we have to keep our fingers crossed.'

As we made towards the door, the tall, lean driver tapped the pocket which held my sheathed knife.

'Please leave it here,' was all he said.

As we neared Schiphol airfield Jock muttered: 'My God. . . . What a smart organisation these Jerries must have to handle such a volume of air traffic. I've never seen anything like it.'

Nor had I. Aircraft were everywhere, some nose up in take off, others nose down for landing. Fighters in profusion roared all over the sky, dodging in and out of lumbering Junker 52 transports in formations of three. It was a revealing picture of Luftwaffe strength and organised activity.

'Steady, boys, don't flutter,' Mr X commented. 'There's a German road block coming up.'

On either side of the road stood formidable concrete gun nests, and lowered in position across the road were two white-painted poles. A squad of German soldiers in square steel helmets decorated the scene. Their jackboots were bright and shiny, and across their chests they hugged tommy guns in a most professional manner. The tommy guns pointed at us in concerted movement as we halted twenty yards from the barrier. A tall officer with a Hitler moustache detached himself from the group and strode towards us.

'Good day, officer, *heil Hitler*,' Mr X said.

'*Heil Hitler*,' the German replied with automatic guttural precision, clicking his heels and giving the Nazi salute. His face was a mixture of pompous importance and hard efficiency.

'Papers,' he snapped. 'Where are you going? What is your business? Who owns this vehicle?'

Without a trace of confusion, Mr X answered as he handed over our papers, 'We are workers at Philips Radio Factory, Section Four, *en route* for Leyden. The Military Technical Control has ordered us to the coast to carry out repairs on a beacon transmitter. This car is factory registered, and we have all the necessary papers from the Amsterdam movement control office.'

A careful scrutiny of our papers followed, and then the driver was asked to show his licence and authorised petrol vouchers.

'*Ach* . . . so you are *deutsch*?' remarked the interrogator to our driver. '*Ja*,' answered our man, and for the next few minutes animated pleasantries were exchanged. The masquerade of our Dutch driver as a German national was a well-planned move. It made the officer less formal.

'How are you liking your duties in Holland?' the officer asked.

The driver retorted with a wry grin, 'Oh . . . much better when I get my *Frau* along to join me from Duisberg.'

The officer winked and rasped out, '*Quatsch*' (an Army term for piffle), chuckled, and continued: 'You are young. Do not forget *in der Nacht sind alle Katzen grau.* [In the night all cats are grey.] Mix your love, my friend, while you have good opportunity.'

We all chuckled as naturally as possible.

Without further comment the officer strode off towards the concrete guard-room. The guns covering us never wavered for a second. He was absent five minutes or more with our papers and as each minute passed I felt as though I was sitting on a high-voltage plate.

Even the imperturbable Mr X showed signs of uneasiness as the minutes ticked by.

'Anything at all rather than he should phone Leyden,' he muttered to the driver.

At last the officer reappeared, and ordered us all to climb out of the car. A personal search was conducted, and we were adroitly patted for arms.

'Please get back into the car,' instructed the officer, satisfied that we were not in the possession of any weapons. He examined our papers for half a minute longer. 'All is in order,' he announced, 'except that you have no voucher authorising the conveyance of German tools from the Amsterdam Control Office, whereas the Technical Control Department say you have been loaned two boxes of instruments, thirty-seven pieces in all. Show them to me.'

The boxes were removed from the boot. Each individual tool had the German insignia stamped upon it.

'In future,' the officer rapped, 'check up and see you carry all necessary papers.' He strode back to the blockhouse without another word.

'Phew!' murmured our driver. 'We nearly missed out with the tool business.'

A sergeant appeared and motioned us forward. He handed Mr

X a green paper. 'You will pass through Numbers 2, 3 and 4 barriers on presentation of this document,' he said. 'If you have any mechanical reason to halt between posts on no account leave your car. Remain seated until you are approached by the motor-cycle patrol. Drive at fifteen kilometres an hour.' He stepped back a pace and gave the Hitler salute.

'Heil Hitler,' we proclaimed as we drove off.

In spite of the paper handed to us at the first post – the most important one of the series – at each subsequent post we were again asked various questions. Each post seemed to be vying with the other in efficiency.

At the final barrier we were asked to give the name of the place at which we were scheduled to stay in Leyden. Mr X handed over the official vouchers entitling us to board at factory workers' Hostel Number Five. They passed us, and the last obstacle cleared, we breathed more easily.

'Here,' Mr X exclaimed heartily, 'what we have just experienced merits a cigar.' He took four from his pocket and handed them around.

About seven miles from Schiphol aerodrome, three Messerschmitt fighters were doing low-flying aerobatics. The centre one, showing yellow wing-tips, streaked down on us in the same kind of crazy mock attack that so many British fighter boys gloried in performing despite all Air Ministry instructions to the contrary.

The German pilot skimmed across our path with a frightening roar, and then he heaved the joy-stick back too sharply. The nose of the aircraft pulled up almost to the vertical, climbed a short distance and stalled, lost all speed, and nosed straight into the ground. There was an explosion, and a sheet of crimson flame.

'Keep moving fast,' yelled Mr X to the driver. He turned around and grinned at us. 'That,' he commented, 'adequately offsets our embarrassment at their confounded guard posts . . . a German pilot less as the result of our journey to Leyden.'

The road veered to the right, and a pall of smoke from the burning machine was visible above the trees. The driver took a side-long glance at it.

'Burn, you bastard, burn,' he said.

CHAPTER 3

ARREST!

We arrived at a small dwelling in a suburb of Leyden in broad daylight. I was not too happy. There were too many neighbours' windows scowling down on us.

The man and his wife charged by the underground to get us off the coast that night were introduced. Our young host was full of smiling affability; his wife was of a quiet and serious disposition. The husband, before the war, had been a well-known figure in horse-training circles, and we were given to understand from Mr X that his gay and flippant manner belied an iron character and keen energy for activities against the Germans.

'You are in good hands,' he told us with assurance. 'Others have been safely launched to freedom. It will be done again.'

I was prompted to view the weather with increasing anxiety.

'Conditions outside are not too rosy,' I remarked.

Drake, as we had been asked to call the young man, replied that he would get us off no matter what rain conditions were, but if thick fog descended it would be completely impossible to contact the submarine. Signal and counter signal had to take place, and the safety of the submarine must not be jeopardised by impatience.

Quietly I implored the favour of Heaven, but Heaven must have been in a bad mood because my silent request was unavailing. Fog wreathed about the houses and up the street when Mr X and the driver left us. I felt sick at our bad luck. Jock hardly spoke a word.

Outside it grew dark, and the fog deepened. With difficulty Jock and I assumed a brave air of complacency. Then we were suddenly startled by the sharp ringing of the front door bell.

'Open the back door,' Drake said quickly to his wife. 'If need be, take the boys to M's, and lock the room door before I open the front door.'

For five minutes we listened to the dull drifts of conversation from the hall. Then Drake called out, 'O.K., dear . . . all's well.'

He came back and told us about the interview in the hall. 'The submarine cannot rendezvous in the area tonight, but that's only a temporary setback. If the weather permits, tomorrow night it will return. It has happened before. Once we had to wait around for six nights before contact could be effected. You will remain in this house.'

We nestled about the fire, but it required a strong drink to foster a little cheer. Conversation was not very animated. Then Drake struck his thigh, and brightly exclaimed: 'Boys, what about a cinema show tonight?' He insisted that the risk was negligible. Of course, Germans would be all over the cinema, but we would be unmolested. We would sit inconspicuously between him and his wife, and there would be no need for any conversation.

Drake's breezy assurance bolstered our morale, and we all walked to the cinema some fifteen minutes away. Drake got tickets for seats at the back, and Jock and I sandwiched ourselves in between our host and his wife.

Enemy personnel were scattered about everywhere, and it was interesting to observe German reaction to what was going on on the screen. A film about the Eastern Front was running, and one could detect winces from them as they saw German soldiers hanging grotesquely from Russian trees on Russian ropes. There was a feeling of bewildered hate in the atmosphere, and the place was electrically alive. The revolting Russian incidents at first aroused a buzz, and then a whirl of vocal fury; many loud and distinct imprecations could be heard.

The main feature film revealed a German sense of humour as weird as it was wearying. Into the structure of the film the British were dragged and I flushed at the Jerry's depiction of an effete race and squirmed at the coarse, contemptuous chuckles from the German onlookers.

Unwisely, we left the cinema before the show ended. We should have remained and joined in the anthem: *'Deutschland über Alles'*. Nearing the house where we were staying, a heavy man hurried around the corner and murmured *'Goeden Nacht.'*

'I wonder who the hell he is?' Drake muttered uneasily.

Jock and I were shown to our quarters after a bite of supper. In the attic, a mattress and blankets had been placed on the floor.

'Keep smiling,' Drake said as he bade us good night. 'All being well, by this time tomorrow you will both be fathoms under the surface ploughing your way across the North Sea to Britain.'

I did not undress. I felt far too uneasy. Neither Jock nor I spoke of our personal misgivings. Across the length of our experiences together a subtle understanding had developed.

A variety of town clocks chimed the hours . . . one, two, three, four. I resisted sleep. In my mind I was acutely apprehensive, and sleep savoured of unpreparedness. Even the medley of chimes from the clocks echoed my concern. But with dawn I was falling into snatches of drowsiness.

A confusion of voices brought me out of bed with a start. Commotion had suddenly broken loose outside. Yelling guttural voices were accompanied by battering thuds on the outside door.

I looked out of the window. 'Christ!' I yelled to Jock. 'Quick!'

75

The entire street was guarded by steel-helmeted Germans, rifles and sub-machine-guns poised at the ready.

'We're trapped like rats!' Jock croaked. 'Quick . . . let's try the other side of the house . . . maybe the roof.'

But we were too late. The street door splintered and feet pounded along the passage downstairs.

'Into bed . . . pretend you're asleep. Don't move,' I said, just before a black-uniformed German burst into the attic.

A Mauser pistol covered us. 'Out of that bed,' the German screamed and fired two shots into the wall between our heads. 'Stand up against the wall, you pig-dogs,' he bellowed, 'and raise your arms above your heads.'

We got up and pressed our backs to the wall. The German was sheet white with suppressed emotion, and his trigger hand was shaking alarmingly. I realised that if that jittering idiot uncontrollably squeezed the trigger, it was shrouds for us. I also noticed that the captor was more scared than the captives, and I felt a glow of a challenging anger.

'*Verdammt*, you dumb-headed fool!' I blared. 'You're making a mistake. Point that pistol downwards . . . point it downwards! Where is the *Fuehrer-Offizier*?'

Intentionally I spoke to him as I knew German soldiers were addressed by their superior officers; hysterically, scornfully and with eyes aflame. It worked. He was like a fish out of water, and his twitching gun hand steadied as if by magic.

'*Deutscher Soldat!*' I spat. 'Use your head and report us to your commanding officer, or it'll be a *Straflager* for you.'

The soldier looked stunned. I had played my ace card. In a subdued voice he replied: 'Please will you walk ahead of me, and I will take you to the officer?'

On the landing below, two Germans were posted by the room occupied by Drake and his wife. We were led to the lounge. Drake entered after us with a gun pushed in his ribs. He raised his eyebrows slightly at us as if to say 'Sorry . . . bad luck.' His wife was grey with anxiety but superbly collected.

The officer addressed us. 'We have grounds for believing that you are spies,' he announced. 'You are under close arrest.'

We were searched for arms. Off came our jackets and shoes. My coded book was strapped to my thigh up in my crutch. I was sweating as the searcher started patting my legs upwards from the ankles. I knew I was a certainty for a firing squad if they discovered that book. When the searcher's hands were close to the book I did a wet sneeze on his forehead. He jumped up wickedly, and I mustered up the most amazed stare as I exclaimed '*Mein Gott*, aren't you like Rudolph Hess!' I could feel the beads of perspiration pricking me.

'What are you trying to get at, you blasted *engländer*?' the German snarled. 'All of you stand over by that wall. If you move, you will be shot.'

Luftwaffe police appeared on the scene and took guard while the Gestapo searched the house. We could hear them thumping about overhead, and pulling out drawers.

A small, scholarly officer started the interrogation. We stuck to the story we had been primed to give in the event of capture and told him that we were British fliers who had crashed on the border. He was surprised and wanted to know where and what we had been doing since the crash. I told him that we had been wandering all over the country, stealing food, clothes and money, and sleeping where we could. I gave him names of towns and villages which had never seen us, and explained that it was impossible to furnish any names and addresses of the few folk who had given us food as we had never had them.

I was lying with cold cunning, and the officer knew that I was lying. He kept looking up from his notebook and nodding his shaven head in a mocking, disbelieving manner. Until the end of the questioning he never disputed our statements.

'How did you come to this house?' he asked. 'How did you come by the excellent civilian clothes you are both wearing?'

'We stole the clothes from a shop,' I answered. 'In desperation we came to this house early in the morning asking for food.' Turning to Drake I continued: 'These people advised us to hand ourselves over to the police. I gave them our promise that we would after sleeping. But we were so tired.' Glaring at Drake, I added as scathingly and as realistically as I could: 'You might have given us a bite of breakfast before bringing the police in.'

Drake informed the officer that he would have told the police of our presence sooner, but as his wife was sick, and as we were threatening and demanded to stay, he dared not leave her alone with us. He was pleased that the police had arrived. Doubtless some neighbour had seen him signalling, and had brought them along.

'My wife wanted me to lock them in the attic,' he went on, 'but I didn't want to arouse their suspicions and create any danger in my home.'

The officer wrote on in silence, then closed his notebook with a snap, and carefully pocketed his gold pencil. Turning to me, and looking full into my face, he remarked leisurely: 'You are a lousy English liar. You are all treacherous swine. You professed English fliers have been arrested in civilian clothes. You, therefore, have no recourse to prisoner-of-war protection.' He chuckled. 'Doubtless

we shall shoot you all tomorrow. Of course,' he added as an afterthought, 'if you provide truthful answers to our questions, and tell
us where you have lived and what you have been doing, it is quite
likely that we will permit you to live on. It is up to you.'

We were ordered to sit down, facing their revolvers. I studied
everything, the Germans, the room, the window, the coal shed
outside and the possibility of a rapid plunge through the glass and
away. But one thing curbed my desire for any window hurtling. If
I were dropped by a bullet the coded book in my groin would be
discovered and such condemning evidence would spell disaster for
us all.

Somehow I had to dispose of that code-book. But how? The
problem was maddening. Then I got the answer. The lavatory, of
course! Humbly I asked the officer if I could use the lavatory.

'Can't you wait?' he asked.

'I've waited since early this morning,' I replied meekly. 'It is
urgent, please . . . I appeal to your gentlemanly understanding.'

Addressing his comrades he rapped out: 'Guard him carefully.'
He beckoned me to rise. Outside the lounge he opened the closet
door, examined the interior carefully for a window and, satisfied
that there was no opening for escape, he gestured me to go inside.
The door was closed to within a few inches, and the officer stood
by watching my movements.

Slowly I unbuttoned my pants, and as I slipped them down I gripped
the thin code-book in my right hand under the cloth of my breeches.
I sat there, realistically bent on the urgent business for which I had
supposedly come, and smuggled the book into the water of the pan.
But, somehow, I had to get my hand into the basin and ram the papers
up the bend in the pipe.

'Close the door, please,' I said to the smirking watcher, 'it is most embarrassing you standing there. Are not the Germans gentlemen?'

'Hurry,' was the reply. 'You English are not so constipated with your tongues.'

The door was pushed closed, just short of the latch clicking. With the German's face no longer visible I thrust both hands between my legs as I sat in a crouching position. I ripped the pages of the code-book into small pieces, and then still smaller pieces, and then fragments. It took about thirty seconds. I turned and scooped up handfuls of the bits and rammed them up the slimy closet pipe as far as my hand and forearm could reach and stuffed all of it out of sight.

Then I heaved on the chain. The water swirled, flushed and started to build up in the basin. I had jammed it too tight, and it was not dispersing. I forced my arm so far up the pipe I thought it would snap. There was a sucking intake, and the water and the paper pieces of the tell-tale book had returned and were floating on the water. My dry mouth was an encouragement to ingenuity. I scooped up the remnants of the paper and stuffed them into my mouth.

I was bent over the lavatory pan, gulping and chewing, my trousers round my ankles, when the German opened the door. In a flash he knew full well that I was up to some mischief, and he charged me with a hiss of dumbfounded fury. He lashed my chewing mouth with his fist, but this only expedited my swallowing the cloying mass. Berserk, he fired into the lavatory pan and scores of porcelain splinters flew off. A piece of paper, one piece, floated on the water, and he stooped to take possession of it but I beat him to it by jerking on the chain. Water gushed over his tunic sleeve, and the last piece of evidence hastened towards the sewer.

Fuming, white hot with rage, the German drove his fist into my Adam's apple. Mistily I listened to a hell's tattoo of blind rage screams and an avalanche of noise from the street as half a dozen guards tore into the house to investigate the shots. Now what, I wondered. The thwarted officer glared at me. I instinctively ducked as he raised his arm and fired. The bullet smacked into the plaster.

Luckily, the other Germans crowding in saved my bacon, and two of them ushered me into the living-room. Drake, his wife and Jock were ashen. I readjusted my trousers and managed to sneak a grin.

When the officer re-entered the room he had adopted an expression of icy calm. 'Swine!' he snapped. 'You have chosen for yourself the choicest agony.' He waggled his gun, and added: 'No, not this clean, quick, bullet agony.' His eyes glared at each one of us in turn.

Now he was taking no chances with me. I was moved from my chair to a position with my back hard against the wall. Then the heavy dining-table was pushed up against my ribs, and I had to rest my hands, wide apart, on its polished surface.

Meanwhile, the Gestapo carried on with their house searching, after which they had in their possession evidence which would certainly sentence to death my civilian friends. The cellar produced about four hundred rounds of ammunition, and papers in tins. From upstairs, the snoopers excitedly spread out papers on the table and made notes.

Drake was deathly white, almost green about the eyes, and his wife kept her head bowed.

'What a find,' tittered the officer.

Guards were brought into the room and given strict instructions. They saluted and departed. An hour later two of them returned

81

with a young Dutchman who showed a bruised eye and a bleeding lip. He was a solicitor, and a member of the underground organisation. A few minutes later the postman delivered letters which were promptly opened. The officer hissed and chuckled and gave immediate orders for the street to be cleared of guards.

'No suspicion must be aroused,' he ordered. 'A very important caller is due here with a motor-car to take away our English guests.'

The officer ordered that certain things be done to the front window as detailed in the letter – obviously a pre-arranged safety signal. Guards were also instructed to commandeer the house opposite, to cover our front door and to fire if any stranger attempted a break away in a motor-car.

A little later, we heard a car drive up and stop outside our door. A loyal underground worker strode into the room. Tense with despair and sickness, we watched him challenged and arrested. He was searched and a pistol and papers were taken from him. He was a tall, handsome man, and as he looked around his eyes smouldered in a white face. He refused to answer a single question put to him by the officer.

'Revolvers are forbidden to civilians,' purred the officer. 'I am sure you must know that our penalty is death. You will die unless you explain your position.'

Some hours later there arrived at the house four military staff cars, bringing eight Gestapo officials, who entered the room with a certain formal grace. The cocksure little officer who had been the high and mighty kingpin since our early morning arrest, now appeared as a mangy, grovelling underling. He stood rigidly to attention before his superior officers, a scared and frightened rat before his faultlessly attired chiefs, all of whom seemed to bear the same implacable expressions on their faces.

It seemed crazy to me that I was actually face to face with the infamous Gestapo in a tiny parlour in Holland. I had read of the Gestapo back home long before the outbreak of war; I knew of its terrifying powers; its cruelties, how this pitiless force of men had subjugated a nation of 88,000,000 by fear and threat, but it had all been a world away. Now they had grabbed me also, and I felt hopeless and sweaty.

After a brief conference with the squirt of a little officer in the next room, one of them addressed me in perfect, soft, refined English.

'You and your friend are to be taken to The Hague for further questioning,' he remarked. 'And may I remind you to behave yourselves and cause us no inconvenience. I learn that you have been disorderly and abused a privilege which was kindly accorded to you in respect of the lavatory.'

Another member of the holy order had a say also, and his accent was almost Cambridge. 'You must realise,' he said, 'that no military respect or grace is possible as neither of you is officially related to any British military section or unit. You have no identification whatsoever and your word is hardly sufficient to qualify our treatment of you according to the Geneva Convention. You are classed as espionage agents.'

Into the rear of a staff car we were herded, a guard on either side of us. Pistols were attached to the wrists of our escort by small chains. The civilians piled into a second vehicle.

As we moved away from the ill-fated little house, the swastika pennant on the bonnet fluttering in the breeze, neighbours looked on, scared and frigid, from surrounding windows. Motor-cyclists took up escort positions when we turned into the main thoroughfare, their wailing sirens clearing a patch for us like a scythe, and we tore off towards The Hague at high speed. No other civilian transport was allowed to move, and many vehicles were pulled into the roadside under armed guard.

It struck me that the Germans were on to something of importance, and in the general sort out had somehow dropped on us; or else our capture was treated as a major operation. We were halted at six different road blocks, at one of which a German major sneeringly commented to the driver: *Kröte* [toad] *engländer.'*

The Hague was guarded by marines, and as the cars pulled up before the big front door of Gestapo Headquarters they sprang to attention. We passed through the big entrance, and were escorted upstairs, where Jock and I were separated.

Under the scrutiny of an armed guard I was taken into a small oak-panelled room. I was ordered back against the wall, and my arms were outstretched, my fingers easing the weight of my arms by gripping the beading of the panels above my head.

Directly in front of me there was a large portrait of Adolf Hitler, and I was compelled to stare eye to eye with it for three-quarters of an hour. The perspiration ran off my chin and my arms seemed paralysed. The guard neither moved nor spoke, the tommy gun in his hands flickering slightly about my head. Hitler seemed to possess more life than the German in the room. The picture had uncanny stoat-like qualities; I gazed transfixed. Even the Fuehrer's ears seemed to twitch. Had it not been for the roar and reverberations from German dive-bombers pouncing on the building in low-flying mock attack, I felt as if my brain would have melted. Balls of red danced between my eyes and those of Hitler, and apart from the clarity of the painting the rest of the room seemed misty.

But roaring aircraft engines spelt reality, and I seethed and writhed against the wall. I was determined that no Hitler painting was going to blur my senses in this original Gestapo technique for lowering morale. I closed my eyes.

'Open your eyes, and obey the Fuehrer,' snapped the guard standing by the window.

I opened my eyes and gazed again at Hitler. A red light flashed in the corner of the room, and I was ordered to lower my arms and march.

I found myself in the sanctum of a Gestapo investigator, a small man with piercing eyes, grey hair and, to crown it all, a Hitler moustache.

'Well . . . well . . . Mr Civilian Englishman,' he said in perfect English. 'I have lots to say to you, and I know you have lots to tell me.' He invited me to sit down. 'Now let's forget animosities,' he continued, 'and enjoy a friendly pow-wow. You will have a good meal when we are finished . . . if you speak the entire truth . . . and I must remind you that in so doing you will best be serving your own interests.'

For a few minutes he stared at me with half-closed eyes, and I stared back unflinchingly. What kind of process was being applied now?

'You smoke, *engländer?*' he murmured, as if drowsing off to sleep. 'Then you must try one of my cigars.' Almost gently he took from his pocket a cigar case, flicked it open and with suave politeness offered it to me.

'No, thank you,' I answered.

'But,' he said, 'I insist you smoke with me, my English friend. I assure you they are not poisonous.'

I took a cigar, and as I slowly removed the band I tried desperately to work out what was likely to follow.

'And here is a light for you,' he said, and an outstretched arm came across the desk.

The cigar was good, and I inhaled deeply.

Leisurely the German rose and walked round the desk to my side. He was narrow shouldered, and his cheek showed sabre slashes. I felt big by the side of him. Without any warning his hand cut across my face and sent the cigar flying across the room.

'But, my English friend,' he said. 'You forget that you have told me nothing. How can you expect to smoke in peace with me. It's not done, is it?' Measuring his steps and puffing his own cigar, he returned to his chair and pressed a bell button on his desk. A soldier came into the room instantly. 'Bring this gentleman a carafe of water and a glass,' he ordered. It was duly brought in and placed by my side. 'Do drink,' the German said, almost imploringly.

My gullet was dry and parched but I replied: 'I am not thirsty, thank you.'

'I request, nay I order you, to take a little water,' was the next remark. 'You look uncomfortably warm.'

I raised the glass to my mouth, but barely had I time to swallow any of the contents before his fist crashed on the desk. In a very different tone of voice, he screamed: 'Put that glass down!' I obeyed, and in his former oily way I was told that I could hardly expect to refresh myself on German hospitality when I had not told him anything.

I realised that this was a plan to break my nerve, and that cut the danger of folding up by half. The interrogation lasted for two hours at least. I gave rank, number and name, and the names of the other members of the crew, explaining that they could be checked up on somewhere in Germany. I lied and continued to lie about my movements and activities in Holland, and stuck to the story I had given to the interrogating officer when I was captured. I avoided all names of people and places where we had actually stayed.

The interviewer alternated his questioning between slimy cajolement, dire threat, screaming hysteria and silky enticement. I was given a final slanging and threatening before I was led off to another room along the corridor.

The second interrogator was a very tall German, impeccably smart, and possessing a strong handsome face with very thin lips. He plied the questions fast and furious about the Stirling which I had navigated, and I was astounded at his technical knowledge about aircraft, especially about four-engined units in Britain. At that time the Germans were anxious to know all about Britain's first multi-motored bomber.

I maintained an inscrutable face, but some of his disclosures were shattering, and after listening to him for a while, I concluded that somewhere on or about my aerodrome at Wyton, in Huntingdonshire, there was a German informer. If my Wing Commander could over-hear these remarks, I thought, wouldn't he just comb out the personnel and make them keep their mouths closed when they hit the liquor bottle!

For some unaccountable reason, the subject of conversation was abruptly switched to matters political and economic. The man opposite me seemed to know his facts well, and his words were carefully weighed and measured. After talking for a while on a specific subject, he would fire a series of questions at me. I replied slowly, thinking hard all the time. I was baffled; obviously it was some smart game. I was told of Britain's meekness when she nodded to the Germans' repudiation of the terms of the treaty of Versailles. I was asked to explain why the Bank of England issued huge sums of capital to a former enemy when Britain must have known that such money would never be repaid.

'Please tell me,' inquired the German, 'why did your country act so detrimentally to her prestige?'

After about ninety minutes of this discussion, suddenly I rumbled that the smart German was assessing my general knowledge in order to see if it was in keeping with the mental versatility of a British agent.

'In this war,' I was informed, 'we shall not make the same mistake as in 1914. We have ignored the principle of respecting the neutrality of lesser countries. This conflict sees the whole of Europe harnessed for employment for Germany – one vast workshop in the interests of our war machine, and the food production potentiality of the entire field forced to ensure against starvation. If your country enters into bacteriological warfare we shall do the same. But we are in the fortunate position of decentralisation.' Without a pause he fired the question: 'Will Britain in your estimation resort to this?'

The sonorous, testing, searching voice went on and on. I was tired, hungry and thirsty, and the effort at caution was being strained to the limit. How much longer was this bloody business going to last?

'You must realise that the roots of all wars are economic,' droned on the voice. 'You British monopolise most of the earth, and yet you restrict legitimate immigration from my country. When victory is achieved a new scheme of world order will come about, and the worthy German character will do vital work out of uniform in moulding a more perfect economic world, freer and happier.' Sure enough, there came another volley of questions. 'Do you not think it intolerable,' he asked, 'that democracies are permitted to seal their ports to German goods and immigrants?'

He lit a cigarette and rang the bell for black coffee. I envied him as he drank it. He emptied every drop of the liquid down his throat, and started off again! For the first time he lost his temper. I must have been drowsing, because a heavy smack on the table preceded a harsh command. 'Listen to me,' he roared, 'or I will have you suspended by your ears!'

I came to life with a jerk. My head was ticking like a clock.

'Now tell me,' he said smoothly, 'when will America come into this war?'

This form of questioning was clever, a psychological torture. After a few hours of it all the facets of a man's mind seemed to tug in opposite directions. At last he raised himself from his chair and towered above me.

'Come over and inspect this wall map,' he instructed. 'There you see the face of Europe. From the Baltic to the Mediterranean, from the Ukraine to the Atlantic wall, the map virtually shows the same colour of red. Red *deutsch*, and Greater *Deutschland* is the new Europe. Now tell me, *engländer* . . . What hope is there for Britain to oust us from what we have conquered?'

I pulled myself together and replied: 'Before you can ever claim all this you must conquer Britain.'

The German looked at me closely before answering. 'Britain will be conquered within a year by scientific superiority as well as by numerical weight,' he announced. 'Our plans are complete.'

When I was asked to challenge this statement, I said: 'Britain has never been overpowered or beaten.' I found that I had to take a grip on myself from becoming too informative. 'My country is famous for its last battles.'

I knew that I was talking too bluntly, but I was so tired that I was almost asleep on my feet. I had experienced more than enough, and I could do nothing about falling forward in a whirl of giddiness. I clutched wildly in front of me and brought the whole of the red-coloured map of Europe tumbling to the floor.

In answer to the officer's ring, a guard pushed me outside. 'Put the swine into the cells at the military prison. He'll talk,' was all he said.

I was put into a van and taken to a prison about four kilometres away, the clang of the door sealing me in a cell. I did not trouble about the bed of three wooden planks; the floor was too luxurious to bother about moving. Hours later someone threw a bucket of water over me. Unknowingly the person gave me what I most wanted. Like a cat, I licked up some of the water.

In the tiny prison cell, vast tracks of boredom and desperation glued the ensuing days together. The date and the hour of day or night ceased to have any meaning. I had only hope left, and to offset it was a series of brutish incidents of hate and cruelty by interrogators and guards. My only satisfaction was in being able to resist and mislead them. But the star of hope hung very low.

I found myself talking aloud at random. I hungered for a friendly voice. The solitary confinement and the foreign hate which encompassed my cell were soul destroying, and I had to grip hard at the edges of my nerves to prevent hysteria from welling and bursting through. A hideous dread had to be mastered every time the bolts clanged back to allow a uniformed German thug to enter, bent on extracting information. The only thing to look forward to was the extinguishing of reality through sleep; but sadistic guards begrudged even this small escape. Frequently they spied through a peep hole in the door and, seeing my body inert, would enter the cell and let fly with their jackbooted feet.

One guard was a terror with his boots and would add insult to

injury by screaming: 'Until you speak the truth, you are not entitled to any sleep, you British pig-dog.' He would have a go at
Churchill, too. 'You are a Churchill swine,' he would add, 'and
neither you, Churchill nor London will have any sleep until you
surrender.'

Sometimes an interrogator would enter the cell at dawn and
start questioning. I never knew when they were likely to enter,
crashing and cursing.

One evening I was seated on the wooden bed when my hand
paused in its aimless wandering along the edge of the boards as it
felt a deeply imbedded nail. Patiently I worked this little piece of
metal from the timber. I wanted it badly for it represented the
finest drawing instrument in the world. Standing on the boards, I
scratched into the plaster wellnigh all night. I had to break off a
number of times when I heard the guard's feet pause outside my
cell door, but he did not spot my work. I was cunning, even if a
little crazy, and by dawn I had countersunk in the plaster a portrayal
of the Union Jack with Adolf Hitler swinging from his neck on the
flagstaff rope. I also imprinted the Royal Air Force cap badge.

Almost immediately after completion of my masterpiece I was
removed from the cell, and taken to a German staff car in the
courtyard.

The man whom I was to come to detest most, because he always
wore the traditional German monocle, addressed me. 'We are satisfied that you are not a British agent,' he said. 'We have checked up
with the other members of your crew in Germany as to your identity. Headquarters in Berlin instruct that you go to the Luftwaffe
intelligence centre for prisoners at Frankfurt for further interrogation.' He looked at me threateningly before finally commenting:
'If you give any trouble, you will be shot at once.'

I was in the car when Jock was led out into the daylight. I shuddered when I saw him. He had changed terribly in the short time since I had seen him last. His jaws were sunken, and his eyes burned like hot coals in a deathly white face. He did not see me for a while as I looked at him from the window. As he joined me on the back seat I whispered joyfully, 'God . . . it's good to see you again, Jock!'

'Thank Heaven you're alive,' he murmured. 'I was told you'd kicked the bucket.'

'Silence,' roared the German with the monocle.

I nudged Jock's leg encouragingly as we moved off to the station. Two armed guards accompanied us, with hand-grenades tucked down the sides of their jackboots.

BOOK 2

EAST TO POLAND

CHAPTER 4

BARBED WIRE FROM
THE INSIDE

(1)

The train twisted on its way leisurely through the winding Rhine Valley. The scenery was lovely with vineyards carpeting steeply rising slopes in a series of steps. The whole picture was washed in the richest of tones. But all the loveliness of the landscape outside the carriage window was in sharp contrast to the beastly specimens of armed guards opposite me.

The journey to Frankfurt took many wearisome hours, providing me with ample time to speculate about 'Dulag Luft', the notorious Luftwaffe Intelligence Headquarters which specialised in the grilling of British airmen. Our *bona fides* was apparently accepted, otherwise we would not have been released from the Dutch gaol and transferred to Dalag Luft.

Nevertheless, on the face of things we were still civilians. We possessed no p.o.w. registration, and we could not expect any protection under international law. The Gestapo still reserved the right to hand us over to a firing squad if they unearthed any clues about our mode of existence in Holland. It was not comforting to reflect that we would receive small mercy if they traced us down to the Dutch underground movement and got wise to some of our escapades and activities. We were far from being safely out of the fire, and Dulag Luft would demand extreme caution. I was dependent upon Jock's ability not to crack; he was likewise dependent upon me.

'Before we get our p.o.w. discs,' I whispered, 'it's likely we shall have to stand up to a lot of hammering from these rats. Hold out to 'em for all you're worth.'

Jock grinned, and answered under his breath: 'Ginger, trust a Scotsman. Those identification discs are as good as round our necks.'

At Cologne we changed to another train for Frankfurt. It was getting late and the connection was behind time. We lounged about the platform waiting. Some inquisitive German marines paused to inquire who we might be from our guards, and what we had done? The guards informed them that we were captured in Holland in civilian attire, and that we professed to be British airmen. The news spread among the civilians on the platform and a crowd assembled. We were gazed upon with hate, and openly cursed.

An old woman in the crowd raised her voice almost to a scream. 'Shoot the pig-dogs. Shoot them for the *luft* gangsters they are.' Her voice broke into sobs. 'The *engländer* swine killed my husband and two sons home on leave two weeks ago . . .' The mob sympathised as the old woman sobbed and croaked. 'They were such good men,' she kept on repeating. She faltered in her wailing and moved forward. The crowd opened up for her. Without any hesitation she lashed me over the head with her umbrella, and the crowd applauded and snarled.

Two young women in the audience were inspired to follow her example and three weighty tin cans were hurled at us.

But the nearest guard promptly restored order with a drastic intervention. It was not pretty to watch. Savagely he rammed the steel butt of his tommy gun into the face of one of the excited females. She curled round on her feet, stiffened rigidly and slumped unconscious to the ground. Her mouth was smashed to a bloody mess.

Nobody moved and not a word of protest was uttered by any member of the mob. Where the woman had slumped a flow of bright blood from her mouth ran into a hollow in the concrete and a small pool formed.

Police were soon on the scene and the crowd was ordered to disperse. Quickly they moved away. The still unconscious woman was carted away on a stretcher as guards and the police sadistically chuckled together. One of the guards viciously rubbed his jack-booted foot across the puddle of blood.

To sit opposite the two uncouth guards hour after hour in the train was exasperating and nerve-racking. It had grown dark and I was hungry, but somehow I managed to fall asleep and forget both the guards and grub. Jock awakened me as we approached Frankfurt.

'Brace up, Ginger,' he said. 'The music's about to begin.'

We were met by Luftwaffe officers. After a few minutes' conversation, the two guards who had accompanied us from Holland were dismissed with a 'Heil Hitler'.

Without anything being said we were bundled into a waiting staff car and driven at speed to Dulag Luft, just outside Frankfurt. The car had a thick glass screen separating us from the three men in the front seat. Two sliding openings permitted a gun to be poked through if necessary. The two back doors of the car were locked.

'Wonder if they'll be decent enough to feed us before they start grilling us,' Jock commented, with a forced air of casualness. 'What wouldn't I have given for a piece of that train guard's sausage . . . The bastards stuffed themselves stupid and didn't even have the decency to offer us a drink of water.'

Searchlights could be seen cutting the darkness with rhythmic swing as we approached Dulag Luft. We advanced on top of them, passed through a formidable wall of barbed wire and elevated sentry

97

boxes and drove up to a timbered building perhaps four hundred yards clear of the wall of wire.

Doors were unlocked and, covered by revolvers, we were bustled into the building. Jock and I were immediately separated. My eyes caught his for a fleeting second as he was taken along a corridor, a glance which expressed quite clearly his confidence.

I was led into a small room and, wonder of wonders, it contained a pukka iron bedstead, blankets and a white pillow. The guard left the room and locked the door. An hour passed before I was disturbed, and then a tall, good-looking blond officer and a dwarfish monkey-like guard came in. Immediately the officer was inside the room he instructed the monkey to leave. He did so without a word, locking the door from the outside.

'Good evening,' the officer said, in perfectly charming English. 'How are you?'

'Hungry as hell,' I replied.

'Don't worry,' he answered politely. 'After we get through the initial formalities a reasonably solid meal will be coming along to you.'

I had heard that one before – and cynically reminded myself of the fact – but the German's friendly, polite approach rather took the wind out of my sails.

'I little doubt that you have experienced a rough time,' he said. 'P.o.w. travel can never be on a par with Thomas Cook's, but things will be less trying here at Dulag Luft. This place is noted for its international aviator *esprit de corps*. But do have a cigarette.'

From his tunic pocket, he took out a packet of twenty Players. I goggled at it.

'You look surprised,' he commented. 'As a matter of fact we

captured as legitimate booty of war about twenty millions of these when we overran Dunkirk.'

I promptly took one. Noticing my somewhat greedy eagerness, he remarked: 'Here, take the packet . . . there are stacks more of the same brand if you want them.'

After I had smoked half, the German said: 'Do take a glass of wine with me. It will restore you. I'll bring a bottle and some glasses at once.'

'I really don't want any wine,' I answered, perhaps with intentional suspicion.

He laughed. 'Oh rubbish!' he exclaimed. 'You may pour it yourself. Actually it's quite funny the number of you Englishmen who have strange notions that Dulag Luft wine is drugged.'

Chuckling, he left the room. The door was left wide open, but the monkey-like guard was framed in it. The officer promptly returned with the wine and suggested that I should fill the glasses and take my pick. I did. I drank a couple of glasses of very good light sherry.

The officer, glass in hand, seated himself in friendly manner on the edge of my bed and proceeded to discuss most amiably issues far removed from any suggestion of direct cross-examination. No defiance was hurled, I made no complaints, but it was patently obvious that this was all part of some plan or other, and I never relaxed my caution.

We discussed Yorkshire. He had travelled all over my county. In fact he had travelled in every county in England. We switched to Cornwall. He had stayed at Penzance, and had often visited St Michael's Mount.

'Know Cambridge at all?' he inquired.

Quietly, I told him that I had studied astro-navigation at Clare College, that I knew the town generally, and the pubs in particular.

'Interesting,' was the reply. 'I spent some time at Trinity College, reading law. I liked Cambridge as well as any German university town.' He chatted freely about Cambridge. 'I often took a punt up the river and stayed for tea at the Red Lion,' he told me. 'Hot buttered scones and fresh strawberries and cream, eh?'

There was a pause in the conversation while we pulled at our cigarettes.

'Where were your quarters in Cambridge?' he inquired.

I told him rooms S.2, Memorial Court, Clare College.

The German's eyebrows shot up in frank amazement. 'How very odd!' he exclaimed. He poured himself another glass of wine. 'Often I sat in those rooms and drank coffee and talked with colleagues,' he exclaimed.

I laughed disbelievingly at this rather tall statement.

'You think I'm lying?' he asked, a little tartly. 'All right . . . I'll describe to you the exact layout of that ground floor suite of rooms.'

He did it, too! He gave me an exact description of the place, even to the old tree a few yards from my former window at Clare. Then suddenly he seemed to have had enough of Cambridge and he rose to his feet, held out his hand and graciously remarked: 'I am most inconsiderate. You must be very tired. Forgive me. I will have food sent along immediately. After you have eaten, a quick personal search must, of course, be made. Then you can sleep. Good night.'

That was the last I ever saw of him. When I eventually reached the main camp I frequently looked out for him and made inquiries. Nobody knew of him. Today, I am still intrigued by the blond German who was an ex-Cambridge undergraduate, who gave me wine and cigarettes and disappeared as quickly as he appeared. He kept his word too. A most admirably cooked meal was brought in to me, the best for a long time, and while I was eating someone switched on a radio outside the room, and strains of music from *Tannhäuser Fantasie*, and *Der Fliegende Holländer* made me chuckle at the change in my fortunes. I lit a cigarette and then the door was unlocked, and a Luftwaffe sergeant with a fine specimen of a beak nose descended upon me and ordered me to undress immediately. I discarded all my clothes, whereupon I was thoroughly and embarrassingly examined in my birthday suit. Satisfied that I had not got anything hidden away some place, I was forthwith ordered into bed. Collecting all my clothes, the guard made for the door.

'My cigarettes,' I hurriedly exclaimed. 'Your officer gave them to me personally!'

'Rauchen verboten,' was the curt reply, and banging the door he locked it behind him.

The window was strongly barred on the inside, but it was possible to swing it open for ventilation. I climbed into bed and wondered if Jock had fared as well as I had with wine, a smoke and a decent helping of boiled beef, spuds, carrots, cabbage and bread.

I slept solidly, and was awakened to reality early the next morning by a slap across the bottom.

'Eat,' a guard informed me, and pointed to a jug of coffee and two slices of black bread which he had placed on the floor. It was barely daylight and shiveringly cold. I wrapped a blanket around myself, and inspected the landscape from the window.

The building was at the foot of the mountains and pine trees covered the slopes. But the pleasantness of the scene was soon dispelled when I moved my head in the other direction, and observed the camp of Dulag Luft proper at a slightly lower level. I scrutinised the long, low wooden barracks for some sign of prisoner of war life. It was still too early and the morning roll-call was an hour away. I watched the guards in their elevated, pine-log sentry boxes moving restlesly from side to side in the chill morning air. I saw that each box had twin machine-guns, and that any part of the surrounding wall of wire could be promptly raked by cross-fire.

I was still assessing the camp layout and wondering just how far the Swiss border might be in a south-westerly direction when the stillness of the early morning was shattered by a strong English voice. It came from a position almost immediately above me and sang *Waltzing Matilda*, the favourite marching tune of the Aussies. I listened intently and after the first few lines gripped the window bars in excitement when I realised that a message was being conveyed to me.

'Waltzing Matilda, waltzing Matilda,' the voice sang on, 'who'll come a-waltzing Matilda with me . . . and I warn you below, Mist—er English maaan, don't fill in any Red Cross fooooorms . . . tra, lah, lah lah, dideedlum, dideedlum . . . they are phoney, chum . . . diddle diddle de dah, dah, dah, dah.'

The singer paused for breath, and then burst out again. 'Waltzing Matilda, waltzing Matilda, who'll come a-waltzing Matilda with me . . . and microphones are planted all over the place, who'll come a-waltzing Matilda with me.'

Quickly I replied by singing 'O.K., O.K., O.K., who'll come a-waltzing Matilda with me.'

The voice-paused, and then continued at a quicker pace with increased gusto. 'Waltzing Matilda, waltzing Matilda . . . watch your bloody step, give only rank, name and number . . . who'll come a-waltzing Matilda with me.'

The unseen singer had barely mentioned rank, name and number when a guttural voice intervened. The window above was slammed, and all was dead silence again. I, too, closed my window and quickly clambered back into bed.

102

But I did not have long to wait before the guard re-entered the room carrying my new clothes. God . . . what comic opera sartorial splendour! I donned the clothes, and looking myself over felt mad enough to take a running jump at the smirking jailer. I had on a pair of old French cavalry trousers with a red piped seam down the sides, a Polish infantryman's tunic with a pair of aluminium buttons boasting the Polish eagle, and a pair of oversized Dutch clogs with leather bands to fit across my feet. In lieu of socks I was given foot cloths about the size of ordinary dusters, and my shirt was of a rough, dirty grey material made principally from wood pulp. On the front of it was stamped in large black letters KGF, an abbreviation for *Kriegsgefangene*. The pantaloons finished about mid-calf, being of the lace-up variety intended to go with riding-boots.

Attired in this outfit, I was taken to the chief interrogation officer who, in good English, told me to be seated. I watched him carefully as he doodled with some papers on his desk. He was an elderly man with an impressive face and grey hair.

First I was asked my name, rank and number. These were precisely written down by my questioner. He looked up and in a suave voice said: 'Now let me tell you a few facts and figures about the squadron to which you were attached.' I was told my squadron number, its location, the C.O.'s name and description. I was told where the aircraft of my unit had been dispersed the day before I was shot down. He drew out a book from his desk and it was disconcerting to read a list of the names of men who had failed to return to the squadron over the preceding months. He gave me the names of men who had received the 'big chop', men who were not prisoners but six feet under. All the time he was passing over this information he scrutinised my face intently. It was a grim personal struggle to avoid betraying surprise and emotion, especially when he gave names of my squadron buddies who were in the land of the living when I myself was shot down. The accurate facts and figures my interrogator knew about Bomber Command were staggering and amazing.

But when he asked me to confirm these facts and to enlighten him further, I told him that I could neither confirm nor deny anything . . . that all I could give him under the international p.o.w. laws was my name, rank and number.

Then he resorted to Gestapo methods. Twice he spat at me, and vented his anger and annoyance by slinging his ink bottle at my face. The ink dripping from my face struck him as exceedingly funny, and he guffawed.

My efforts at lying were taxed to the limit. Twice I had to go over the Dutch story and time and time again he tried to dissect and confuse my statements and ram them down my throat. I was told that newspapermen the world over were effective as a means of obtaining information for a nation preparing for war and engaged in war. The German Intelligence had reason to suspect anybody associated with the Press in any way as secret agents.

'But,' I explained, 'I've confessed truthfully my civilian work. If I were playing a double role I would obviously not inform you that I was associated with newspaper work.'

He wanted to know what I had flushed down the lavatory. I told him the same old story, that it was nothing more than a map which I had stolen for escaping, and photographs of my family.

'Why did you not retain the map?' he asked.

I replied that I thought that its possession might get me into trouble. At the same time I secretly prayed that Jock's yarn would match up to mine in all details.

After a couple of hours of cross-examination I was returned to my room. I lay on the bed and puzzled over all I had said. What did they know that I was not aware of? They knew only too well that I was an airman. I had described each member of the captured crew, and when I was captured the Germans must have requested my crew to give some description of me for identification purposes. The German intelligence officer knew, of course, that I had flown in a Stirling, but he did not know the details and number of my squadron, at least not from me.

I concluded that it was my Dutch sojourn that had them worried and uncertain. Who had taken us under their wing? What had we been up to? Were we mixed up with the underground movement? One point which had irritated the Germans no end was the fact that I had had my hair dyed. I had told them that I had purchased the dye from a chemist as I passed through a small township, and that I had performed the hair colour transformation myself. Which chemist? . . . where? . . . when? . . . and scores of other relevant and irrelevant questions were levelled in an effort to trip me up.

A couple of hours passed before I was again visited by a guard and taken before the intelligence officer. I was grilled minutely about my home, my schooling, my civilian work, where I had taken my holidays over the previous eight years, and details about my parents, their parents, and my great-great grandparents. I learned for the first time that my name was an old Prussian one of some repute. Hell . . . I nearly spun through the floor when I was pertinently asked if I was any relation to Claus von Pape, a name among twelve listed on the dedication page of the Fuehrer's book, *Mein Kampf*.

'Do you know that there is a railway station called "Pape" Bahnhof outside Berlin, and in Berlin there is a main thoroughfare called General Pape Street?' my interrogator asked.

'I am one hundred per cent. Yorkshireman,' I replied. 'My family is traced back along a line of pure British descent.'

This latest business was quite upsetting. My God, I queried to myself, surely they don't think I am a traitorous German? What are the bastards getting at now?

Next a Luftwaffe photographer was called in and I was photographed from all angles with a cine-camera. The officer informed me that my case would be thoroughly checked. Before I left the room I was told that a Red Cross official from Geneva would see me in my own quarters.

'These Red Cross people are international,' said the German in a changed and gentle tone. 'What he takes down from you is confidential to the Red Cross organisation, and if all you say is true, p.o.w. concessions and registration will be given to you.'

It was not until the following morning that the Red Cross fellow arrived in my room. He was tall, sallow and exceedingly bright and breezy. He started off by presenting me with a bar of Swiss chocolate all done up in special p.o.w. dress, together with half a dozen cigarettes stamped with the Red Cross in the middle, and then he wasted little time getting under way with his line of patter.

'My boy,' he said, almost lovingly, 'you must clearly bring yourself to understand the great mental agony which your disappearance has brought to your family. Have you a mother?'

I told him that I had.

'Ah . . . the poor . . . poor mothers,' he continued. 'What fearful burdens they have to endure in the name of war, irrespective of who they are, where they are, to which side they belong.'

I interrupted him to ask for a match. Undaunted he carried on.

'Creed, ideology, rank or nationality makes no difference, because a mother's noble love is internationally the same. Think of your dear mother, now, think of her suffering during the long time you have been living in Holland with friends. Tell me . . . couldn't your helpers have got in touch with her?'

I was on the alert immediately. The damned fool was trying out the sob stuff to get me goofy and make me squawk. I did not answer. I was too busy polishing off the chocolate while Mother's Joy prattled on. I was not going to risk losing it like the packet of cigarettes the Cambridge man had given me.

'Think of the unfathomable joy that will be in your mother's breast when she learns from the Red Cross Society that she can safely trust that you are safe, alive, well,' proclaimed the stooge.

I maintained a strict silence, and he continued with his blarney.

'Within less than a week she will learn of your positive safety,' he said, ingratiatingly, 'if you will fill up the official Red Cross form from Geneva which I shall give you. It will be despatched tonight. It is my duty and the duty of my organisation to act speedily and allay all needless anxiety.' He delved in his briefcase, and handed me a white form, accompanied by another touching outburst. 'You owe it to the finest and most humane Society in the world, to your own honour and loyalty to those of next of kin, to complete the form and quickly end suspense and agony of mind.'

For at least a further twenty minutes I was regaled with heart-searing mewing. I was given edification as to my duty time on end. I let him ramble on, but after the Waltzing Matilda episode, this spurious son of a bitch couldn't have given me a heart throb or brought a lump to my throat in a year of Sundays.

'I will call and collect the form in an hour's time,' he said as he walked to the door and knocked for the guard. 'Oh . . . take this pen.'

I looked over the printed form. It was a cleverly compiled ques-
tionnaire, and I squirmed as I wondered how many of our chaps had
filled it in following the big goof's pep talk. Obviously, the phoney
Red Cross officer must have twanged the heartstrings of many
captives, worked them to a soft and sorrowful pitch, made them
forgetful of caution, so that they unsuspectingly filled in all the blanks
with teardrops splattering the paper. Boldly I printed rank, name and
number, and in all the other spaces wrote 'irrelevant'. Had I completed
that form in its entirety I would have divulged to the Germans important information about my Squadron and Bomber Command.

An hour later, the Red Cross officer returned. Decorously he
placed a bottle of lemonade on the bed. 'Ah . . . you've completed
the form,' he remarked.

I handed it over to him and promptly unscrewed the stopper on
the bottle and started gulping down the contents. Again, I was not
going to risk the chance of the gift departing with the giver.

'My boy,' was the terse comment, 'why all this nonsense in
writing "irrelevant"? I assure you all the questions must be answered
for our filing and sorting departments at Geneva.'

I cut him short, as I belched fizz. 'Explain to me,' I asked, 'who
else sees this form in addition to yourself as a Red Cross officer?'

'Nobody,' he replied. 'I am trusted with a special despatch to
Switzerland. The whole of this written matter is absolutely confidential. This incomplete form is useless . . . it would not be accepted
by the Swiss Red Cross.'

'Sir,' I said, with difficulty being polite, 'I shall never fill in
anything but my rank, name and number, and you must know that
that is according to the terms of the Geneva convention. If another
system operates now I am afraid that the Red Cross must go to
hell, and my mother must weep on. Sorry.'

108

With a face flushed and tight the masquerading Red Cross officer, without a further word, walked to the door and rapped for the guard. He slammed the door behind him.

After this interview, food changed, courtesy changed, and they even took away my pillow. I was confined to the room for almost a fortnight and the fact that I was not interrogated further had me worried. I saw nothing of Jock, and longed to know how he was faring. From my window, I could see the R.A.F. prisoners strolling around the camp at the bottom of the hill, and I longed for a healthy pow-wow with them. I longed to have their news, views and companionship. It was hellishly monotonous in that little room with no books, no friendly faces, no cigarettes and precious little food. Day after day there was nothing to do but pace the room or pause at the window.

One evening I was stretched across the bed with a big ache in my belly, fed up to the back teeth and indifferently watching the flickering reflections from the nearby searchlights dancing on the wall. Suddenly an air-raid siren on the roof shattered the silence. I almost went through the ceiling with the shock. Other sirens in the area started wailing, and these, in turn, were accompanied by one vast rising and falling of sound from Frankfurt. Up the valley, down the valley, from over the hills on two sides, German sirens heralded the approach of their enemy.

A little later, above the confusion of siren noises, it was possible to pick out the drone of heavy bombers, particularly after the siren on the roof had panted itself to silence in a series of raucous sobs. The camp searchlights and wire lamps flicked off. The advancing noise of the bombers stirred my blood like the wail of the bagpipes to a true Scotsman. I thrilled as the rhythm of the concerted bomber strength droned louder and louder. The boys must be almost over the target now, I told myself.

109

Alsatian dogs were released inside the camp wire, and they were barking excitedly. They were there to prevent escapes under cover of darkness.

The German anti-aircraft guns on the pine-wooded slopes opened up with a thunderous roar. Simultaneously searchlights probed the sky, and vaguely illuminated ground outlines in the distance as they swept across the mountain range. The guns from Frankfurt and all about the outside area put up a deadly wall of bursting shells.

The first stick of bombs burst somewhere in the city. Looking along the corridor of the hills I saw a succession of flashes and heard the slightly delayed crump of explosions. Then the main force of the attack arrived on the scene and bombs came down in a deluge. Two bad bomb-aimers unleashed their respective loads less than half a mile away. My room was brightly illuminated, and shuddered.

Before the last formation of bombers had set their noses for home, even before the sirens blared out the All Clear, three steel-helmeted guards with tommy guns burst into the room and ordered me outside. I was hurriedly escorted to the *Grossen Tor* (the big gate) of the camp; it was swung slightly open, and I was booted inside and left to my own devices.

At last I was in the cage with the other prisoners and it was heaven after that rotten little room up the hill.

(2)

I ferreted out the camp leader and linked up, at long last, with British prisoners. There were 200 men in the camp, all aircrew – fighter pilots, bomber pilots, navigators and gunners. I was promptly tipped off about concealed microphones and the need for absolute caution during conversation when indoors – a few days after my arrival the incessant searching unearthed a microphone behind the thin wall boards. We connected it to the main electric light wires and switched on!

Wing-Commander Douglas Bader, the legless pilot, was in Dulag Luft at the time, and we talked together in walks around the perimeter wire during the day. Bader told me of a tunnel that was being built, but it was extremely slow work because the wily Germans had seismographs planted all over the place to record the slightest earth tremors. Digging took place mostly in the daytime, and it was calculated that the tunnel would be under the wire in about fourteen days.

I was proud to know that when it was time for the break I would be allowed to string along with Bader, and I took my turn in tunnel excavating. But rotten luck set in. We struck a thick layer of rock when we were quite well advanced and had to burrow over it, thus rising dangerously near the surface of the ground. We did not know this part of the tunnel was directly under the guard's beat, and one afternoon the guard, a heavy specimen, paused to stamp his cold feet almost on our heads. The wooden reinforcing gave way, and we managed to fall back just in time. The whole structure collapsed and the weighty Jerry dropped plumb into the hole.

'Murder . . . murder . . . murder!' he screamed. His comrades raced to the scene and dragged him from the hole.

The only good point about the incident was that the guard fractured a bone. It resulted in rapid German reprisal. Wing-Commander Bader was picked out as number one instigator and removed at once to a camp on the Baltic. It was a sorry departure, because he kept the R.A.F. personnel on tip-toe the whole time. A dynamic leader, he would not tolerate any flagging or weakening.

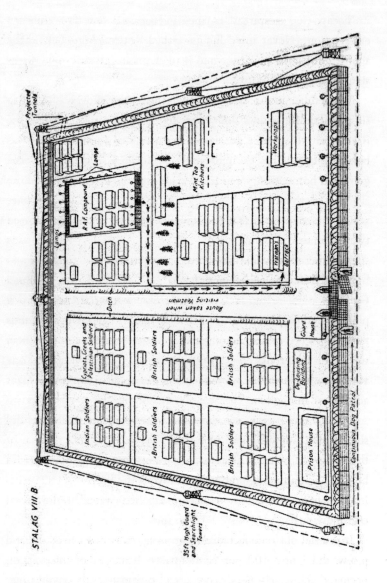

STALAG VIII B

'Escape . . . escape . . . escape . . . by God!' was his constant exhortation. 'Never mind hunger pains, discomfort or any other agony. Let escape become your passion, your one and only obsession until you finally reach home.'

I remember him tearing a strip off one airman who elected to sit apathetically around doing nothing until the war closed down. Repeatedly this man told his room mates that it was madness to risk getting killed in escaping when a few years of patience would get them home safely.

'Blast you and your kind!' yelled Bader. 'You're getting paid while you're in captivity. Earn that money! If you get recaptured twenty times you're helping the war effort by making the Germans spend time, money and manpower in organising manhunts.'

What Bader preached he practised, in spite of his tin legs. The Germans admired him even though they knew that he never stopped plotting and planning. They felt that he was only safe when his artificial legs were removed and locked in safe keeping at nights. And whenever Bader played deck quoits at Dulag Luft, the Germans would gather around, watching with incredulity and awe at his adroitness and agility.

Dulag Luft – as in any other prisoner of war establishment – sorted men out in quick time, and soon revealed the pattern of their true characters. Of first importance were truth, integrity and honour, as it affected in all ways the basis of communal existence. In every camp there existed certain suspicions about the loyalty of odd individuals.

It is a sad but true fact that in no camp in which I lived while a p.o.w. did I find 100 per cent. loyalty. Leakages of information occurred about prisoners' secrets, and it was patently obvious that German stooges were planted in our midst. Men of dual loyalties made overtures to the enemy, disregarding all decency and honour, and often caused serious trouble for their fellow prisoners. Men in the camps bent on escape worked in constant dread of a collapse of their enterprises through treachery. When it was more or less absolutely established that a man possessed such weakness, and was safely named, he was immediately 'fixed' without delay or conscience.

In Dulag Luft it became necessary to deal with such a character, a man who had been kept on as a member of the permanent staff in this otherwise transit camp. Three of us waited for him one dark night. As he crossed from one barrack to another we fell on him with bricks. A roving searchlight saved his skull from being fractured beyond all repair but his enforced stay in hospital made safer the secret activities on the inside of the wire.

Treachery was Crime Number One. Personal dishonesty came second. Men were treated ruthlessly if they attempted to cheat the rule of share and share alike. Because of one act of dishonesty I discovered, I was embroiled in a mean fight before I left Dulag Luft. A man stole two sardines. He had been entrusted with the job of dividing a tin of sardines equally among four men. He effected the share-out when the others were out of the room, sneaking for himself an extra two fish and most of the oil. I discovered the loss and resorted to the only effective method of camp justice – a beating up.

(3)

A few days after that fight I was marched to the station with some others and herded into a truck. We each received one loaf of bread and a little *Leberwurst* – rations for three nights and four days of train travel. We were *en route* for Upper Silesia, to Stalag VIIIb on the Eastern German border.

114

It was a long and slow journey. The train was halted for wearisome periods in countless sidings. We were all hungry, thirsty and dirty, and for the first time in my life I realised that I was well and truly lousy.

It was on this journey that I vowed to escape at the earliest possible opportunity. It would be less agonising to be hungry and hunted, than hungry and insanely tormented by scores of disgusting lice. I became fanatical about escape. Nothing would stop me, the independent optimism of my spirit told me. In that way the trials and tribulations of the journey became less tiresome because my mind refused to digress from the inspiring thought of escape.

When we finally alighted from the train at Annahof, near Breslau, we were a sick, stinking company of men. The camp was five miles distant, and in groups of four, strongly guarded, and with heavy feet and heavier hearts, we trudged off into the growing dusk. Drizzle was falling, and this only helped to make the situation even gloomier. I was on the outside of a section of four, and keeping pace with me was a steel-helmeted guard with a fixed bayonet. My comrades dragged themselves along, too preoccupied with their private thoughts for any conversation.

As we neared what appeared to be a black field, I noticed that it was full of small dirty crosses. On the left there was a similar field, and beyond that other fields crammed with dark wooden crucifixes, an interminable vista of cemetery. I asked the guard if the crosses had any military significance.

'They are dead from the last war,' he replied. 'They are British, Russian, French, American, Canadian. They died in captivity in the same camp to which we are taking you. Stalag VIIIb was the biggest p.o.w. camp in Deutschland in 1914–18. In this Second World War it is still the largest.'

I walked by the rows of little crosses with mixed and sickening feelings, and the camp in front of us appeared even more menacing and deadly. I saw each cross as a man who had once worn a uniform to uphold a cause for the decencies and dignity of existence. Only God would ever know of their sufferings, pain and anguish over the weary months and years as they rotted to the grave in the War to End War. The wind blew gustily over the serried rows of crosses; the drizzle fell on them as it had done over the last twenty-five years; and my party slithered on up the road.

The camp stood out in relief against an indigo sky, and patrol dogs bayed in the dusk of the evening. Barbed wire seemed to grow out of the ground in symmetrical profusion.

We advanced through the main gate, and then we were halted and counted. We passed through a second wall of fifteen-feet-high wire and were checked again. In front of the guard-room we were patted and searched. For ninety minutes we stood silently 'at ease', shivering and cold, before we were finally marched to the barracks. We were soaked to the skin. After we had marched only a few hundred yards underneath the brilliant lamps, a German officer screamed at us to halt.

'You ill-mannered pig-dogs!' he bellowed. 'I am an officer, and all German officers must be saluted.'

Half a dozen times we were ordered to salute him until he was satisfied that we had done it smartly and correctly.

The Royal Air Force compound to which we were conducted was commonly known as 'the prison within the prison'. Stalag VIIIb was an Army camp, and at the time of our arrival accommodated almost 20,000 British and Allied captives, the majority of them from Dunkirk and Crete. Separate camps for the R.A.F. were being erected by the Germans, but until they were completed it was necessary for captured airmen to muck in with the Army Stalags. The Germans, however, did not allow the flying types to mix freely with the soldiers. As a result R.A.F. compounds were stoutly wired-off and isolated. The German authorities loathed and hated British airmen, but at the same time were compelled to respect them for their virility of spirit and unquenchable passion to escape. Such acknowledgement found expression in harsher discipline and a keener guard.

The prison-within-a-prison had six long, low barrack blocks, and when I set foot in barrack 17b for the first time I stood aghast. The newcomer behind me summed up the situation tersely.

'Christ!' he exclaimed. 'The Black Hole of Calcutta!'

Beyond the doorway the air was thick and polluted with smoke, and the stench of burning wood, sweaty flesh and stagnant air all mixed in the worst offensive odour. Small fires burned in open tins – home-made contraptions – and crouched over them, coughing and spluttering, men wielded herring tins with improvised handles – the camp frying-pans. The few electric light bulbs, vague and dim, catered for a barrack approximately eighty feet long by thirty feet wide. They were hung on the left-hand side near the open fires. The other side of the room was in gloom and shadow. The length of the barrack near the cooking devices was a seething mass of humanity as most of the 180 inhabitants jostled, yelled and cursed. Bedlam in a dustbin!

I wiped my eyes, which had started to smart and stream. It was bewildering witnessing such a crazy scene, and trying to associate the men in the milling throng with Royal Air Force personnel. No wonder Stalag VIIIb was generally known as a Hell Camp. Staggered and scared the new arrivals stood grouped in the entrance and watched the dirty, raw and sullen faces dodging around the fires.

It was flesh pots evening. We had linked up with the barrack on a red-letter day. That evening a distribution of Red Cross parcels had been made, one parcel between two men. We had intruded when the precious contents of the cans were being frizzled and tried over the open fires in the barrack. The Germans provided no cooking facilities so the barrack inmates had to resort to camp fires indoors to have their brew of tea and fried meat roll. It was out of the question to start a fire in the compound outside the barrack, as the guards had informed the men that they would open fire at the sight of a blaze.

The barrack was indescribably dirty, untidy and wretched. Lines carrying clothing criss-crossed everywhere, and near the walls there were piles of twigs, used Red Cross cardboard containers, tin cans and junk. Two-thirds of the barrack space was made up of a solid phalanx of three-tier wooden beds. The first layer of sixty beds was slap bang on the concrete floor; three feet six inches above them was the middle layer of sixty more; thirty inches from the ceiling was the top layer. Eighteen-inch alleyways divided blocks of twelve beds and allowed, just allowed, the men to ferret into their respective sleeping compartments.

This was to be my hotel *de luxe* from now on, a sardine-packed chamber of fantasy and sweaty flesh. I forced a laugh and said to one of the other newcomers alongside me: 'Well . . . what do you think of this stinking closet?'

One of the regular residents happened to pass us by at that moment with a handful of twigs. Sharply he retorted: 'No one guffaws at this Ritz, chum . . . it's not done. If you think it insanitary, speak to Hitler about it.'

I glared hard at the seasoned barrack dweller and told him that we had just arrived. 'Do you expect us to weep with joy at joining this stinking hovel?' I commented. 'We've got to get pig happy the same as you had to, so kindly respect our feelings and shut your bloody trap.'

The man with the twigs let out a mighty bellow of enthusiasm. 'Quiet, everybody!' he yelled. 'New arrivals up . . . new arrivals up . . . latest news . . . latest news!'

The Barrack Commander introduced himself, smiling broadly as he gripped my hand. 'Sorry about the reception,' he said. 'We weren't told new arrivals were due in. Come across and have a mouthful of tea. Then you've all got to give us the latest news from home.'

It was always the same when new arrivals joined the barracks. Almost immediately they were placed on the table and briefed by the old lags, with men posted at either door to warn of prowling guards. Lots of the men in the R.A.F. compound had been shot down soon after the opening of hostilities and were starved of news. In between the arrival of new prisoners with pukka information, the camp was a centre of incredible rumour. Questions came fast and furious, and cooking and eating were postponed as the men grouped around us.

'Is America in the war? . . . Was Coventry really smashed up? . . . Is it true that the Russians are falling back without a fight? . . . How is the food situation? . . . Is Rommel really bashing us in the desert? . . . Are we in a better position at home to carry out much bombing? . . .

Questions were answered as reassuringly as possible, but the really burning question of the evening among the men was: 'Has such-and-such a town or city in Britain been bombed?'

Apparently only German news was released in the camps, and horrific details were relayed about certain British cities being virtually wiped out. Men from those towns, or who had relatives living in them, lived in dread and fear, especially when mail was delayed.

One of the other newcomers was being bombarded with questions about the desert campaign. He was a twenty-year-old fighter pilot who had baled out after months of desert warfare, and had actually landed on top of German Headquarters. Rommel had treated him magnificently, and had wined and dined him personally without any subtle motive of interrogation. The German commander had even gone so far as to inform British forces by radio that Sergeant-Pilot Thomas, number so-and-so, was safe and well and a prisoner of war.

I was listening as interestedly as the rest of the gathering to this young fellow's 'desert intelligence' when a tap on my shoulder brought me face to face with George Kingley, an old school friend. He had already done almost a year's service behind the wire, and had undergone a great change since the last time I had seen him in Yorkshire. I remembered reading in the local paper all about old George being shot down, and I had assumed that he had well and truly bitten the dust. But George's chuckle at the sight of me was by no means dusty.

After the news session the Barrack Commander distributed Red Cross parcels. He warned us not to devour the entire contents at one sitting, as was the general practice among new arrivals.

'It's got to last you a week,' he said.

I linked up with a New Zealander, and together we set about cooking our first camp meal. George Kingley supplied the necessary items from his kitchen utensils: two plates (oval herring tins), two mugs (cocoa tins with improvised tin handles) and a frying-pan (a biscuit tin opened up and turned up at the sides).

'You'll have to eat with your fingers or use bits of tin,' George remarked. 'The lousy Germans won't give us eating irons.'

I opened a tin of salmon and mixed it with the contents of another tin marked mixed vegetables, and into this mixture I managed to induce a little heat from the fire. We scoffed the lot, and still felt hungry. The tin of meat roll and biscuits appeared excellent food from the labels, and I did not offer any opposition when my Kiwi friend said: 'Let's whoof 'em, eh?'

Somehow the chocolate also disappeared, and the cheese. In fact, after we were replete, little was left for the coming week.

'We'll have to subsist on 350 grammes of black bread and a daily litre of cabbage soup,' remarked the New Zealander stoically. 'Never mind . . . a chap tells me that hunger doesn't worry you much when the stomach contracts.'

The Barrack Commander showed us our bunks, and gave us an armful of wood straw to fill sack palliasses. The top covering comprised one and a half dirty threadbare blankets. My bunk was a lower one next to the concrete, and to keep from actual contact with the floor I received four thin bed boards. The Germans had originally provided ten such boards, but the severe shortage of fuel had compelled the barrack dwellers to use the timber for the fires, leaving just sufficient to prevent the bodies of middle and top bunk sleepers from dropping through.

It was a hell of a night. The windows were opened to clear the smoke and stench of the atmosphere, and the temperature was below freezing. The chap in the middle bunk above me sagged dangerously between his boards, and every time he turned over I got eyefuls, mouthfuls and earfuls of filth, straw and, not to be surprised at, a few lice and fleas. I was cramped and frozen rigid, and about four o'clock I couldn't feel my feet. Lice soon singled me out as new meat, and I tore and ripped at my skin as they nipped at me from one end to the other.

It was still dark when armed sentries stamped through the barracks screaming at us to leave our beds and get outside on the parade ground. With surprising alacrity the prisoners bounded from their beds. I soon learned that it was wise to throw off sleep at the voices of the guards as turning over for an extra few minutes of shut-eye was a certain invitation for a bayonet prick. If the delinquent occupied a bottom berth, as I did, a slam in the face from a German jackboot was the rule.

The sharply awakened captives, strangely and wonderfully garbed, tumbled out of the building into the shivering cold for early morning roll-call. The majority of the R.A.F. boys wore clogs and, instead of socks, loose foot cloths; and about every head there was some oddment of material to guard the ears from frostbite.

The Germans who carried out the roll-call were nicknamed 'goons', a popular expression among the prisoners. These goons counted, recounted and rechecked again, sometimes prolonging the roll-call over two solid hours. When dismissal was finally given the men would totter back indoors, sick to death with cold, the only thing to look forward to and restore their circulation being the German ration of mint tea.

Every morning after roll-call four men would bring a dustbin full of this liquid from a central kitchen outside the compound. It held enough to provide each man with a Lyle's Golden Syrup tin measure. It was an odd liquid, brewed from the scalding of what appeared to be chopped twigs, leaves and the like, and flavoured with mint essence. No milk or sugar was added by the Germans. When Red Cross parcels arrived and were distributed regularly, and providing that a little fuel could be scrounged to make a fire,

Red Cross tea was made and the enemy mint tea ignored; or at least, ignored for drinking purposes. The German liquid would then be used for scalding the lice out of the seams of our shirts, or as shaving water.

I had been a member of Stalag VIIIb less than a week when it started to snow in earnest. From then on the stuff descended more or less continuously until the Germans were compelled to erect boards in front of the wire to prevent drifts building up. The temperature at that time in Upper Silesia was invariably well below zero, and conditions were Arctic and soul destroying. At no time during my sojourn as a prisoner of war did I witness such a sag in morale as in 1942, when the temperature dropped so severely. Clothing was quite inadequate to cope with the severity of the weather, and the Germans were trumpeting their certainty of an early victory.

We existed at that time on 350 grammes (four slices) of black potato bread a day, and a litre of the watery muck of cabbage soup. At week-ends, the Germans magnanimously gave us a piece of fish cheese, a spoonful of turnip jam and a piece of *Wurst* made of raw meat. In size the cheese and *Wurst* were no more than half an inch thick by one and a half inches in diameter. I shall never quite forget that fish cheese. It was coated with a thick slime as if half a dozen snails had been crawling over it for a couple of months, and it stank to high heaven. In spite of my hunger, I just could not take it. The sausage *Wurst* was filled with minced raw meat. Maybe it was genuine pig offal, but the lads had another name for it. Whatever it was, the British camp doctor instructed the men to subject it to heat treatment at all costs before eating it. Apparently it was infested with tape-worm germs.

If you happened to collect a worm in Germany you invariably

got a prize one. One fellow, a Greek, parted with a snorter eighteen feet long. I actually saw it in a bottle, a pure white, wrinkled length. The German camp doctor was so tickled by this magnificent specimen that he sent it off to a medical research laboratory at Breslau. The poor devil was a mass of skin and bone when he was admitted to the camp hospital. One night he was in great pain and had to be assisted to the lavatory by two Britishers. When the tape worm was spotted the two fellows formed a cradle under the Greek's legs and raised him to allow a natural down-drag on the worm. They persuaded him to strain his bowels slowly and consistently so as not to break the tape, and they moved forward foot by foot. Before the trail of white worm ended the Greek had been carried out of the lavatory and across the corridor into the ward. Eventually the Red Cross medical people in Geneva sent special medicine to knock out these intestinal suckers in the early stages.

During the cold winter most of us developed Eskimo habits. At that time in Stalag VIIIb hot showers and clean linen were only a dream. We hardly got enough water for cooking purposes. Every morning the Germans turned on the water after mint tea, and a football match took place in the wash house. Eight sprinklers supplied the flow of water for twenty minutes, and during that time desperate efforts were made to fill up tin cans and snatch a face clean at the same time. When we had no Red Cross soap we had to use the piece which Jerry issued once a month. It was the size of a matchbox, as hard as a board, manufactured mostly from lime and possessed no lathering properties whatsoever.

But in spite of the lack of washing facilities we did all in our power to oust the lice from our clothing and bodies. Each day we would run lighted paper over the seams of our shirts in an attempt to frizzle hell out of the nippers. The big black lice were less impervious to a roasting than the little red ones, irrespective of their greater surface area.

We always tried to get to work on the lice before the Germans took us outside for our marching practice of at least sixty minutes in the snow. The exercise heated up the blood and the lice sprang into action on warm flesh and bit furiously. But the Germans eventually had to abandon this health marching, as they termed it, because so many of the chaps folded up at the knees from lack of strength, and toppled headlong into the snow.

The cabbage soup came at noon, and the bread ration four hours later. In between these important hours we mooched idly about the barracks in limp and languid conversation. Bored with talk and listening to rumours, we would climb into our bunks and attempt to escape from the hell of reality. Day after day it was monotony and hunger, lice and snow.

I noticed that my flesh was leaving my bones. My thighs had lost their solid packing and my legs were spindly. I realised that I had to get out pretty soon if I hoped to stand up to the strain and rigours of escape, and from then on I applied all my thoughts and determination to the idea. I lived, I sustained myself, on escape ideas and planning. But I never talked escape. I knew that as long as I kept the cherished planning of escape secret, I was master of that secret. Once I shared that secret, it was my master. The other fellows talked escape, escape, escape, but I *thought* escape; and worked for it.

Then something else happened to strengthen my determination. The day after I had been officially registered as a prison of war, finger-printed and given a disc to hang round my neck, I was collected from the camp and taken to the Interrogation Officer.

He subjected me to a long and clever grilling which gave me the idea that the shadow of my Dutch record was catching up with me. I sweated this latest examination out with the greatest caution, but I was scared, and I realised that the sooner I escaped the sooner I would feel safe again. I was a marked man, and would be an immediate suspect for any activities against German discipline, camp law and order. As I turned for the door after the interview, the Deputy *Kommandant* rapped at me: 'Pape, I warn you. No tricks in this camp or you will be despatched immediately to a *Straflager* [punishment camp]. We are not wholly satisfied with your statements.'

I returned to my barracks determined to gather together my escape kit in double quick time, and to hop the wire. But certain things are necessary for an escape: maps, food, a compass, knapsack and clothing. I had none of them, so I set out to get them, and a few other things as well . . .

CHAPTER 5

PLAN FOR ESCAPE

The map, fortunately, was easy. I overheard a fellow telling the others that he had managed to smuggle a Royal Air Force silk escape map into the camp in his clothing. A few rations of bread persuaded him to lend it me and, working for many hours a day, I made careful copies.

To accumulate a store of food I saved a little each day from the meagre bread ration, crumbling and compressing the black stuff into tin cans. I also flung myself headlong in a poker school. My stakes were sums of money from my accumulated pay at the Air Ministry. It was done on promissory notes authorised by the camp leader and doctor. An official note would be sent via the Red Cross in Switzerland to R.A.F. accounts in London, where money would be paid to the winner's next of kin. I carefully selected as opponents those whom I knew had hoarded chocolate and raisins from their Red Cross parcels for escape purposes, or against the day when conditions got worse. I played for their supplies and I played with harsh unscrupulousness. I played fanatically, and I won. I often backed £20 back pay against a quarter-pound slab of broken and stale Cadbury's chocolate.

Next I had to have a compass, and night after night I played with the idea. Only one thing was missing: a small, ordinary magnet. Then, like an answer to a prayer, I got a new bloke in the bed alongside me.

The previous occupier had moved to another bed space because I used to lean across in the middle of the night and bash him with my wooden clog. Every other night he would blub like a school kid who had lost his toffee apple. I did not mind him saying his prayers in whispers which I could distinctly hear, but when he started reprimanding God for having done such a thing to him, I got mad. The night before he ceased to be my bunk companion, he had persisted in whimpering and whining until I could stand it no longer.

'Oh God . . . Why must I rot in this prison camp?' was his audible prayer. 'Why must you bring misery to my home when I have always lived a decent and Christian life?'

His ranting aloud to the Almighty brought him some well-placed cracks, and the resultant noise also brought along the Barrack Commander to investigate the trouble. He detailed a more solid type to share the bunk alongside.

A few mornings after his arrival, the newcomer lost his precious one and only needle. Lazily I watched his efforts at recovery by dragging the stem of his razor up and down the floor. Then I almost whooped with joy. His razor possessed a magnet, as many razors do, for lifting up blades!

That same day I got to work on my compass. First, I placed an old razor-blade in the fire and de-tempered it until it had lost all its brittleness and flexibility. I then punched in it three holes, carefully spaced, two small ones on the outside of a larger centre one. Next I cut out from one half of the detempered blade an elongated diamond shape, the larger hole being dead in the centre. I scrounged around and pinched some brass, which was non-magnetic, from an electric light fitting. This I cut to shape and fastened it to the blade through the two small holes after careful trimming to give correct horizontal balance and suspension when placed on a pivot. The actual pivot was also cut from brass and possessed a needle-like point which fitted into an indentation punched in the centre dome of the brass pendulum. Taking possession of the razor containing the magnet, I went outside and located the Pole Star for true northern direction. Thereupon I stroked into the de-tempered piece of razor-blade the correct polarity and magnetism.

This home-made compass was superbly accurate, and swung easily to north without hesitation. I used the inside of a matchbox for a compass rose plate, marking on all quadrantal angles between the cardinal points. In fact, the whole thing fitted quite compactly inside a matchbox. I subjected my compass to searching tests, but without any trouble it swung to north, and the magnetism did not weaken. I made four spare compasses, and concealed them by sewing them into my jacket.

I was feeling satisfied with my progress until one morning I was again collected by guards and marched off to the *Kommandant's* office. I was asked many disturbing questions about the time between my crashing and my being picked up at Leyden. A horrifying moment came when I was asked if I had ever travelled in a private car with three others past Schiphol Aerodrome from Amsterdam to Leyden.

I was told to wait outside in an ante-room. On the walls of this room there were four quarter-inch-to-a-mile maps. One was of Eastern Germany and Western Poland. I promptly pinched it, folding it up and stowing it in the flat of my clog. In its place I substituted a picture of Hitler, and I had to suspend the frame on two drawing-pins. The wall, fortunately, was tough and the frame stayed put.

Then I noticed a double row of heavy black twill curtains hanging by the window. I pulled a set down and in a jiffy had them wrapped neatly about my middle. I had only just patted out the bulges and done up my fly buttons when I was recalled to the inner sanctum.

'Pape,' I was informed, 'it is likely that we shall have to return you to Holland for further questioning.'

I was escorted back to my barracks, and it was lucky for me that some twenty other men followed me for interrogation, all soldiers returned from working parties and suspected of sabotage. While their sentences were being considered they waited, as I had done, in the ante-room. The stolen articles were not missed for three days, and when the loss was discovered every single man who had been interviewed was summoned back to the German officer for questioning, together with their respective guards. I got away with it because my guards, so scared were they of being sent to the Russian Front as punishment for neglecting their duty, told the investigating officer that they were in attendance the whole time I was in the room.

From the curtain I made a stoutly reinforced knapsack, and mittens lined with blanket for barbed wire scrambling, together with a neat black jacket.

I was now short of only one thing. The one article to make my escape easier and safer was a pair of wire cutters. I realised that it was going to be no easy task scaling two walls of wire rising fifteen feet with lashings of the stuff entwined in between. With wire cutters I would be able to cut the lower two strands and burrow unobtrusively in the snow.

Anxiety about cutters cost me not a few sleepless nights, until one evening the hubbub of the main barrack got on my nerves as I tried desperately to think of something to avoid clambering the main barbed wire barriers. I wandered out to the wash room at the end of the barrack block in an attempt to think in peace. In

130

the corner of the wash house was a built-in set-pot or cauldron, and underneath it a brick fire box with an outer steel door about sixteen inches long. I gazed through the broken windows at the stream of falling snowflakes. Watching it for twenty minutes or more I resigned myself to a full-scale barbed wire assault. There seemed to be no alternative. I was about to retrace my steps to the hut when the wind started to howl as if in protest. A particularly violent gust shipped the snow against the broken panes, scurrying a number of snowflakes into the wash house. As they fell downwards a few were arrested by the iron bar across the fire-box door. As the flakes lightly came to rest on the flat surface my wire-cutter idea was born.

I knelt down and immediately disconnected the flat iron bar. It was eighteen inches long, three-quarters of an inch deep, half an inch wide. Five inches from one end was a quarter-inch screw pivot bolt with a stout butterfly nut head. When this was fully unscrewed the bar was easily detached from the holding gadget. Where the metal bar was halted by a steel attachment affixed to the brick-work, a clean-cut recess was cut in the bar which would easily take two strands of barbed wire. Now I needed a second bar of flat steel to make up the other side of the snippers.

I climbed through the window and scurried across the snow to the next barrack and located the corresponding wash house. In a couple of minutes I had stolen my second bar of tempered steel, machined dead flat, straight and smooth. The two screwed together perfectly with a strong pivot bolt and worked with a scissor-like smoothness. My improvised wire cutters were actually better than any orthodox pair because they offered a tremendous leverage owing to their length. I could not have wished for anything better.

I slept little that night. My excitement was at high level. First opportunity next morning I pulled from the compound rubbish dump some old pieces of wire for test purposes. There was not the slightest need to doubt the efficiency of my clippers. I snippered and severed strands of double wire with childlike ease. Now at last I was all set for the big breakaway.

I decided to cut my way through the wire at a carefully selected spot on the night of December 24. It was just possible that the guards in the boxes might be a little drunk, and it was more than likely that the boisterous Christmas singing from the prisoners in the barracks would serve as a useful distraction. But on the morning of December 23, the Camp *Kommandant* had the entire R.A.F. compound paraded and personally addressed the prisoners. He told us that as a special concession he had given instructions for all barrack lights to remain on until 10 p.m. on the nights of December 24, 25 and 26. Barrack celebrations would be permitted, impromptu concerts could be organised, but on no account must there be any wise-cracking or derogatory insinuations against Germany or Hitler. Pompously the *Kommandant* informed the prisoners that the Wehrmacht had sanctioned the distribution of an extra thick soup on Christmas Day, plus an additional gift of 100 grammes of black bread. But when we were told that a special consignment of Red Cross Christmas parcels had arrived in the camp that morning from Switzerland, and that a distribution would take place on Christmas Eve, the whole assembly cheered enthusiastically, threw headgear into the air and danced in the snow. Then came the warning that if any breach of discipline occurred, or if any attempts were made to escape, total reprisal would be made against the whole Stalag, and no privileges would be accorded for a long time.

For me it was a hellish predicament, especially when each

individual Barrack Commander spoke to his men about sportsman-ship, asking them to refrain from escape until after the 26th, to keep noses clean at all costs until we had safely whoofed all Red Cross supplies and used up all German Christmas concessions. Escape, therefore, I could not until the 27th. To violate a promise would never be forgiven by the men. To sling my hook before the Christmas festivities would spell hunger for 20,000 prisoners, and I would, if I were caught and returned, be branded the lousiest stinker in the world. In any case, my conscience would smite me for the rest of my life if I cancelled out the men's Christmas dinner.

On Christmas Eve it snowed with great force. Just my luck, I mused, but there was compensation in the grand collection of canned food and chocolate which I received in my Red Cross parcel. I decided there and then that I would eat almost nothing of the contents, but pack the lot in my knapsack for sustenance on the other side of the wire.

I had never seen my comrades in happier mood. The main interest was Christmas dinner on the morrow. Home-made stoves were repaired, and cooking contraptions renovated; and each man subscribed one of his precious bedboards to ensure an abundance of fuel. Christmas puddings had to be heated, baked beans hotted-up and canned pork prepared piping hot. The rugged, toughened, half-starved men of the Royal Air Force were as happy as a bunch of school kids and each man was the possessor of more grub than he had seen for a long time!

For Christmas night, the long, low barrack room was decorated with typical p.o.w. sentimentality. Empty cartons and bits of coloured paper, saved over a long period, were threaded together and arched across the room. Bits of fir trees, taken when the dogs were not looking, also played their part. Glamour pictures were drawn on the walls with home-burned charcoal. The lines of washing in the barracks were forbidden and for once we were able to gaze with uninterrupted view across the closely packed three-tier beds. At long, bare tables sat the groups of prisoners. They were feeling happier than they had felt for days. They had eaten more at dinner-time than they had for many a long day.

There was a hum of conversation. Then a door banged. The Barrack Commander, a fine-featured Australian called Ian Sabey, who was sitting at the top of the table, jumped to his feet as a German officer and a heavily clothed guard entered.

'Barrack room, 'shun!' the Barrack Commander exclaimed.

The German saluted and spoke in German.

The barrack interpreter, a Palestinian, detached himself, and faced the German. '*Das Licht muss um zehn Uhr ausgelöscht werden,*' he was told. It was understood that the lights would be out by ten o'clock.

'We understand,' the Barrack Commander replied. '*Es ist gut,*' the German said. He saluted, clicked his heels and walked out, accompanied by the bull-necked guard with his tommy gun.

The Barrack Commander remained standing, and then he offered a toast to the company of quiet and pale-faced prisoners. Outside the snow was falling thickly, and faintly from another barrack room there could be heard the singing of *Silent Night*. As he read out each line of the toast which the Barrack Commander offered to the company, the man representing the country mentioned slowly rose to his feet and raised his tin mug. Turning his eyes to the Barrack Commander he put the can to his lips and sipped his cold tea. No other word was spoken. Thoughts were of home, of distant battlefields, of former comrades who perhaps died when the aircraft exploded and dived to earth.

The dogs bayed in the distance and the muffled tread of the guards could be heard on the pavement of snow outside. Searchlights slashed great yellow streaks on the curtain of densely falling snow as they swung to and fro.

I tossed about in my flea-pit, the common term we used for a bed. This was the night that I should have been up to and cutting at the wire, and oh! what a perfect night it was for a breakout! I prayed that the same weather would hold until the night of the 27th. For weeks I had watched the searchlights swing over and search the miles of barbed wire, and patiently I had evaluated the overall wire fences and marked the best spot.

For the actual belly crawl through the wire defences I had acquired by theft a strong, coarse white sheet which I had stolen from the hospital. I had managed to gain admission to the hospital for swab tests a week previously, and I was given a bed minus sheets. Only men who were on their last legs received clean linen. In the bed next to mine lay a New Zealander ballooned up with frostbite and the colour of dirty whitewash. He was in hellish pain, and the German doctor decently pumped him full of morphia. When the medical orderly told me that the New Zealander had snuffed it, I promptly pulled away the sheet from under the corpse. When the body was cleared away the next morning, and the bedding sent to the de-louser, the sheet was not missed. I shuddered when I considered the unlucky Kiwi, and how frostbite had murdered him with pain, but his sheet was going to get me out into the snow too. With it I would not stand out against the snow as a black target for German marksmanship.

About 7.30 p.m. on Boxing Day the escape sirens suddenly shrieked from every point in the Stalag. Machine-guns crackled and sprayed the wire, and the dogs barked frenziedly. There was no need to guess what had happened. I knew immediately, to my intense disappointment, that an escape had, or was, taking place. But I had little time in which to bemoan my ill luck. The Barrack Commander came racing into the room. 'For God's sake, fellows,' he bawled. 'Hide everything you've got to hide . . . quickly! Hundreds of guards are in the camp conducting a search. Two Syrians have cut through the wire and cleared off. They cut a gap big enough to take a horse and cart.'

Men scattered like ants to hide odds and ends which they knew the guards would take. I dragged out from under my bed my heavy knapsack. I oozed fright. Months of painstaking labour, my pliers, my home-made plus-four suit and a bag full of grub for which I had hungered and gambled for weeks were in danger. Guards and dogs were kicking up a hell of a noise outside.

I made for the wash house at the end of the block with the bright idea that I would stuff my possessions out of sight in the fire box, or if I could reach out of the window and scratch a hole in the snow, better still! But the fire box was stuffed with old cans and full of burnt rubbish, and as I leaned out of the window on the side nearest the compound gate a flood of soldiery entered by it. In a whirl of panic I leaped through the window on the other side and shot across to the opposite bar-rack, barely reaching the safety of the window-ledge before a big Alsatian dog was prancing about below, trying to get a bite at me. I found to my joy that the fire box was clean and into this I rammed all my grub and escape clothing. The wire cutters I hurled as far out as I could into the snow.

The bellowing of the guards swept through the barrack as they entered the doors. The prisoners were immediately herded to emergency stations outside for check-up. It took repeated counting and three hours passed before the Germans were satisfied that the escapees were not from the R.A.F. compound.

The searchers, we found on our return to the barracks, had ripped everything apart. Our bed straw was scattered all over the place, and every nook and cranny had been explored. Un-consumed contents of Red Cross tins had been scattered and spilled in a sickly mess and trampled underfoot. In one such container one of the chaps had hidden a wad of twenty Reichmarks, and the finding of these by a German proved disastrous. An order came through from the *Kommandant* that all tins in the future had to be pierced in front of the guards. For a long time afterwards everything was tipped into one dixie – tea, sugar, rice, coffee, chocolate, meat-stew, cheese, biscuits – all were toppled in and given a vindictive stir by a German bayonet. Even cigarettes were suspected and snapped in two in case they contained messages.

Upon my return to the barrack I hardly dared breathe, and the suspense was intolerable. Whatever would I do if my precious escape kit had been found? The doors were locked upon us, but next morning I raced across to the wash room opposite to investigate. Everything had gone: they had nabbed the lot. My work of months was destroyed.

After the first hollow shock at the destruction of my plans my immediate thought was for the barrack next door. It might unfairly take a rap for my hasty attempt at concealment, so I at once visited the two Barrack Commanders and told them my story. My good Australian friend Sabey gave me a cigarette before answering. 'Ginger,' he said, 'I guessed you'd make a break for it sooner than later, and last night, when the sirens yapped, I instantly assumed you'd floated and let me down. I've watched your quiet preparations, particularly your gambling for food, and it was pretty easy to work out that you were determined on a quick wire scramble.'

Sabey gave me some of his Red Cross stuff, even to some of the contents of his Christmas parcel, and some blankets to offset suspicion when I explained that all my things were stacked in my captured knapsack.

Twenty minutes later along came officers and guards. Six men in the barrack were called out – those earmarked as suspects and violators, inciters and hard cases – and our bed spaces were minutely examined before we were marched off to the camp intelligence officer. The interrogators made me try on my own home-made suit. I struggled into it, doing every muscle-expanding trick I could think of to make it appear anything but a good fit. Fortunately, the five other fellows fitted into it quite snugly. The tins of food in the knapsack had been fingerprint tested, but by some piece of good luck my own did not match up. Finally, we were all returned to the barrack and got away without any further trouble.

After a search I found my wire cutters, but to attempt a wire scramble in the near future would be courting certain death, so I dismantled them and reaffixed them to the fire-box doors in the event of further unexpected searches.

A week later I worked out the structure for my second escape plan. It originated from idly watching a party of soldiers working in our compound erecting new wire posts. Each day twelve of them came along under guard as a working party. One of the twelve was extraordinarily my shape and stature, with a certain facial similarity. I prayed that he was a true sportsman, for I was going to ask a lot of him. I was going to make him myself!

After a few days the guards slackened off and I was able to speak to him. I learned that he was a New Zealand private soldier from

138

the 5th Field Company, and that his name was Winston Mearil Yeatman. He had joined up in Christchurch, his home town, and after a spot of slogging in the sand of North Africa had quickly been despatched to Crete when the trouble started there. German parachutists captured him at Sparkia Gully, Crete, on June 1,1940. He was flown to Salonika and from there entrained for Germany and Stalag VIIIb. For some months he had worked with a labour commando on sugar beet in Poland, but owing to sickness had been returned to the main camp for lighter duties.

I told Yeatman about myself, and of my ambition to escape, and point blank asked him to exchange identities with me. As a soldier I would be able to join a working party and leave the camp, and from the working party it would be easier for me to depart.

'You'll take a hell of a personal risk,' I warned him. 'But if the worst comes to the worst you'll have to divulge everything to the Germans and save your own skin. They'll not take too drastic reprisal against you when they know that you are the wrong guy.'

Yeatman listened interestedly. 'But,' he inquired, 'will you inform the Camp Leader of everything?'

'Yes,' I assured him, 'I'll leave a document with the Camp Leader in my own handwriting giving rank, name, number, nationality and all details.'

Before the soldiers finally completed the pole-erecting work, I sneaked many chats with Winston Yeatman. On the day before he left our compound for the last time he said: 'O.K., limey, I'm game . . . I'll do the swop-over. I'm not married, and never cared a damn for consequences. You've got to promise me one thing if we go through with your crazy scheme.'

'What's that?' I asked.

'My old Ma,' was the reply. 'She relies on me a lot, and should

I catch the sticky end of the stick and not get home again through this business, promise me that you'll see that she has her dearly beloved cup o' tea.'

I gripped his hand. Yeatman was the finest Kiwi, the grandest sporting fellow, that ever came out of New Zealand. The only thing which really caused my friend anxiety was the fact that I possessed red hair. He did not.

'Anyway,' he said. 'You're the brains department in the matter, and I rely on you to work out all solutions and effect the change-over.'

I carefully noted his barrack number and relevant details and told him to do any damned thing to avoid being sent out on a working party.

'I'll get in touch with you,' I told him, 'as soon as I have everything cut and dried.'

I watched him stride off through the R.A.F. compound gate with the other soldiers. A few weeks later he re-entered the same compound no longer as a soldier but as Dick Pape, and for almost two years he masqueraded as me as a model prisoner to allow me to carry out escape and other subversive work.

CHAPTER 6

TYPHUS, A CODE AND A COALMINE

(I)

The days following my association with Private Winston Yeatman, and the knowledge that he would change over when the time was ripe, hastened my efforts in co-ordinating plans for Escape Attempt Number Two.

I lost no time in deliberately cultivating friendships with a dozen or so Poles domiciled in the same compound. These Poles had reached England by devious routes in 1939 and had enlisted in the R.A.F. In British aircraft they had crashed with British crews in Germany. Under the guise of good fellowship I critically screened and analysed these Polish airmen until I was satisfied that I had selected the best one as a future escape partner.

Mieteck C——, aged twenty-six, was a man of solemn and cadaverous countenance, who before the war had lived at Lvov. He possessed a phenomenal patriotism for his homeland, and utterly loathed the Russians. In fact, he hated the Communists far more than he abhorred the Germans.

The inclusion of such a fervent Pole in my escape scheme was essential towards ultimate success. Mieteck C—— was possessed of a genuine escape-mindedness. He would never rat against odds, and his spirit was tough and elastic. The strange tautness of his pale face, and the deep burning look in his eyes, told me that here was the man for me.

Finally, I put my proposition to him. I would arrange and organise a change of identity for him so that he could accompany me when I changed my name. Together we would get outside of the camp in a working party, and I would arrange it that it was close to the border. If our escape proved successful and he reached his own stamping ground, Poland, he would assist me from there on with his knowledge of Poland and the Polish language.

Mieteck promised with deep emotion that he would do this. I found that his general knowledge of English was passable, but his pronunciation very defective. So each day I set him lessons in phonetic pronunciation, and made him grind away at them for not less than four hours at a stretch.

My next move was to get out of the R.A.F. compound and link up with Winston Yeatman. His barrack was at the bottom of the camp, about 500 yards away, and the only solution was to cut through the encircling wire of our prison within a prison.

It was now urgent that the New Zealander and I should meet at the earliest opportunity to prepare the ground for the exchange of identities. For instance, our respective next-of-kin would receive mail from the prison camp in unfamiliar handwriting, and the contents of the letters, by their lack of domestic intelligence and homely intimacy, would arouse alarm. The people back home in Britain and New Zealand would know that the senders were not their sons, and doubtless approach the Red Cross at Geneva in their bewilderment and concern. This would give rise to official correspondence between Geneva and the German authorities, and possibly lead to our undoing.

But the most pressing of all the problems at this juncture was to find a reliable soldier who would agree to exchange identities with Mieteck. Free association with the soldiers in the camp was strictly forbidden, and the only alternative, and an extremely dangerous one, was to wriggle through the wire. It was imperative that I should never miss roll-calls in my compound, but more important was the fact that I should never run foul of guards, while departing or returning through the wire.

I set about the task of preparation by first collecting from the fire-doors in the wash-houses the flat strips of steel for my wire cutters, and reassembling them. I did not leave this indispensable instrument hidden in the barrack in case the Germans put on a search. Unannounced Gestapo searches often took place at odd hours, and the most wary of captives were frequently caught out. I took the cutters to the large communal fifty-seater lavatory building where I concealed them on a ledge under the seats.

During this particular period, discipline in the compound was relaxed a little, and during the daytime prisoners draped their washing on the wire. The prisoners had told the guards that by leaving their clothes to freeze, the lice eggs suffered considerably. For six days I, too, hung out my washing on the wire, but always at different points. By this manœuvre I selected the ideal location at which to snip out my escape gap. It was a position on the lower fence, closest to the soldiers' compound, and hidden by the corner of a barrack building from the view of the guard box. At this position I suspended my washing for a number of days, at the same time putting my full weight on the two lower strands of barbed wire. This relieved the tautness, and caused a sufficient sag for an escape gap which could be used repeatedly, requiring only a single snipping operation.

At last all was ready, and I informed the Pole that the big day had arrived. 'If any of the fellows spot me going through,' I told him, 'instruct them to keep their ruddy mouths closed. Not under any consideration must they stand about watching my movements and so give rise to suspicion. I've got to get back into the compound by the same way I left.'

The next day, when all had quietened down after roll-call, I set to work on the wires. I prised open the staples and severed the bottom two strands of barbed wire immediately behind the timber post. I wriggled through, and from the other side restored the cut and loose ends back under the staples, tapping them into the post to grip the two wires at a reasonable tautness, and to present a normal appearance. On returning I jerked the doctored wires free from the staples, entered and reattached them.

Once through the wire, I belly-dragged myself along a deep drainage ditch at the side of the camp roadway. The ditch lay some fifty yards from my escape gap in the wire and, always awaiting my return as I wriggled out of the ditch, was a casually strolling Pole on the inside of the wire. When he spotted me he would drop his handkerchief as a signal of danger. If the coast was clear he would pause and use four matches to light his pipe.

After the third trip to Winston Yeatman I had satisfactorily completed all negotiations for my swop-over with the New Zealander; but it was a nerve-taxing disappointment at not being successful in finding a suitable person to make a changeover with my Polish friend. Yeatman worked loyally on my behalf in selecting fellow New Zealanders, and bringing them along to meet me whenever I paid a secret call. But after listening to the set-up they all arrived at the conclusion that an exchange with a foreigner – particularly a Pole – was altogether too risky. Several would have seriously considered a changeover with a fellow-countryman, but the idea of taking personal risks to help a Pole on his way to freedom did not excite them.

'But, damnation!' I exclaimed. 'Don't you realise that a Pole is part of my scheme to achieve freedom? I'll certainly have a bang at Poland alone if I have to, but with the aid of an interpreter and someone knowing the ways of his native land I stand a far greater chance.'

'Don't trust a Pole,' was the general consensus of opinion. 'Break solo.'

I was not at all ready to abandon my original plan, and the Pole, so easily. A solo escape into Poland would offer a remote chance of success. It was not quite the same as a run for it in Switzerland, Holland or elsewhere to the west, where I could speak English or German. The average Polish mind, I had learned, was highly suspicious, and although strange travellers without a knowledge of the language occasionally contacted the underground, more often than not they vanished.

I decided to wait a little longer and risk a few more wire-wriggles in the hope that something would turn up. The Pole himself made a contribution by offering £200 to any soldier who might agree to our plan. It would be paid from Mieteck's accumulated back pay in Britain, and a letter of authorisation would be arranged through the Red Cross at Geneva.

Feeling more confident that I might be able to engineer a swop, I decided on my fourth wire-wriggle. The night before it was to take place, however, a fellow airman in my compound was shot dead, and the visit to the soldiers' compound was out of the question for a time.

This death excited a wave of vigilance, and intense security measures were levelled at the R.A.F. prison within a prison. The airgunner who had met his death at the wire after dark had died 200 yards from my escape gap. While walking around the wire in the daylight he had spotted a useful length of timber slightly beyond the fence. He was short of fuel with which to light a fire to boil water for tea, and under cloak of darkness he crept up to the wire to reach through for the wood. A guard, a fiendish brute nicknamed Ukraine Joe, was biding a short distance away. Sneaking up to the airman, he shot him through the stomach. The victim writhed on the ground and screamed, 'Mother, mother, mother!' But such plaintive cries meant nothing to Ukraine Joe. Stepping back a few paces he pumped three more bullets into the helpless man, two into the head and one into the chest. This cold-blooded murder was passed off by the *Kommandant* as 'an incident'.

Days passed, and the guards maintained their watchful patrols. I imagined that Winston Yeatman would back out of his promise at my non-appearance, believing that I had lost my nerve. I was greatly encouraged one morning when I was handed a note from him. One of the airmen had rubbed shoulders with the soldier in the sick bay outside the compound.

'Dear Ginger,' the note read. 'Don't panic. I'm still waiting. Realise the great difficulties of late. Take it easy. Got a fellow N.Z. to definitely swop with the P. Seeing you when possible. Yrs. W.Y.'

This was great news, and Mieteck was jubilant.

Some few days later another compound flare-up occurred when Russian p.o.w.s were brought into a camp next to our own. Due to some misunderstanding, we were not given the *Kommandant's* orders to remain indoors. The R.A.F. men flocked to the wire to see the Russians, and the Germans opened up from the boxes with a hail of machine-gun bullets. The *Kommandant* called us all out on parade as a result of crowding the wire and scaring his guards, not caring that his guards had scared the life out of us with their crazy fire. He informed us that punishment would take the form of no issues of Red Cross parcels, no inside camp entertainment and no mail for a month.

The Russians and their arrival, in spite of the unjust punishment meted out to us for watching them, indirectly aided the perfection of my exchange-of-identity plans. Or to be more exact, it was the lice which the Russians carried into the camp which solved the problem of my having the reddest of red hair, compared with the dark colouring of my New Zealand partner.

The Russians literally teemed with body vermin, and in an incredibly short span of time typhus raged throughout the Russian and British camps. Our Stalag was a magnificent playground for the black Russian lice, a Slavonic species with a red stripe on their backs. The Russians, overcrowded in their barracks and sick with vermin, died like flies. British and Allied prisoners also died; and even the Germans were affected. A man would feel seedy and feverish, as if he had caught a common cold. He would ache all over, and his body would tremble and shiver, then crash, and he would be out to the world while typhus flowed through his body.

The entire Stalag was put into quarantine. Each compound was segregated, locked and closely guarded to prevent men from mixing and spreading vermin. The cemetery I had passed on the road outside the camp, and which boasted thousands of little wooden crosses, daily grew in size as new crosses marked the resting places of victims from typhus of World War II. Daily this burial ground was feasted with uncovered Russian corpses, while the British dead at least got a coffin, a cortège and a firing squad.

The Russians presented a ghastly, inhuman spectacle – despair at its worst. They had no Red Cross aid, they received nothing but a mouthful of bread and a paltry portion of what the Germans had the nerve to call cabbage soup. We were luckier. We had special serums flown out from Switzerland, and other valuable medical aids. And the Germans did at least attempt to save British life by treatment. Compared to our Russian allies we were treated with kid gloves.

The Germans avoided entering the Russian compounds as much as possible. The soup was invariably pushed through the gate, and the Russian bread rations pitched over the wire into the snow. The Russian captives, when feeding time came round, fought like savage animals. I watched once, but never again, 300 wasted, feverish and dying Russians crawl, totter and fight towards a dustbin of cabbage soup. In the furious scramble the container was toppled into the slush and snow, and the prisoners flopped on their bellies, lapping up the liquid, screaming, clawing and biting. One almost living skeleton bit off part of his comrade's ear in the mêlée. Even the guards could not stand the ghastly spectacle and opened fire into the seething and writhing ant-heaps of humans. But this was only partly effective. Those Russians not maimed or dead still clawed and lapped at the now crimson-tinted snow-mush where the container had spilled its food.

For a time the typhus epidemic was right out of control, and the Germans soon panicked when it struck at villages and civilians in Upper Silesia. Alarmed, they invaded the camp with portable de-lousers and fumigators.

The prisoners, however, did not view the spread of the disease to the outside with any regret. On the contrary, they felt it was their duty to aggravate the epidemic as an act of sabotage. A lice dissemination scheme was thought up which became the rage among the thousands of prisoners in the camp. Every louse showing the deadly red stripe on its back was carefully conserved in a matchbox instead of being killed. The compound enthusiastically responded to the 'Lice towards Victory' Saving Scheme, and many matchboxes were filled. Men would lie low and unobserved in the shadows on the top bunk of the three-tier beds, poised at the ready with their boxes containing the crawlers. Fellow conspirators would halt the barrack-patrolling guards on some phoney pretext, while the man aloft would play his part. Lightly, the lice would descend over the Germans to be carried back on their clothing to the German quarters, and, we hoped, wider afield to the civilian population.

The *Kommandant* finally ordered all prisoners' heads to be shaved, and the Germans worked through each barrack with automatic hair clippers. The whole camp was shorn, and after the shearing free razor-blades were issued with which to shave the skull. Hair on every part of the body also had to be shaved off.

My own hair fell from the whirring shears to add to the pile on the concrete floor. After shaving my skull to a glistening whiteness I was delighted at the transformation which the mirror showed. The Pole stroked his shining pate gently with an air of satisfaction.

'Fate has proved generous and timely,' he commented. 'Our present appearance is going to simplify identity imposture a great deal.' It was going to be easy for two bald soldiers to swop with two bald airmen. I had often worried about my red hair, especially as the guards had got used to seeing it wandering about the R.A.F. enclosure. Now, thank heaven, the absence of my red thatch would excite no curiosity.

Next day after roll-call I reopened the hole in the wire and reached the New Zealander's compound. I was introduced to Yeatman's friend, also a New Zealander, named George Potter, the man who was prepared to change places with Mieteck.

I could hardly blame Potter for thinking of all the direst possibilities in taking on a foreign nationality. His was a perilous swop, but I strove to make light of the dangers. George Potter was a solid and stubbornly courageous soldier, a man of honest principles, but he had learned in the hard school of life never to allow those principles to enslave him.

'Suppose the German Intelligence get suspicious and grill me in the Polish lingo?' he inquired. 'Good God, man, I can't speak a word of the ruddy stuff, and I don't think I've the patience or aptitude to ever learn it!'

I assured him that the other Polish airmen were enthusiastic about helping him, and would act as his mouthpiece in all possible circumstances.

'What if the Polish personnel are moved?' was his next question. 'Suppose they are taken to some stinking *Lager* where there are no Britishers and no contact with the Red Cross. Don't you think that is asking a bit too much of me?'

For a while I thought he was wavering, but my fears were dispelled when he put his hand on my shoulder and said decisively: 'O.K. I'll swop with the Pole so that I shall be in the same compound as my friend. Neither of us will be sent out to work and that suits us fine. But, if the Poles are told to pack for some other destination I quit on the spot. I'll play the game to the limit and take all the raps that come my way as long as my obligations to you both are confined to the R.A.F. enclosure and this camp in general.'

Laughing, he turned to Winston Yeatman, and said: 'Winny, old son, I guess we can keep our noses clean until this Yorkshire bird and Polensky Potter-to-be get clear of this ruddy hole, eh?'

'O.K., Kiwis,' I said as they helped me through their compound wire. 'I'll get to work on plans for the swop and be down to see you both soon.'

150

But in my excitement I had forgotten the clock. Only one hour remained to roll-call. Getting back was a prolonged and difficult business. Twice I had to sprawl into the muck of the gully as guards strode by only two feet away. And when I finally popped up from the drainage channel at the nearest point from the R.A.F. compound I experienced the most devastating shock. A guard was patrolling the stretch of roadway parallel to the wire in which I had my entrance gap concealed. I dug in, not daring to move, and as time passed I went through the most agonising moments of panic. The roll-call whistle sounded and I watched the boys turn out of the barracks for checking. Each section was counted, and when the Germans got to my own group I waited for the balloon to go up. But nothing happened, and it was a glorious relief when the whistles blew for the men to disband. The twenty special guards who attended every roll-call in the compound shouldered their arms and marched off through the gate. The last roll-call of the day was over, and by some smart ruse the boys had covered up my absence. I doubled low across the intervening space and manipulated the barbed wire, wriggling backwards, feet first, as I always did on return. This enabled me to reset the wires with neatness and tautness in case of German scrutiny.

I had made all readjustments and had my head poked through the two lower strands, giving a final quick check on the camouflage of mud over the staples, when the Pole's voice behind me screamed: 'Look out, Ginger.'

A German voice barked: 'Don't move or I shoot.' Pistol in hand, the guard crossed over to where I lay and hacked at my face with the toe of his jackboot. Flat in the snow, I dared not move. The guard kicked on. My nose crunched and poured blood, my eyebrow opened and spurted blood, my lips burst in three places and dripped blood. I rammed my head hard into the snow, but this did not deter the boot from smacking at my bare head.

A group of airmen on the inside of the wire reacted quickly to the situation. A few paces to my right they scrambled at the wire like a pack of monkeys, cursing the German and telling him to lay off. Others, spurning personal risk, let go at him with snowballs.

The guard, startled by the turn of events, ceased to hack at my face. Disregarding me, he dashed off to confront the others. I pulled my head clear of the wire, and Mieteck got my feet. Luckily I had remained conscious during the assault, and even when my face was buried in the snow I had strained on my arms to prevent my chest from dragging the rung of wire from the staple.

The pack of yelling prisoners relaxed, and the German, raving and on the point of apoplexy, screamed at them to stay where they were until he entered the compound. He sped off to cover two sides of the squared compound cage to reach the gate.

As soon as the German left the wire I gave urgent orders to Mieteck to get the wire and remove the bloodstained patch. I told him to scoop it up and carry it to the second post on the right and to throw fresh snow over the spot where I had been caught.

'Here . . . take this pipe,' I added. 'Place it just beyond the wire near the transferred blood patch.'

The Aussie Barrack Commander joined me, and together we watched the German admitted by the guard on gate duty. When he was half-way across the compound, Sabey and I stepped forward to meet him. Sabey took no notice of the pointed revolver, and in acid tones he addressed the German soldier.

'I shall report you to the *Kommandant* for brutally kicking this man's face because he tried to retrieve his pipe. It was flung over the wire accidentally and in horse play.'

'*Quatsch*,' snapped the guard. He strode over to the group of prisoners near the wire. The men opened a way for him to the blood-stained snow, two posts away from the original place of assault, and at the same time made sure that the German's view in either direction was hemmed in.

'See,' said the Aussie, 'there's his pipe, and is your confounded barbed wire any the worse for its owner trying to get it back?'

The guard stooped and picked up the pipe, and without a word examined it. Then he pitched it at my feet. He turned again to the wire, and taking hold of the lower strand tugged at it with both hands. The second, third and fourth were similarly tested. Sweat mixed with the blood on my face.

The German slid his revolver into its holster. 'It is forbidden for any man to retrieve anything which has passed over the wire,' he said. 'A guard must be called. I was entitled to shoot to kill.' Pointing at my face, which was dripping with blood, he loudly informed the other men: 'Let this dumbhead be a lesson to you all. Next time there will be no leniency.' He turned on his heel, and it was an almost overwhelming relief to see him go.

The Aussie tittered, the men quietly cursed and Mieteck's face showed an expression of mingled relief and hate.

''Struth,' the Aussie laughed, 'that was the greatest quick-action piece of hoodwinking scene-shifting I'm ever likely to see!'

I tried to appreciate the funny side of the situation, but somehow I finished up in the snow horizontally, out cold, and so stained another patch.

The face battering I had received kept me quiet for three weeks. But despite that unnerving experience, another wire wriggle was absolutely necessary. It was snowing hard when I made my last departure through the compound wire. Linking up with the two

New Zealanders I wasted no time in arranging for the foursome swop, next morning. It was to take place at the Mint Tea Kitchen. I gave George Potter the Pole's identity disc, and pocketed his for Mieteck. I had Yeatman's Stalag disc about my neck, and he had mine.

The Mint Tea Kitchen was in the centre of the camp, and every morning parties of four men, accompanied by an armed guard, left their barracks in their respective compounds and collected from the kitchen a dustbin full of the hot liquid. The Germans did not permit too many parties to assemble at the same time, so times were staggered and barrack personnel took it in turns to act as carriers. Two of the four men whose turn happened to be next morning dropped out to allow Mieteck and me to fill their places. Our time at the kitchen was 6.20 a.m. The barrack housing Yeatman and Potter was due there at 6.30 a.m. The success of the change-over depended on the two parties of carriers synchronising, and the ten minutes' difference had to be whittled down.

At dawn the next morning, the guard duly prodded us out of the bunks, and the first few minutes' delay was organised by one fellow not being able to locate his trousers. The guard angrily marched us at double speed through the compound gate and along to the kitchen. Without delay the scalding liquid was run off into our dustbin. There was no sign of Yeatman and Potter. Just before the bin was full, No. 1 carrier of our party assumed a half-faint in the play for time. As he tottered his hand passed through the gushing stream of boiling mint tea. Crying out aloud with pain the scalded airman staggered a few yards away to a low stone wall and was sick.

At that moment Yeatman and Potter, with two other carriers and a guard, crunched through the snow and stopped only a few feet away from us. Their escort went across to our guard and the retching airman. In a flash positions were changed. Our mint tea brew was collected, and calmly we swung off towards the army quarters, the scarves about our heads pulled low over our eyes. The change-over had been safely accomplished.

(2)

In our new barrack, Mieteck and I soon fell in line with altered circumstances and different faces and, with time enough on hand, I busied myself with coding activities. I wanted to send off some secret information to my folk in Britain and headquarters in London, but before I could send off the code proper I had to let the receiver know that I was coding, and acquaint him with the key so that he could unravel later communications. I had not arranged for any code system in Britain before I became a prisoner, so had to work up a code from the enemy's camp and in his country, and the key to this code had to be made known to my friends in my own country.

For days I struggled with what appeared to be an impossible problem and then, suddenly, I got it.

The *Yorkshire Post*, my old paper, had a racing code which was known to me. Friends of mine still on the staff also knew it. A particularly close friend was Alfred Willcox, a subeditor, a man with a keen analytical brain. I felt sure that if he received a letter from me full of nonsensical ramblings he would realise that I was trying to deliver veiled news.

Willcox was a crossword puzzle compiler of no mean ability, and virtually a one-man brains trust in the competition field. If anyone was capable of understanding what I was getting at, and who would painstakingly plod away until he found the key, he was my safest bet. But two heads are always better than one, and in the certainty of a good second to Willcox, I decided to write to another old Press friend, Miss Lilian A. Rowe, an experienced newspaper woman.

I decided to make Miss Rowe my wife, because I would get away with a lot if my information was framed around the ramblings of a love-crazed heart. The many prisoners with wives, and those zany over sweethearts, invariably devoted nine-tenths of their mail to expressing lush and loving sentiments. The German censors, I assumed, would be less exacting with such blarney. Alfred and Lilian would undoubtedly put their heads together, and in the hallowed precincts of my old newspaper thrash things out and eventually decipher my real meaning.

I sent two letters to each, built up in such a way that I hoped they would realise that I was using racing code. The second letter was actually assembled to give a message in reverse alphabet. To Alfred Willcox, the coded letter consisted of simple statements and dry harmless accounts, but to Lilian Rowe there was a gush of love-stricken bilge. Hell, I chuckled, as I handed them in, I would love to see old Lilian's face when she gets this! I could well imagine Lilian expressing herself most forcibly to Wilky in her cold, practical manner when she received my protestations of love!

My friends in Yorkshire caught on immediately and they quickly replied in the same code. This gave me the chance to explain the workings of a better code, the letters I proposed using, alternatives, groupings, and when changes would occur for safety. I had signed my letters, as I had to, of course, Private Winston Yeatman, No. 7490. But my handwriting would convince them that I was no stranger.

It was a great thrill when I received a letter from Lilian Rowe to see that she filled in the addressee space 'From: Mrs Yeatman.'

In simple racing code, to the tune of love and undying affection, she replied: 'We've got racing code. Tell us all. Give instructions. Be careful. Yours, L.'

Alfred Willcox also replied in racing code. 'Thought you had gone barmy,' he wrote, 'but all is fine. Contacted London instantly. Explain. W.'

Paving the way with this simple code, I gave more instructions to my friends, and gradually a more involved cipher was arranged and came into operation between us. Everything was explained about the swops and promptly wheels started turning between Britain and New Zealand. Our parents were contacted by special security police and advised what they should do. They continued to send next-of-kin parcels just as before, and in the case of poor old George Potter, who was now a Pole and had no parcel despatch, special arrangements were made with an organisation to ensure that he was not left out.

In a short time my code was working beautifully, and through it I told the story of Holland and gave full details of the life and happenings in the camp. Whenever I heard of military information which might be of value to British Intelligence, off it went at the first opportunity.

(3)

Mieteck and I soon became part and parcel of the soldiers' barrack and the men surrounding us, roped in from Crete, from the beaches at Dunkirk, from North Africa, were protective and loyal. Our masquerade was running perfectly and we both felt a new sense of security when suddenly most of the young and regular guards were transferred to active service units. Their places were filled with older German soldiers, most of whom had sustained wounds on the Russian Front. They were less trigger happy, and after experiencing the Russians, looked upon us more humanely, realising that we were by far the lesser of two evils.

The typhus epidemic was slowly dying out as German thoroughness and determination mastered the Russian black lice. But camp conditions were still too serious to allow working parties to leave the Stalag. In our compound a number of stout-hearted fellows laughed with us one day, and the following day were stricken and delirious with the disease. I joined in some of the burial parties and shouldered the coffins with other barrack dwellers, transporting them through the fields of wooden crosses to the cold dark graves. After such goodbyes we would quietly return to the barracks, almost as cold as the graves we had left, and if our reveries were broken, we would jest and curse to mask the terror of our true feelings.

As a private soldier I could, under the Geneva agreement, be called upon by the Germans to earn my keep by labour inside or outside the camp. Since my arrival in the soldiers' quarters, however, I had managed to avoid being selected for manual work, and my soldier comrades had purposely undertaken duties on Mieteck's and my behalf to protect us from coming into contact with the guards. But one day on parade, without giving the Barrack Commander a chance to compile his own list of men for camp duties, a German major detailed the nearest six soldiers for immediate work. We were to assist in burying dead Russian soldiers.

Along I went with five New Zealanders, accompanied by two guards, to the Russian camp next to our own, and with bayonets behind us we entered. It was with strained feelings that we entered the Russian barracks, cesspools of typhus, and abounding with lice, on duty as undertakers. Inside the barracks, case hardened as I was, my stomach heaved. I had never realised that human life could be so debased. I never imagined that the smell from human beings could be so horrible. Through the barracks we passed to the respective wash houses at the ends, morgues full of emaciated and presumably dead Russians, their faces like white, dried, fatty bacon, limbs like sticks and the mockery of flesh which covered them riddled with big blue scabs.

We slung about a dozen of these sickening corpses into the ox wagons outside, and agonies of imagination made us scratch like the devil, and thumb under our armpits to crush any crawlers. A German guard standing alongside laughed and exclaimed: 'These swine were fighting your war. At least help them when they're dead.'

A young New Zealander turned on him angrily.

'We'll all be dead, too, after this!' he snapped.

'Don't worry,' the German said, quite seriously. 'The major told me to take you all to the de-lousers and showers before returning you to your barracks.'

We filled four wagons, and as they trundled along to the large communal graves, we tramped in the rear. I was looking at the ground when the New Zealander next to me struck me on the arm. In a scared tone he exclaimed: 'Christ, Yeatman, some of these Russians are not dead! Look!'

I looked at the young Kiwi's white face and trembling lips, and followed his finger to the bodies on the last cart. He was right. The top Russian was slowly half raising his arm in repeated effort, while another Russian's protruding head revealed the ghostly opening and closing of eyelids.

'Stop!' I screamed at the guards. 'Some of these Russians are alive. See for yourselves.'

A guard closed in on me and prodded me in the back with his bayonet.

'Silence!' he screamed. 'Mind your own business.'

Alongside the big holes we had to sling the not-quite-dead Russians in layers. Putting our hands on them was like picking up stenching, rotten, maggot-infested meat. Thump, thump, thump . . . one Russian body after another struck those below.

A few feet from the top of the crater the Germans started up their lime-spraying pumps, and we watched the white foam being pressure-forced over the carcases. The German who did it was as unconcerned as if he was icing a cake. It was only when the lime swished over and permeated through the rows of bodies that we realised that not a few of them still possessed life. White-covered corpses bucked, jerked, twisted and trembled, but the noise which the lime burned out of them was most terrifying of all. It was a concerted hissing throat-grating. But what could we do? Guns covered us and had we panicked bullets would have sent us toppling into the white lime to burn with our allies.

We covered the craters with earth, building it up into a mound, and steam-rollers compressed the earth. I put my arm around the young New Zealander on the way back to the delousers. He was unnerved and ashen.

'Take it easy, kid,' I tried to comfort him. 'Those poor devils are better off.'

'What I've just seen,' he whispered, 'will haunt me for ever. I don't know who's to blame . . . God or the Germans.'

(4)

It was a red letter day in the Stalag when it was announced by the *Kommandant* that all compounds would be thrown open, excepting that of the Royal Air Force, and that prisoners would be free to mix and merge with the men of other enclosures. The typhus plague was under safe control and Mieteck and I felt optimistic about working parties being resumed by the Germans in the near future.

It was a source of great interest to me to wander through the many compounds of the Stalag, and study the thousands of widely varying residents. The camp represented an amazing conglomeration of humanity of more than twenty-five different nationalities. Stalag VIIIb mirrored the world. It was an international pulse-beat of human values and emotions, frailties and strength, a drama of masculine life in all its moods. Habits, religions, traits, tastes and instincts varied considerably. I witnessed unforgettable dramas of courage and patriotism, desperation and frustration. Dominating everything was the personal loyalty to those at home which could not be dissipated by the darkest days of hardship and hunger. It was not surprising that the effect of any unfaithfulness of women back at home made men rapidly deteriorate.

The number of soldiers who received letters informing them that their wives or sweethearts had gone off the rails was staggering. In Stalag VIIIb, as in all other camps, hundreds of divorces were put through the camp office via a special International Red Cross Department in Geneva. As the months and the years passed by, soldiers sued for divorce in ever increasing numbers after they had been informed by mail, either from their wives or other people, that their womenfolk had let them down.

I read many cruel letters from wives who openly admitted that they had erred and changed their affections, even that they possessed children by other men. Such disloyalty took on sharper definition and stabbed more deeply through the impotency of separation, and because prisoner of war life was attuned to a loyalty code of the greatest meaning. Stern, tough soldiers, sailors and airmen were strangely and strongly affected.

The love for a wife or a sweetheart which they silently possessed was the food that fed their hearts, the fuel of their enthusiasm and optimism in the unswerving purpose to live. It was the love in a prisoner's heart which, more than anything else, prevented him from swallowing the bitter pill of hopelessness and defeat. Many fellows who received the fateful news went to pieces, internally torn to ribbons. Some burned themselves to insanity, obsessed with a gnawing lust for vengeance; others just withered, rotten with the disease of apathy. Stupidly they would wander the compound, thinking of the woman who had proved disloyal. Their eyes would become queer and they would bark and snap if anyone tried to help or advise them. Some men took the easiest way out by committing suicide.

Bluey slept in the bunk alongside me. He was a fellow who just laughed at the hell and hardships of prison camp existence. He was the jolliest fellow in the barracks, and a creator of optimism, until his wife threw him over for being too long a prisoner of war. Bluey thought his wife a pearl and smiled his way along looking forward to the day when he would be reunited with her and all the decencies of happy family life. He often said to me as we lay on our bunks: 'I've got the world's grandest wife. She'll wait for me for ever. And my little boy will be talking and romping all over the place now. Boy . . . wait until he sees his daddy!'

The night before Bluey hanged himself he turned and spoke to me quite naturally when the lights went out. For almost a fortnight since he had received the shattering news from home, it had been impossible to get more than good night from him.

'Yeatman,' he said, 'all is unfair in love and war, after what my

162

wife has done. I really believe infidelity is a failing in all women. When separation takes place, a war especially searches out weaknesses, and women become as cheap and disgusting as war itself.'

That was the last time I heard Bluey's voice . . .

Mail from home was our greatest joy; the token of reality and sanity in an insane and unreal world. Whenever mail from home came into the barrack for distribution a rallying yell penetrated to every corner, a clarion call of 'Mail up . . . Mail up!' by the Barrack Commander. Confusion and noise ceased abruptly and as if by magic a tense silence gripped the 180 men. Precious letters from wives, mothers, sweethearts, from those near and dear, were handed out. Hard countenances and grim expressions relaxed, anticipatory feelings too strong to conceal appeared. Younger prisoners made no effort to mask their excited expectancy, and older faces, lined and tired, revealed an ingenuous look of brightness and hope. Smaller fellows of the throng strained forward on tiptoe, their eyes attentive as their ears, as they watched the pile of letters grow smaller. Then hopes began to fade and faces registered the disappointment.

It was the rule to pin up on the 'mess pot' board, as we termed it, for the general scrutiny and amusement of the barrack dwellers, 'mess pot' letters and photographs. One company boasted four such boards crammed with female photographs, placed there by fellows who had treated their love affairs as of no great importance, and by others who had philosophically worked disappointment and shock out of their systems. Many of these 'mess pot' letters which adorned the boards were pricelessly amusing, and many others left a nasty taste.

One letter, which a sergeant received from his best girl, very cryptic and summarising a situation in five words, was the laugh of the camp for days. It read: 'Sorry. Married your father. Mother.'

One airman captive, twice decorated for gallantry, was badly burned when his bomber crashed over Germany. He remained at the controls so that his crew might jump clear with safety. His *fiancée* wrote him: 'I don't want anything further to do with a cowardly airman who chooses to play safe by becoming a p.o.w. I would rather be married to a 1941 dead hero than a 1941 prisoner.'

Then there was the soldier who received a Red Cross sweater. In the pocket there was the name and address of the person who had knitted it. He spared one of his precious letter-cards and wrote and thanked the donor. The reply he received, and which was pinned on the board as a 'mess pot' letter, read: 'I'm sorry you got it. I wish it had gone to someone on active service.'

One wife openly admitted, in another 'mess pot' letter, that she had unfortunately borne two children to an Italian prisoner of war, who worked as a labourer on the same farm. The prisoner husband was shell-shocked from the Dunkirk beaches, and not mentally capable of grasping the enormity of his wife's infidelity. His mania before the war had been motor-cycles, and the wayward wife thought she would enlist her husband's hobby as a good approach toward eventual forgiveness. She offered to buy him a brand new machine when he returned home from the prison camp. Permanently dazed, he toyed with the letter, and after a while his face brightened and he remarked: 'I hope she buys me a Norton.'

Another 'mess pot' letter from a wife revealed a most original way of putting it over.

'Darling,' it ran, 'I am sending you more cigarettes than ever. The other night, by the way, I visited the cinema, very good show, too, and stepping out into the blackout a very queer thing happened to me. A perfect stranger came up to me and pushed into my arms a baby in long clothes. Naturally, I was astounded and quite speechless. When he made off I didn't know what to do. The baby is a beautiful child and I know you will adore him. I have without fuss adopted him and I am sure you will not offer any opposition. I call him "Blackie". Praise God, darling, for our wonderful "blackout babe".'

(5)

At last came the news Mieteck and I had been waiting for. The *Kommandant* ordered that all fit soldiers under the rank of sergeant should be sent out on working parties. At last we could make our big move towards escape.

Next day the German *Arbeitsoffizier* demanded from our barrack a party of four men for immediate duty in a coalmine at Beuthen, just over the Polish border. Mieteck and I promptly volunteered; such a location was right up our street. But of the rest of the barrack company no other men stepped forward. It was not to be wondered at. The prisoners had seen the injured men returned to the Stalag from the mines, and had listened to their stories. In the repatriation compound there was a number of soldiers with broken backs and amputated limbs incurred, not through battlefield action, but because of accidents in German coalmines.

The German *Arbeitsoffizier* snarled at the unresponsive men, and instructed the Barrack Commander to detail two more men before morning. In sympathy with our plans, the sergeant major picked two men, an enormous Turk and a puny, snivelling, cringing Greek. This was to my liking. The two foreigners spoke poor English and would hardly enter into a lot of personal and revealing conversation.

The Turk was a soldier of fortune, a stern and merciless individual who had been captured on Crete in British battledress and with a British rifle. The mangy Greek had been arrested in a brothel in Athens and accused of touting and leading German officers towards venereal disease. He was the personification of all that is associated with a spiv, a drone and a pimp. When he learned that he was to become a miner, the big Turk shrugged his wide shoulders, and spat on the wall derisively.

The yellow-skinned Greek, panic-stricken at the prospect of coal heaving, implored the sergeant major to select someone else. He complained of T.B., weak heart, faltering kidneys and other afflictions, and he even went so far as to swallow soap to make himself ill.

It did not work. Next morning Turk, Greek, Pole and Englishman were marched out of the camp gates under an armed guard and off to the station. As the train pulled out of Annahof I nudged the Pole and whispered: 'So far so good. Now for the Hohenzollern *Grube* [mine] and whatever lies ahead.'

It was dusk and snowing hard when we pulled into the station at Beuthen, and tramped off under escort to our new quarters. We were like snowmen when we finally entered the doors of an old church hall, right next to a pub. To our surprise we were greeted by fifty solemn Britons, toilworn, their skins ingrained with coal dirt. These men had been captured at Dunkirk, and since their arrival in enemy country after their long march, had laboured in the mines. Red-eyed and pasty-faced, they had already lost some of the original number in underground fatalities. The last accident had accounted for four, and the Pole, the Greek, the Turk and I were filling their places.

We were all classified by the Germans as heavy workers, and thus received 500 grammes of black bread instead of 350 grammes, extra sausage and jam ration, and one extra and thicker ration of soup a day. On this quota of nourishment we had to work like horses for nine hours a day, six days a week. For our labours we received the magnificent payment of 2 marks and 70 pfennigs weekly.

This money was not the real coin of the realm, but token or monopoly money, printed on special vouchers and called *Lagergelt*. It was next to useless. All we could spend it on was rubbish at the mine canteen such as cheap haircream, note books, pencils, combs and imitation Bavarian pipes. It would not have been so bad if we could have bought any kind of cigarettes.

The first few days after our arrival some of the other prisoners looked closely at my Polish mate. Some queried his halting speech and peculiar intonation. I cooked up a yarn that he was the outcome of a marriage between a half-caste Maori woman and a half New Zealand, half French, father; and that he had lived in France most of his life. This was easily substantiated by Mieteck's fluent French. I kept constant vigil, and never permitted Mieteck to be drawn away from me so to enter into serious conversation with the others.

One thousand five hundred feet below Beuthen I hewed coal with the wildest conglomeration of humanity conceivable. I dripped sweat alongside Russians, Frenchmen, Cypriots, Slavs, Rumanians and other emaciated people from across the face of Europe, all recruited as slave labour. The Germans forced this slave labour to turn out staggering quantities of coal. Twenty-four hours a day the mines were beehives of activity, and bayonets, the lash, threats and the dynamic energy of the Germans achieved stupendous results. All day and all night trains pulled out of the yards laden with coal. Every kind of truck was employed. Some bore French and Italian markings, others Norwegian and Rumanian. Accidents in the mine were frequent but the Germans paid little heed to safety or decent working conditions.

The Russians bit the black dust with the greatest frequency because they were forced into the most dangerous warrens to extract the smallest pockets of coal. When the roof collapsed the Germans casually sealed the section off and left it. It cost time and labour to extricate men, and Russian life did not merit such trouble. There were plenty of captured Russian soldiers to take the dead men's places.

The tremendous production pace was increased week by week, and there was not a word said about strikes, no petty bickering, and no open discontent. There was always a firing squad ready.

The Turk and the Greek did not fare too well as coalminers. Electricity, as I nicknamed the Greek, lost four of his toes through a passing wagon. Whether it was done accidentally or intentionally I do not know, but he was returned to the parent Stalag. The tough Turk was sentenced to a year's hard labour in a civilian prison by a German civilian court. He spotted a Russian stealing his two slices of bread, and a fight started. The Russian picked up a cob of coal and hurled it full into the Turk's face. Roaring like a maddened gorilla, the Turk swung his big heart-shaped shovel with a tremendous force at the Russian. It contacted low on his neck and lopped off the Russian's head as clean as a whistle.

The Germans merely laughed and it was not because of murder that the Turk was imprisoned. He refused to pick up the dust-smeared head and coal-blackened body and take them to the furnace. The German overseer screamed at him and threatened him with punishment if he continued to stand there like a statue. Slowly the Turk turned his head, faced the German overseer and then spat twice into his face.

I was sorry to see the massive Turk end up so ingloriously. I liked him and he liked me. We had many chats together, and in his broken English he often told me that after the war he would give me a free holiday in the only decent land in the world.

'You veree great happy in my house in Turkey,' he said. 'Me have five veree nice sister, all veree sweet sleeping girls for you all time.'

CHAPTER 7

FLIGHT ACROSS THE PLAINS

(I)

The Pole and I were detailed to work in a tortuous tunnel which rose and fell for the best part of a mile. Its average height was five feet. Branching off from it were scores of other passages, and from these, many other offshoots and forkings. Had it been possible to look downwards with X-ray eyes, the workings of the Hohenzollern coal-mine would have resembled the vein formation of a leaf.

For more than sixty years this veteran Upper Silesian pit had yielded a continuous output of rich coal from its three separate levels. Hundreds of miles of tunnel had been hacked out between rock layers in all directions, extending for miles around the pivotal point of the shaft's base.

Our tunnel was two and a half miles from the cage, but fate favoured our escape plans by directing us to work in this remote section of the pit. In this easterly underground location there were many gangs of Polish miners in the adjacent labyrinth of tunnels.

Mieteck's job was rail laying, and this gave him a first-class opportunity to meet them. His masquerade as a New Zealand private soldier was carefully maintained, and whenever he was compelled to open his mouth he spoke in English or halting German. At every possible opportunity he listened to his countrymen and their whispered conversations, watchfully assessing every man. Eventually he was sure that a certain man was trustworthy and would help us when our story was revealed.

170

Mieteck's choice was a middle-aged Polish miner, who, we learned, was a key man against German interests. To all outward appearances, he was a model worker, but Mieteck had observed from careful judgment that he was some kind of a secret leader who stealthily imparted orders and information to selected Poles.

After the day's work, Mieteck would relate to me all that he had picked up while laying his rails. He had learned of a great many things connected with activities against the Germans, and German atrocities against the Poles. After a couple of weeks of such listening, I noticed that Mieteck returned to his bed dreadfully upset and unusually quiet. Somehow I sensed that he was slipping. He was in a terrible situation, a fugitive and an impostor in his own land and among his own countrymen, but patience and diplomacy were vital. I had to pitch into Mieteck many times when in despair he told me that he intended to reveal his nationality and talk in the Polish language.

'Watch and wait,' I told him. 'For God's sake don't go and spoil everything for a ha'porth of impatience. The snow in Poland is still too thick and the weather too foul for an immediate and successful escape. Wait a while longer for the quick thaw, and then tell your story to these countrymen of yours. As long as you are master of our secret, we are masters of the situation.'

I sincerely felt that if Mieteck revealed his true identity prematurely, the sudden companionship and inevitable excitement it would cause underground might well lead to disaster. I sympathised with, and consoled him, about the tragedies of his people; but I cherished in my mind only one thought: avoid all sentiment and sentimentality to achieve one purpose.

It was now obvious to me that Mieteck possessed some kind of a dual personality. He was tough, brave, reliable and determined, away from Poland; but on his own stamping ground his spirits tended to oscillate widely and unpredictably.

My work at the coalface was more severe than my companion's. Throughout the long shift I shovelled coal into wagons with two Poles, three Russians and a Frenchman. Four Germans supervised the explosive blasting and the erection of the pine props. At the start the heavy work contracted my back, arm and leg muscles into knots, but once the stiffness had worn away, the continuous daily labour tempered my limbs and muscles into flexible steel, in spite of inadequate food. My body gained in wiry strength week after week: good preparation for the big escape.

I was involved in one bad mishap. Towards the end of a shift, just after the German in charge had detonated his explosive and loosened a quantity of coal, a shower of heavy rocks hurtled down without any warning. A German had a leg broken and a shoulder fractured, a Russian had his skull fractured and two of the Poles were badly crushed. I escaped with the least injury by diving hard against a steel tub which narrowed at the base. Nevertheless, in spite of the protection from the tub's upper flange, my back was lacerated and the lower part of my spine bruised. I was taken to the hospital with the others but was discharged after only three days, the doctor informing me that I would be given a light-duty voucher which would keep me on the surface for ten days.

(2)

During my rest from heavy underground work, I met six others who possessed light-duty chits. We were assembled by the officer in charge of the slave labour, a diminutive rat of a man we nicknamed 'John the Bastard', and were told that one light duty would be among captive Russian women in the nearby briquette factory.

'You will understand,' he snarled, 'that you will see all you ever want to see of half-naked women. But remember . . . that is the limit of your association with them. If you had been Germans instead of foreign pig-dogs you would have been entitled to Russian flesh sport.'

Daily we marched to the briquette factory, through the strong barbed wire fences and into the two long black sheds. Daily we stacked and trundled coal briquettes on barrows, and in the yards outside restacked them into 15-feet-high squares.

Within the black corrugated metal sheds laboured and perspired two hundred Russian women. When their homes had been overrun and their native earth scorched by their own retreating armies; when their families had been either annihilated or hopelessly separated, the invaders had herded them into cattle trucks and brought them into Germany as slave labour. The average age of the women was about twenty-eight and, like the coal briquettes they moulded daily from pitch and coal dust, they also were moulded in a filthy and disgusting communal existence. They had to contend with harsh discipline and the unrelenting pressure of manual labour. They writhed under physical and mental starvation, and clamoured for food and friendship in a world of suffering, fear and loneliness. The younger element found lack of peace even after a day's toil, for the guards made a habit of visiting their quarters. For ten days I watched, walked and worked among these wretched women.

Inside the factory only middle-aged Germans supervised the briquette manufacture and attempted to enforce discipline. Evidently they had been specially selected. Two possessed an artificial leg apiece, while Number Three was bent almost double with

173

rheumatism and apparently immune to the steaming bodies about him. His fanatical enthusiasm for greater coal briquette production for domestic German heating made him completely unsexual. But that was not quite the case with the two other guards. Both derived crude, erotic gratification through continually pinching, patting and prodding the Russian women as they moved among them. The misery of those women's lives, the privations they suffered, their unnatural segregation, their normally crude peasant make-up, created in them a feverish flood of desire for grotesque exhibitionism whenever the six young and reasonably virile Englishmen moved among them.

At first the whole set-up was repelling and obnoxious, but not for long. Close proximity became a physical torture. When would such opportunity occur again? Conscience and fear of consequences dispersed as impulses and instincts inspired the means to cheat the supervision of the guards. The German crippled with rheumatism soon became pro-British after he had been bribed with a few odds and ends of Red Cross items. He nodded acquiescence to forbidden love between the Russian women and British men, enacted behind the high stacks of coal briquettes in the yard outside.

Some of the women were tall and stooping, some revealed Mongolian features, others were short and appeared oddly misshapen in their ragged and wretched attire of unfashioned sack cloth. The boiling vats of tar and pitch stoked up the temperature, and the interior of the sheds became sticky, sickly, stifling. Heat and fumes were choking as the huge cauldrons spewed and bubbled, and oddments of sacking garments were discarded for freedom and coolness. Lack of underclothing was as common as lack of decency. Breasts and bodies were coated with shiny black coal dust, glistening and gleaming on the underlay of ever-rising sweat globules.

Over the moulds the women stooped, their swaying breasts hanging and rivulets of perspiration trickling to the floor. Faces were sullen, gaunt and vacuous, but even such cow-like expressions failed to obscure a leering lust whenever we passed them by or inadvertently contacted their hot and steaming bodies. It seemed that two hundred ravenous women were magnetised by the young Englishmen. All the women knew that ways and means existed, and this made each man a hunted quarry.

In those sheds of rising and settling coal dust and heat it was a life beyond relief. Some of the women were already padded with pregnancy; those who were not begged us to fertilise them. Pregnancy meant relief. At the approach of the birth of the child the camp doctor would order the women away for light duty and prescribe for them additional rest with extra rations. That was their relief.

The Germans were anxious to increase their population, including nondescripts. Babies were placed in German State homes at the earliest date to be nurtured as cannon fodder and inculcated with the ideology of the Third Reich. The Russian women cared little what happened to the babies they bore. As far as childbirth was concerned it simply meant lighter work and a decent rest with considerably more food.

(3)

When the shift was over the Germans always left the mine first. Only when the last relay had been taken aloft were we allowed to move towards the cage. We squatted in weary groups at the base of the shaft, sweaty, and thick with Upper Silesian coal dust, talking and patiently waiting. We represented to the Germans so many

175

pig-dog slave labourers. Successive military successes had affected queerly the civilian mentality. We were classed as so much human scum which the proud Wehrmacht had passed on to them. It was the duty of the civilian to enforce duty and discipline; to do otherwise would be to oppose Nazism.

Every day as we waited for the cage I spoke with Ivanov, a young Russian with a face showing character and determination. Speaking in German, he told me about his home town of Minsk, his life, and the annihilation of his entire family. Enthusiastic and proud, he told me of Vladimir Rasumov, the finest friend in the world, the one he honoured most next to Joseph Stalin himself. Vladimir was twenty-five years his senior, and had been the respected headmaster of one of the best schools in Minsk. Ivanov would speak of Vladimir's brain with a certain awe.

'Nobody in the whole province could approach my friend for mathematical ability, philosophy or a true knowledge of economics,' said Ivanov.

I would steal a sidelong glance at Vladimir Rasumov, hunched dejectedly against the dripping wall, emaciated, bent and dirty. The idea of associating him with scholastic achievement seemed incongruous. Schoolmaster and pupil had both been captured together, and now worked together for the Germans as human pit ponies.

'Vladimir never speaks to a soul except me,' Ivanov continued. 'Ever since he saw his wife ablaze inside his fired schoolhouse, he has remained silent.'

I tried to engage him in conversation many times, but it was hopeless. Rasumov only spoke with a look from his deep and searching eyes. In the sanctuary of his barrack, with Ivanov by his side, it was different. He became a totally changed being.

He would monopolise every minute of the young man's time with deep and sober instruction. Mathematics, languages, economics and philosophy were imparted to the young Russian. The schoolmaster was fanatical in the passing on of his knowledge.

'Economics and philosophy are his favourite subjects,' Ivanov remarked. 'He maintains that only by understanding and power can political enlightenment be obtained, and a will enforced.'

Ivanov was receptive to his instruction, and I was staggered when he told me that he was up to differential 'R' in pure mathematics. He would also quote with authority from Karl Marx and Rodbertus. Never had I seen an older man leave such an impression upon a younger man.

When Vladimir Rasumov was killed, it was horrible to see the young man's suffering. The frail schoolmaster had been kicked by Schmidt, the Nazi overseer, for not pushing his trucks to the shaft with greater speed. A short time later he collapsed on the line, and a heavy, fast-moving wagon crushed him to death. Sympathy appeared useless, and during the ensuing days I refrained from discussing the affair. At last Ivanov regained some of his friendliness, but he made some odd remarks with a detached kind of vacancy.

'Economic blows smart longer and disrupt greater. Murder is too paltry, and synonymous of bad education,' Ivanov said contemplatively.

'What the devil?' I said to myself. 'Surely Ivanov is not crazy?'

Occasionally the continuous activities of the mine simply had to cease, and the cages and underground machinery be repaired and renewed. The next Sunday was a stand down. Shifts were always lengthened afterwards, to maintain the output. Coal was vital and fundamental for the Germans' total war, and they got it by threat, fear and explosive. It was explosive that was used to tear out the coal from between the rock layers. The safe and normal methods of production were discarded for greater production.

The day before the stand down, Ivanov asked me with studied casualness how a Zimmer box was connected to a charge. This instrument was the hand-operated contrivance for detonating the explosive charge by remote control. A thought struck me immediately, forcibly. *'Mein lieber Gott!'* I replied. 'Please remember all the slave labour scattered throughout the mine. Please don't do anything stupid.'

He smiled his slow odd smile. 'Stupid, my English friend? Excuse me . . . I don't think I was ever stupid. Nor will Russia ever be stupid again now that Stalin is our mentor.'

Three special roll-calls were held that night by the Germans. A Russian had escaped from the top of the pit while crossing to his barracks.

A guard spat and remarked: 'Russians are so obviously dim and stupid we can tell them anywhere. He'll get caught all right . . . he hasn't a chance.'

It was beautifully timed, an hour before the pit was due to take down its first intake. The explosion occurred 300 yards from the entrance of the main tunnel, in the passage which carried to the shaft all the coal from the many tributaries. What a blockage! Hundreds of tons of rock sealed the tunnel and crashed on the reconditioned trucks, the auxiliary air plant and the sand flowing tubs. It was masterly, studied, mathematical. It took two days to reorganise the routine and production was lost. It was 'economic warfare' with a vengeance! Not a single person was killed.

The Gestapo arrived in force and verified that all prisoners, with the exception of the Russian, had been checked up and safely locked away for the night under careful armed guard. Only the Russian was missing. He had been brought up in the last cage and had been seen escaping from the surface. He was never recaptured.

(4)

Mieteck was becoming increasingly irritable. Listening, as he did below ground, to many stories of the tragedy of Poland's plight was, I assumed, diverting him from his own purpose and ultimate belief in victory. My policy was clear. I advanced the date of escape, disregarding the fact that the Polish plains were still snow covered and the weather far from suitable. We would risk it, for the Pole was my most valuable escape asset.

I told Mieteck to reveal his true identity to the men he thought were genuine. It turned out that his assessments of the Poles in the workings were correct. Mieteck told them everything, and they were greatly impressed. Their first act after our secret had been divulged was to kneel and pray together in the coal dust. They were all devout Catholics and many prayer sessions took place. This only tended to arouse my ire. Perhaps selfishly, I imagined that such devotion might soften up my companion.

The Poles conspired in the bowels of the earth to good purpose. Money, maps and clothing were produced but, most important of all, we were provided with a valuable address in Czestochowa, from which it was more than likely that we would gain entry into the Polish underground movement. The leader of the loyalist miners promised that he would contact Czestochowa, notify the underground of our probable arrival and give them our descriptions.

179

Further, an important password would be given us before we left the mine.

Mieteck was carefully schooled about the circuitous route we would have to follow to avoid the danger spots, and a list of villages was given to us with the names of reliable helpers in each. The distance to our destination, following a roundabout route, was more than 100 kilometres. Instead of heading north-east – the nearest distance between the two points – we would set course due east towards Wolbrom, approximately fifty kilometres away. Fifteen kilometres from Wolbrom we would swing north-west and make towards Czestochowa, some sixty-five kilometres as the crow flies. The whole journey would be completed in a series of treks from village to village. We were told that it was much too risky a journey to be undertaken by train.

We had all our supplies and civilian clothes gathered together and concealed, and the escape date definitely fixed. It was to take place on my birthday. But on the eve of our departure two other captives made a break. They were recaptured only two miles away. Under civilian police escort they were returned to the pithead and handed over to 'John the Bastard'. Instantly, he exploded into one of his violent rages and without hesitation shot the two men dead. Even this did not appease the maniac. He ordered the two bodies to be hung in crucifixion on the barbed wire as a stark reminder of what would happen to others who tried to escape.

'Good God,' murmured Mieteck, shaken. 'Now we know our fate if we're captured and brought back.'

'We're definitely going . . . as arranged,' I replied. 'Fate has merely given us a warning to clear this murder dump good and proper . . . and with no mistakes.' Although I was ill at ease, I was determined not to tolerate any further postponement of our escape.

180

Mieteck, a firm believer in silent supplication, prayed mightily. He told me sincerely that he would stab himself to death rather than give 'John the Bastard' the satisfaction of shooting him in cold blood and draping his body on the wire.

Then, two days before the date fixed for escape, fate again took a hand, but this time to our advantage. The pit authorities decided to change the time of our underground shift so that instead of escaping after our duty, tired, dirty and aching, we would now be able to move off before we went underground. We would be fresh, clean, clear thinking, and we would still have the darkness to cover our movements.

The colliery routine was this: Before lining up in front of the cage each day for counting and checking, the prisoners had to march to the bath house, a large decentralised building. Here we unhooked our mining clothes and boots, helmet and lamp. After changing into underground apparel, the party reassembled in the doorway for counting. Then, satisfied that we were all present and correct, the guards marched us to the platform cage where the military guards handed us over to the civilian overseers responsible for our care and discipline underground. Before the guards moved away, a further count would take place as the prisoners entered the cages two at a time.

The critical minutes of our escape came in the ten-minute interval between the pithead counts. During that time Mieteck and I had to make the break. Further, we had to cross a tricky, fortified bridge to gain the railway sidings. Once among the trucks we would be difficult to spot and hard to hit, but beyond the parked wagons, half a mile from the pithead, a high wire-mesh fence surrounded the mine property. This had to be overcome before we could gain the main highway into the town and collect the bicycles which would be parked at a prearranged spot. Every moment would count until we cleared the town of Beuthen. We presumed that the Germans would fan out and search the precincts of the mine inside the wire before alerting the civilian police in the town.

Every day for a week Mieteck and I had smuggled into the bath house our escape supplies and hid them behind the built-up lockers. On the eve of our escape we got the whole gang together and thrashed out, as scientifically as possible, the most advantageous point at which we could slip away from the column of marching men. We decided on a position midway between the bath house and the pithead, to the left of the pathway opposite a twenty-feet-high stack of pit props. The men who would be leading the column promised to veer gently towards the stack of timber and slacken speed. Two men at the front would start an argument to distract the escorting guards. The tallest men in the coalmining party would be placed to the front, left and behind us to act as a screen.

(5)

When the morning came snow was falling gently. This was Heaven's own birthday present. I was also touched by Mieteck's gift to me: a crucifix on a thin chain. It was a fine and thoughtful gesture.

As we walked to the bath house I asked Mieteck how he was feeling.

'Don't worry,' he replied. 'We'll make it. I feel it in my heart. But please don't swear so furiously if we encounter any obstacles.'

Mieteck never swore, and it was only at this important hour that I realised that my ripe language was distasteful to my religious Polish companion.

'I'll try not to,' I replied, sincerely. 'But just as you derive moral strength from a nice quiet prayer, I get similar satisfaction from a good round of swearing. It does me good. It's only a habit.'

The guards took up their accustomed position at the door. The men primed to assist us safely covered us from suspicious eyes as Mieteck and I quickly donned the pit dress over our escape suits, collected our supplies and, with helmets on heads and knapsacks pressed tightly to our sides, took up our prearranged positions. The guards counted the men, noticed nothing unusual and gave the command to march. The column of prisoners crunched ahead and, like a frontier box between heaven and hell, the black bulk of stacked pit props loomed before us through the falling snow.

The two prisoners in front, a man called Burns and a little Cornishman, began their shindy with gusto. The guards rushed forward. Now the wood pile was opposite me. Ducking, I threw myself flat at the base of the stack. The instant my face touched the snow Mieteck sprawled on top of me. We lay still. The rest of the party crunched ahead into the veil of falling snowflakes. I heard the angry voice of Burns threatening to kick the Cornishman in the ruddy guts.

The narrow bridge we had to cross was forty feet to the left of the woodpile. It spanned an eighty-feet-wide cutting in which were stationed strings of railway trucks awaiting their turn to be loaded with coal at the bunkers. It was a good forty-feet drop from the bridge to the trucks below. The bridge, four feet wide, was of steel girders and guarded by a high, flat, steel door which was always kept locked. To make the barrier additionally escape-proof, the Germans had extended high steel plates eight feet to the left and right of the doorway, presumably to prevent un-authorised persons from clambering around the locked door and jumping over the bridge's parapet. But that was not all. Barbed wire stretched in rows from where the plates ended to points ten feet out on the parapet. The only way out of the mine was to swing along the barbed wire to the parapet. Our only protection against the worst tearing of the barbs were leather-faced mittens. There was no support for our feet and, forty feet below, were the loaded wagons.

Mieteck was first over. He gripped the wire and flung himself outwards, grappling and tearing his way across. The wire squeaked, groaned and sagged but he reached the parapet safely and pulled himself over.

As soon as his weight was off the wire I, too, gripped it and swung outwards. Every second counted. Mieteck's weight had loosened the wire appreciably and my own heavier weight and forceful wriggling made it slacker and slacker. I found it impossible to get over at anything like the same speed. The wire barbs hooked into my chest and I was compelled to jerk and wriggle alarmingly to release myself. It was sickening to feel my feet kicking at nothing. And I dared not wrench and heave too violently or I would have left most of my clothing behind.

I was spreadeagled on the strands no more than two-thirds of the way across when a series of yells told me that our disappearance had been discovered. This wire business had taken longer than anticipated. Oh Christ! What a corner we were in.

Searchlights from the main tower switched on. One swept around wildly, the other centred its beam smack in the middle of the bridge. Demoniacally, I writhed, wrenched, tugged and released myself for the twentieth time. I crabbed along in a muck sweat. And then, even as Mieteck reached over and helped me across the parapet, footsteps raced along the pathway leading to the bridge.

Without a second's hesitation I bent double and hurtled forward, my head just lower than the steel rail parapet, Mieteck on my heels. All fear and hesitation were gone. Over the eighty feet of wooden boards we streaked, our pounding boots kicking up a hellish clatter, as we hurtled through the white cone of the searchlight.

At the barbed wire the pursuing Germans halted and opened fire with their sub-machine-guns. But now the locked steel door and protruding steel walls that had barred our way came to our aid. The guards were compelled to aim on the angle. Had they been able to shoot straight up between the parapets it would have been certain death for us both.

Bullets pinged and spewed around us as we clanged down the metal steps at the other end. In the glow of a small pilot lamp at the bottom stood a watchman with arms outstretched. I was still in the lead and, taking a spring from the last few steps above the ground I neatly contacted the man's crutch with my boot. Every ounce of my strength went into the kick, and he dropped like a log.

We cleared the lines of coal trucks, weaving in and out of at least half a dozen separate sidings, and gained the open. We raced the remaining 300 yards to the mesh fence. It was twelve feet high and so finely woven that there was no grip anywhere. With lungs almost at bursting point we followed the fence towards the main road.

Sucking and gulping for breath, I reached into my haversack for the metal hook and rope which would overcome this last barrier.

It was not there. We must have left it in the bath house.

Mieteck said never a word, but he ran up and down inside the wire like a mad dog. My heart pounded hysterically. To climb the mesh fence was impossible. It was all my fault, and in the turmoil of mental agony I could not think what to do. Mieteck was now out of sight, and I thought he had deserted me. Then I heard him call, and raced up to him. He was on his knees, tearing away at the earth with his knife.

'Help me! Help me!' he sobbed. 'Dig! Dig!'

Here the base of the mesh fence was on sloping ground and revealed a five-inch clearance. With fanatical energy we ripped out enough of the hard earth to allow a belly wriggle under the wire. With incredible speed it was accomplished and one after the other we crawled through.

On the other side we took off our pit helmets and buried them, putting our civilian felt hats on in their place. Then we turned our backs on our prison.

We had made it.

(6)

Casually we strode from the darkness towards the main thorough-fare. Lots of miners were about, some walking, some cycling, some on their way home after a shift, others ready to start the day's work. We had precise instructions about our route and the streets we had to stick to in the town to bring us on the highway which would take us to the hospital at the top of the hill.

We moved off down the road at not too suspicious a pace, tense and without a word being spoken. We had to collect our cycles just beyond a coffee stall lit by a kerosene lamp. But where the hell was the coffee stall? We could see no light and were practic-ally on top of the place before I spotted it. The kerosene lamp had on this particular morning gone sick and the owner had propped a wan candle at the back of his stall in its place.

A group of miners was huddled about the counter sipping their warm *ersatz* coffee in the chill morning air. Nobody bothered to look as we passed by. The cycles were propped against a low wall twenty yards farther on. In fact, there were six cycles. Doubtless four of them belonged to miners taking their coffee. We did not hesitate. Mounting the two first to hand we shot off towards the town a mile and a half away. And as we rode my spirits rallied. I felt like a fighter pilot in a Spitfire as the cold air rushed past my sweaty face. But Mieteck dispelled the mood.

'Faster, faster, faster!' he urged. 'We've got to beat the civilian police to it. Those mine guards will have opened the bridge gate and searched for our bodies by now. They'll phone the town immediately.'

We pedalled faster. We reached the centre of the town and picked up the tram-lines, turned left at the park, right at the Post Office or whatever building it was, and settled down on the main road that led up the long incline to the hospital. Gradually the built-up area dropped away and open fields appeared.

We were well on the outskirts of the town, pedalling like hell, when the balloon went up. A series of police whistles sounded behind us.

'For Christ's sake . . . faster!' I yelled. 'We've just fluked it.'

We were two-thirds of the way up the long hill when Mieteck ordered a halt. 'The hospital is about a quarter of a mile away,' he said, 'but this is the end of our cycle trip. I don't fancy getting too near. It's a military hospital, and the guards will most likely have been warned.'

The sudden roar of a motor-cycle engine, just over the crest of the rise, cut him short. Mieteck hurled his cycle over the hedge. I did the same. We followed them as the lights of the motor-cycle came into view. It roared past us a few yards away.

187

'We deserve a drink,' said Mieteck companionably, and he with-drew from his knapsack a half-bottle of Schnapps given him by his trusted miner friend. The burning liquid was steadying.

'Let's get walking as we've never walked before,' I suggested. 'We must be a mile from the coppice behind the hospital where we're supposed to strike inland. We'll circuit the hospital by a wide clearance and set course, say two miles the other side of the coppice.'

An hour and a half later we were a quarter of a mile from the River Oder, virtually the frontier. We spotted the bridge and could see the moving figures of two guards. We also picked out a pill-box before the start of the trees lower down the bank. Belly flat in the thick snow we cautiously advanced parallel to the river to a point opposite some tall trees. The bridge itself was satisfactorily obscured, but the pill-box remained danger-ously visible. There was no sign of life, and we decided that it would be best to cross at this point. We turned at right angles, and continued our wriggling to bring us down to the river edge.

When we could see the river we experienced the most heart-wrenching disappointment. The ice had broken up, and for at least forty yards, from our side to the opposite bank, massive irregular blocks of ice like the pieces of a huge jig-saw moved almost imper-ceptibly, the water below gently lapping at the multitude of edges.

'It was frozen solid last week,' Mieteck said miserably.

'A lot can happen to ice in a week,' I replied. 'No use be-moaning the fact. There's only one thing for it. We've got to race across . . . dive from ice floe to ice floe. Who's going first?'

Without a word Mieteck rose to his feet and walked back thirty yards. Turning, and almost without pause, he broke into a run. He spurted as he came up the bank, two feet above the big ice block below. He leapt from the solid earth straight on to it and, hardly appearing to touch it, was on the next and the next. His mind worked to split-second timing as he pranced from one ice slab to another. Across the disintegrated surface he swayed, danced and bobbed, his legs literally twirling as they flashed and skipped, left, right, forward. It was only when Mieteck was a couple of yards from the safety of the other side that he paused, faltered and lurched sideways, his arms thrashing as he slipped downwards into the icy water. But when his feet touched the bottom, the water was only deep enough to reach up to his chest.

Spluttering and gasping, Mieteck struggled to the solid earth. Once out of the water he shook himself like a terrier, then he waved hands up and down as a signal of encouragement.

I retreated up the bank, in line with the big ice floe on which Mieteck had wisely touched down on at the start. I faced about, and got off my mark. I made a good leap, a balanced first touch-down, and kept moving, skipping and racing from one piece of ice to the next. Twice I imagined I had placed a foot on watery softness, but my speed and the solid positioning of the other foot maintained my balance and got me almost over. Like Mieteck, I finished up in the icy water a few feet from the opposite bank where the ice was in pieces too small to support the weight of a man.

'God is kind to us on your birthday,' Mieteck shivered. 'Now all we have to do is watch ourselves for a mile or so across the frontier and then walk as we've never walked before. We must get as far into Poland as possible today, and we must work up a heat to offset this wet clothing.'

With extreme caution we pulled ourselves, belly flat, between the sentry box and the guarded bridge. Behind a wood, and reasonably in the clear, we clambered to our feet and set off at a brisk pace. Unswervingly, except to bypass villages and odd clusters of dwellings, we followed, hour after hour, a strict compass course.

We built up one muck sweat after another. We steamed, but nothing daunted us. It was glorious to be free, and possibly nearer total freedom with every step we took. Our spirits and our determination maintained a powerful pressure, completely disregarding the annoyances of squelching boots, numbed feet and wet clothing. On we plodded, on and on across the white plain, ploughing and floundering through deep snowdrifts.

(7)

Dusk was gathering when we made our first real halt. We dropped to rest in the lee of a broken wall, a crumbled ruin of what was once a Polish fort. Using concentrated fuel which we had stored in our kit to be employed in a handy stove, we brewed a steaming mug of cocoa, using melted snow for water. We washed down a portion of our rations, eased our limbs and calculated the distance to the first village which Mieteck had been advised was loyal.

'It is a staunch Polish community,' Mieteck proudly commented. 'There we will spend our first night. Nevertheless, we must not relax our caution.'

We knew that in every Polish village, no matter how small, the Gestapo had an agent planted. The Germans were fearful that Britain would sneak in supplies by air.

For an hour we rested, but the respite only made us aware of our aching bodies and the tremendous exertions which the day had placed upon our minds and limbs. Muscles stiffened alarmingly and it called for a prodigious effort to keep our eyes from closing.

I saw Mieteck's head flop on his chest. 'Come, Mieteck,' I hastily commanded, 'we can't afford to waste any more time. It's almost dark, and we still have ten miles to go to the village.'

In grim silence we pushed forward. Barely had total darkness come down over the flat landscape before a vicious snowstorm swept across the plain. Progress was an agony, walking a nightmare. The wind raged, it was bitingly cold and we could only totter forward yard by yard. The swirl of snowflakes whipped around us, accumulated on our faces and froze. Hour after hour we battled on. Repeatedly we slithered and slumped into snowdrifts yet, despite a weariness that can never be described, we somehow managed to kick and fight our way out.

Once, I dropped the compass through sheer inability to grasp it any longer. By the time we had recovered it and straightened our stiffened limbs I knew that a few more miles would be the absolute limit of our endurance.

Our intense craving for rest and sleep was a mounting agony of torment as we fought the length of each mile. Our minds, thank God, still possessed a dull, warming glow; a glow of mastery and a fearful realisation of our fate if we halted and rested. We knew that once we relaxed we would be incapable of mastering courage or consciousness to rise again, and must die where we lay.

'If we don't reach the village soon,' I reminded myself, 'I shall leave this lousy world on the same date I came into it.'

At intervals, Mieteck whimpered a prayer in Polish. Occasionally he would raise his arm and make the sign of the cross. His head and face were like a large spectral snowball lolling on his shoulders.

We seemed to have walked twice the real distance and I began to fear that we had followed a wrong compass course and overshot the village. Since our departure from the coalmine we had foot-slogged for sixteen hours, a distance of almost forty miles, across a difficult snow-engulfed plain in a temperature well below freezing. With the fall of darkness we had been compelled to use up all our reserve strength in combating a pitiless wind and a raging, blinding snowstorm. We were at our last tether.

Mieteck must have been psychic and read my thoughts. He halted, flung his arms about my neck and prayed and sobbed.

'We mustn't die!' he whimpered. 'It's not fair to let the Germans win after all we've done to escape.'

I did not know what to say. I was even beyond bothering to curse and revile God, the Germans and the Devil. And a few minutes after Mieteck's passionate outburst I began to give prayer more serious thought and respect than I ever had in the past. For, almost as if in direct answer to Mieteck's entreaties, the wind lessened and then dropped away altogether and the snow ceased to fall. Twinkling stars could be seen in the clear sky between gaps in the heavy cloud. But, more important than that, ahead and to the left of us vaguely glimmering lights could be seen, lights that spelt human habitation.

Mieteck yelled deliriously: 'Look . . . Look . . . The village!'

I could scarcely believe my throbbing eyes. It was a miracle that the snow had stopped falling when it did. Otherwise we would have passed the village half a mile to the right.

In a dream of dazed joy we staggered from the plain into the reality of small wooden homesteads. Looking at the warm yellow glows from the oil lamps behind the windows I was seized with an hysterical impulse to rush screaming and laughing to the nearest door.

'Drink . . . drink!' Mieteck urged passionately, pushing into my hands the bottle of Schnapps I had completely forgotten.

192

'I was keeping it for the very end,' Mieteck said, almost apologetically. 'But we made it by our own spirits.'

The strong Schnapps burned sanity into both of us and, squatting by the snow mound at the side of the village street, we discussed our next move. There was nobody about at this time of the night and after reflection we realised that we could not be positively certain that this was the right village. In any case, how were we to find the particular man listed to assist us?

'You pick the house you fancy,' Mieteck suggested, 'and let's hope that your choice leads us to a true Polish homestead.'

'Fourth on the left,' I replied, and without further words we advanced towards it.

Our knock was answered by a tall, ascetic-looking man. He remained transfixed on the threshold as he gazed half scared at our startling appearance. Mieteck spoke to him, and the man nodded incredulously as we were ushered into the warm living-room. The scene inside was one of utter poverty, and the occupants – the man, his wife and their three children – looked at us in stark amazement with thin, drawn faces.

Mieteck explained everything, our presence at such a time of night, our journey and the reason for the long trek. He explained candidly that he was a Polish airman and that I was a British airman. When he had finished Mieteck and the entire family fell on their knees and prayed before the ornate blue-and-gold plaster cast of the Virgin Mary on the wall.

The man of the house spread sacking on the floor while his wife boiled strong scalding coffee, and the stove was charged with fresh logs. We stretched out our limbs, the glorious sense of security and the pleasant warmth of the room sealing our minds in a few seconds against our worries. While we slept the good peasants relieved us of our sodden clothing. Throughout the night they repeatedly wrapped heated sacking around our bodies to kill the stiffness and frost in our limbs, and to restore circulation. I doubt if those villagers will ever again witness such unbelievable weariness as they saw in us when we dragged ourselves from the Polish plain to their door.

We slept until lunch-time. On awakening we were greeted with dry clothes and boots, hot coffee, bread and soup. Before we dressed, the man and his wife massaged our bodies with thick fat. We declined our host's invitation to spend a further night or two in his dwelling, pointing out that it was imperative that we should reach Czestochowa as soon as possible. We were given two bottles of hot coffee apiece and as a gesture of appreciation we left with the tall Pole some of our precious cigarettes and a small gift of money. Then we said farewell to the folk who had befriended us and stepped out into the world of whirling snowflakes.

(8)

At the top of the village we linked up again with the interminable flatness of the white plain. Twenty-five miles separated us from the safety of the next village, a much larger centre than the one we had just left. Hour after hour we crunched forward, passing scattered locations of homesteads at wide intervals, and from the dazzling whiteness of daylight we passed into the early darkness of the night.

On this second leg of our march to the holy city of Czestochowa we were lucky. We did not have to fight a violent wind and a furious snowstorm. Nevertheless, we were semi-rigid with cold and weariness when the lights of our destination finally came into sight across the snow.

194

'Pick a house,' Mieteck laughed, as we approached the village, 'and I will inquire where to find Messrs. Zolonowski.' This was the name of the people we were to contact.

'I think we'll try the first house we pass,' I replied. 'The one in front and to the left of the main group.'

Mieteck banged on the door. It was opened immediately. Framed in the panel of light stood the hornet of the nest complete with jackboots and *Feldwebel* uniform.

'What do you want?' we were asked in Polish, with an unmistakable guttural German accent.

Mieteck reacted instantly. 'We are looking for friends named Kowalski,' he lied. 'Perhaps you know of them?'

The German glared suspiciously. 'Where do you come from?' he snapped.

Mieteck lied again.

The heavy German moved down the single step leading from the house and stood behind us, one hand resting on his revolver holster.

'You have no right to be wandering about at this time of night, after curfew,' he said. 'What is the reason?'

'Our friends are sick,' replied Mieteck, meekly and unconvincingly.

'You lie!' snapped the German. 'Where are your papers?'

I had so far remained silent but now I realised that something had to be done, and quickly, so I took over.

'Here they are,' I answered in German, placing one hand inside my jacket. At the same time I lashed the German a good, solid smack in the groin with my boot.

He gasped and grunted as I gave him two more kicks in rapid succession. Unfortunately, he did not drop but only reeled backwards into the open doorway.

195

'Murder . . . murder!' he bawled.

I sprinted off with Mieteck hard on my heels, pressing on into the darkness. It was quite obvious that the injured German would create hell in the village, and that his friends would quickly organise a manhunt so we dragged on through the snow as fast as possible and for the first few hours the realisation of the danger we had left behind ironed out our weariness.

The next reliable village was sixteen kilometres away, but Mieteck was quite concerned about our footprint trail in the snow, so we hailed with thankfulness the light flakes that started to fall.

'Even at this rate of fall,' remarked Mieteck, happily, 'an hour will completely cover up all signs of our tracks.'

We were soon to experience again the trials and horrors of our first night on the plain. Near to the limit of our endurance we staggered on, tottering and floundering like drunken men. I calculated that we must have covered the best part of ten kilometres, but was afraid to think about how, in such condition, we were going to make the remaining six.

'I must rest awhile,' panted Mieteck. 'I'm all in.'

I looked at his white taut face, and knew that he was. Quickly I got the little stove working and heated up a can of beans and brewed some steaming hot cocoa. It eased the strain, and Mieteck slept. Sitting on guard I was half asleep myself when I faintly picked up the sound of an animal baying in the distance. At first I thought my mind was playing tricks, but it kept on and on, compelling me to stir myself to listening alertness. In the lapses between the gusts of wind the sound of baying was certainly floating out over the plain, and I suddenly remembered the warning we had received about the likelihood of wolves.

I awakened Mieteck, lathering his face with snow. The word

wolves revitalised him more than anything else could have done and, crouched in the snow and the darkness, we strained our ears for a further ten minutes as we tried to identify the sound. Then, suddenly, it ceased. Only the panting of the wind could be heard. I checked on my compass to determine the direction from which I assumed the noise had come. It was about fifteen degrees to the left of our course to the village.

To this day I cannot fathom the reason why I insisted that we should venture those fifteen degrees off track. The baying had suggested to me, for some unknown reason, the one and only course to follow. A partly numbed mind possibly suggested that to walk towards the wolves was the safest tactical means of avoiding them. Acute weariness on that Polish plain was playing queer tricks with my thinking.

We trudged on, Mieteck offering no opposition, and we had covered something like a mile when we again picked up the baying. It was louder and came from more to the right. Listening attentively we now felt certain that it was the lone baying of a dog. We advanced towards the intermittent barking. Mieteck wisely suggested that we rest awhile, and recoup our strength for whatever might lay ahead. Dogs did not usually exist without human beings.

As we lay resting in the snow we suddenly realised the reason for the dog's excitement and restlessness.

'Wolves for certain,' Mieteck whispered hoarsely.

Then, though we could not see them, we heard them close enough. There came to our ears a low, whimpering sobbing from more than one throat, gradually swelling to a dull, concerted growling, with, at intervals, crisp snarling.

I jerked Mieteck to his feet, and we moved off at a fast pace towards the barking dog. We came to a farmstead, and a few hundred yards from it were two large outhouses. The dog was now kicking up a fearful din, and as we circled the nearest outhouse, a lamp was lit in the dwelling-house window. I was almost mad with fury, and determined to stand for no hindrance or interference. In the vicinity there were wolves that would rip us to pieces, and closer to us than the wolves were perhaps human enemies. I unsheathed my long-bladed knife. 'We'll get our sleep,' I reassured my friend, 'and we'll fight it out with anyone who attempts to stop us.'

The shed was built of wide lengths of timber and, heaving on the two bottom strips, we prised them apart enough to permit entry. Inside, the agreeable scent of hay came to our nostrils. I gasped with delight when my flashlight beam revealed two-thirds of the interior crammed to the ceiling with hay. We climbed to the top of the pile and buried ourselves in its warm softness. Through the baying of a dog the most wonderful bed this side of heaven had been given to us. Before I lapsed into oblivion I sheathed my knife and stuffed it down the front of my shirt.

It was afternoon before I was awakened. Mieteck was nudging me. Opening my eyes, I saw that he had a finger over his lips to indicate the need for silence. He pointed downwards towards the floor. Peering through an opening in the hay which Mieteck had made I saw a girl of about twenty poised in the open doorway of the shed. She held on a leash a large Alsatian dog which was keenly sniffing the air.

The girl slowly looked around the interior of our hiding-place, her face half puzzled. Then, suddenly, Mieteck broke the silence and spoke to her. She started back, but did not run away.

'Please do not be frightened,' Mieteck told her. 'I am a true

Polish patriot, and have with me a reliable comrade. We have suffered hardship and distress in escaping from the German occupiers of our country. I pray that we can count you as our friend.'

Without fear or hesitation the girl turned her head towards our hiding-place.

'We knew you were here,' she said. 'My father watched you walk to this barn early this morning and go inside. He didn't want to frighten or disturb you because he knew you must be very weary. A German patrol visited us three hours ago and inquired if we had seen anything of two men, strangers. They are visiting all the farmsteads. My father is here, so please do not be frightened.'

The girl's father, who must have been just around the wall of the shed, approached at her command.

'Please do not run away,' he said. 'Come to the house and have food.'

We climbed down and accompanied the man and his daughter to the house. The girl's parents were elderly peasants, and their genuine pleasure at our entry into their parlour made me relax my clutch on my knife.

Mieteck poured out our story and they listened aghast. Great was their proud joy when he explained his original escape from Poland to Britain where he joined the Royal Air Force and operated with a Polish Squadron against the Germans.

The housewife busied herself with the preparation of a solid meal, and the husband, without question, provided us with fresh shirts and socks. Mieteck and I were far from properly rested. Our nerves were still raw after the trials of the days before, and our muscles were stiff and swollen. We asked the hospitable Pole if we might stay a further twenty-four hours and lie-up in his barn.

199

He readily agreed and this long rest, plus his wife's strengthening broths, greatly improved our physical condition.

The next day our host offered helpful advice and practical assistance. He would go ahead of us by horse and sleigh and talk to our contacts near the church. If all was safe in the village he would return and pick us up on the plain and transport us by sleigh to our destination.

We gave him an hour's start before setting out in the direction of the village. We were half-way there before we heard the approaching sleigh bells in the distance. Darkness was now almost complete. The elderly Pole had assured us that he would pass us on the plain before it grew dusk, but something must have delayed him. I took out my flashlamp and signalled in the direction of the bells. They ceased to tinkle and out of the darkness came a series of answering torchlight flashes. Then the bells began to jingle merrily again and Mieteck remarked: 'More than one sleigh is approaching us.' He was right. Soon we were surrounded by three horse-sleighs and three figures.

'All is well,' said the elderly Pole, as he introduced us to the other two loyalists, and then, waving goodbye, drove off into the night.

(9)

That night we stayed with a man and his wife and two boys of about twenty, placid peasant folk who viewed the German occupation with its miseries and starvation with a profound philosophy of indifference. Suppression and suffering could not dampen the fire of their Catholic faith. I knew nothing about Catholicism, particularly as it was practised and preached among Polish peasants and to whom it was an influence above all earthly considerations. Their persistent kneeling before vividly-painted plaster images amounted in my mind to a fetish. Nevertheless, it gave to these Polish people a magical power of spiritual solace and it would have been imprudent and anything but grateful or diplomatic to abstain from getting to my knees and joining in the repeated prayers. I was never a religious man to any deep and serious intent, nor shall I ever be one; but in the interests of escape I would unflinchingly have become a Buddhist.

We pushed off from the house early next morning on the longest leg of our journey. It had to be completed by nightfall. We were to contact the priest of the district and obtain from him final instructions for our entry into Czestochowa and details for getting in touch with the underground movement.

For six hours we made good progress until the apparently inevitable severe snowstorm lashed across the plain. We approached a small, unpretentious shack and sought shelter from the fury of the storm. I shall never forget the scene of ghastly squalor and poverty within. The one room was occupied by a sick man and wife and an eighteen-months-old baby. Mieteck, in a kindly voice, asked if we could remain until the storm abated. From the trembling in his voice I knew that the tragic spectacle of his countryman's plight had deeply upset him.

'Please abide with us,' replied the sick Pole in a thin voice. 'But we have no food other than a few potatoes.'

The poor devil's face was chalk white, and his hacking cough was never absent for more than a couple of minutes at a time. Here was a man in a dreadful state of emaciation, one foot firmly planted in the grave.

'The poor fellow is in the last stages of tuberculosis,' I whispered to Mieteck in English. 'For God's sake let's open some of our canned stuff.'

The gallant little Polish wife was too weak to lift the iron kettle to the stove, and the whimpering child was a pathetic mockery of a baby, all skin and bone. I could not take my eyes from the infant's face, and I shall never forget its eyes. They burned with an incredible age and intelligence, brown eyes that seemed to have been attuned to the business of living for a century. There seemed to be nothing in the face but eyes.

We learned that their monthly ration consisted of a few kilos of potatoes and one 'cartwheel' of black bread, as the fourteen-inch diameter loaf was described. We gave them a tin of margarine, some beans and a small container of evaporated milk for the child.

Their gratitude was overwhelming. The woman fell on her knees and, raising her outstretched hands which grasped the tin of milk, sobbed out thanks to the Almighty.

The dying man told us that we had an eight-hours march to reach the big house of the priest.

'You will be happy there,' he told us with a certain amount of awe. 'It is a beautiful house inside. The priest has just paid six thousand zlotys for new furniture from a destitute village.'

'Does the priest ever call and see you?' I asked.

'Oh, yes,' was the ingenuous reply. 'Every five weeks or so. We all kneel and pray together in this room for God's blessing and justice and freedom again.'

Apparently the priest toured all the outlying homesteads in his zone and collected what he could get towards the upkeep of the beautiful church on the hill with the wonderful golden roof.

The snowstorm was over, and I wanted to get moving. As we

tramped through the soft snow Mieteck was touchy and unusually quiet. I concluded that the suffering we had left behind had unnerved him. He did not improve with distance, and I was soon made aware of what was on his mind.

'I know you hate Catholicism,' he exclaimed angrily. 'But what right had you to ask so many questions about the priest?'

As we tramped shoulder to shoulder I told Mieteck frankly that I hated nothing about Catholicism, that I just mistrusted any kind of religious creed, that, in eighty per cent. of all religious orders, God was merely an excuse for hypocrisy, graft and greed. I told him sincerely that I was much impressed by the inspiring strength of his people's religious outlook, but at the same time I considered that money expended on furniture or food for dying parishioners would have been more charitably invested.

'What is more,' I told Mieteck, 'frankly, I entertain the most unpleasant premonitions about calling on this priest. I advise that we leave his place alone.'

Mieteck remained quiet for a long time before he turned on me and there was cold hate and murder in his eyes.

'I shall tell him everything you have said,' he remarked bitterly. 'You will have to ask his forgiveness. It is my sacred duty to inform him of the disbeliever you are. We have not used the escape money which my friends in the mine have given us. I shall give it to him for distribution among the poor.'

I looked Mieteck straight in the eyes. 'Tell him what you like about me,' I replied, 'but not a penny of that escape money will go to a bloody soul until we are out of Poland and can't use it.'

The wind howled. We were half blinded with stinging snow and petrified with cold. As we stumbled forward I knew that Mieteck was smouldering. He maintained a wicked silence. Mile after mile

203

we put behind us. The snow ceased and progress was easier but still Mieteck did not speak.

In the early light I was able to pin-point certain features on my quarter-inch-to-the-mile survey map and I realised that we were off track. Quietly I told Mieteck that we were six miles north-east of our destination.

Mieteck turned on me savagely. 'You lousy British liar!' he gasped. Some bee in his bonnet was prompting him to believe that my reluctance to call on the priest was now inspiring me to deceive him about our course.

'O.K.' I retorted. 'Have it your own way. But when you know for certain that I've told the truth, and we are stranded, I demand an apology.'

We trudged on. I was smouldering with fury.

Eventually Mieteck realised that his stupidity was leading us miles out of the way and asked me to revise our course to bring us to the village.

'Apologise first,' I said. 'Apologise here and now for what you said about a British liar.'

We were both stretched to breaking point, beyond calm thought and reasoned action. Half frozen we faced each other, toe to toe, in a small hollow in the snow. We blazed with fury.

Suddenly Mieteck's restraint broke. He lunged at me. At his blow I, too, lost my temper. And there on the desolate Polish plain we fought like murderous rivals. We grappled, smashed and kicked, each intent on killing the other. We both struggled to get our knives free but then, somewhere in the back of my mind, I heard the voice of my long-since-dead Yorkshire schoolmaster. He always preached: 'Fight fair . . . Avoid a brain flash. . . . The first man to go berserk with temper loses the battle.'

I stopped groping for my knife. Instead I managed to wrap an arm about Mieteck's windpipe and squandered his strength and almost his life before I released him. As he crumpled I stepped back and pulled the long knife from his belt.

'You fool!' I said. 'You won't soak *my* blood on your plain, neither will my knife be bathed in Polish blood. I've had more experience of real knife-play than you have, and it's not good for peace of mind. I'm dependent on you in your land, but never under-estimate the British.'

I walked up to him and drove my fist straight into his face. Slowly, with measured force, I repeated the blow three times.

Mieteck never uttered a word. When I had finished he spat out blood and padded his damaged face with snow compresses. Then he rose to his feet and stared at me, his face a tangle of emotions.

'Well, Mieteck,' I inquired, 'what's it to be? If we stick together our fight must be forgotten. If you can't forget I shall leave you.'

Mieteck made the sign of the Cross. 'I am sorry for mistrusting you,' he said. 'My mind was tortured by what I saw in that starving shack. They are my people and I cannot bear you treating our religion and our beliefs with such contempt. You cannot understand us. But I swear I shall never let you down. Neither will the holy Catholic Church of Poland. Wait and see.'

We bent forward and plodded into the wind, arms entwined about each other's waist, and a great brotherly love flowed between us.

(10)

We had been walking perhaps another mile when the village in which the important priest lived appeared on the horizon before us. As we approached, it looked at first like a handful of coal pitched at random about the white snow landscape.

Our bodies jerked forward without pliancy, and the black outlines of the houses seemed to sway and slowly rise and fall. Frequently during our long overland march from the mine, when great weariness overtook us, the surface of the snowed-up plain appeared to lift gently like a milky, swelling sea.

Nearer and nearer we approached, and fear stalked at our heels when we realised that our advance from the plain could be watched from many windows facing us. We knew that all villages had been checked by German patrols. This was a big village, a small township. Would informers or Germans spot us?

We entered the village and we found the priest's house. For half an hour we hovered in the garden, rapping at frequent intervals on the door at the rear. The only response was the barking of a dog.

'No priest and no protection or progress here,' I told Mieteck at last. 'I feel that it is dangerous to remain here much longer.'

'Let's get going immediately,' answered Mieteck with determined resolve. 'I, too, have misgivings.'

Our uneasiness was not unfounded. We learned afterwards that a search party of Germans combed the village at the instigation of someone who had seen us enter.

We were now only sixteen miles from our journey's end, Czestochowa, so we hastily turned our backs on the village and started off. Out in the open again we felt more at ease, and paused to calculate distances and the safest route to our destination. We reckoned that the closely guarded border zone of *General Gouvernement*, beyond which lay Czestochowa, was a few miles ahead of us. To get into Czestochowa would demand our keenest vigilance and resourcefulness for there was a large German garrison in the city. It was an important supply base, apparently for provisioning the troops at the Eastern front.

The landscape took on a happier complexion after the monotony of the barren plain. Large tracts of pine forest spread about us. We had no alternative but to move through the woods. We had covered about four miles and had just emerged from the darkness of a pine forest when we saw not more than 400 yards ahead of us concrete pill-boxes and two patrolling sentries.

'Down!' Mieteck croaked. '*Verdammt!*'

We buried ourselves in the snow on the inside edge of the forest, and for ninety minutes we lay motionless, watching the movements of the guards while the coldness of the late afternoon penetrated our inactive bodies.

'We ought to risk a crossing now,' I said at last. 'If we wait until nightfall the Germans will no doubt be super-vigilant, and we'll more than likely be frostbitten.'

The clearing in front of us up to the next wood was profusely dotted with small spruce and pine trees a few feet high so we secured for ourselves a small pine tree apiece and, holding this camouflage in front of us as steadily as we were able, dragged ourselves across the snow foot by foot until we were close to the guard's beat. The second guard could be heard, but not seen, from this advanced position.

We watched in silence as the sullen-faced, heavily clad German stamped up and down over seventy-five yards of beat. It was not impossible to risk a run for the safety of the wood twenty yards behind the guard without being seen. We could wait until his back was turned and dive for it when he was twenty yards or so from the end of his patrol. Only one factor upset us. Unless he was a rank, unobservant fool he could not fail to notice, when he walked back to the pill-box, two sets of deep footprints running at right angles to his beat.

It was an impasse, and we lay for a further half-hour not keen to advance and not caring to retreat. Then fate took a hand. Two Germans came into sight from behind the pill-box and the patrolling guard walked up to them and spoke.

'The changing of the guard,' Mieteck whispered. 'We should stand a better chance.'

We were all set to go when the three men moved inside the pill-box. No real windows looked out, only narrow slits. Without a moment's hesitation we plunged forward, bent double. We gained the fringe of the wood over the frontier, lay flat on the ground to steady our breathing, and watched the three men reappear. The old guard and a second party strode off without a word, and the new guard wandered slowly along his beat. On his return he paused for a few seconds and surveyed our footprints in the snow. Then, quite unconcernedly, he continued his leisurely strolling.

We decided to press forward as quickly as possible to a small township a few miles ahead of Czestochowa and attempt to find a safe hiding-place where we could dry our clothes before making the final move into the city the next day.

'I hope we are lucky and find a decent place,' I remarked. 'We must shave and make ourselves as presentable as we can.'

We both looked dishevelled and scruffy and it was obvious that our tramp-like appearances would arouse suspicions.

'I think I have the answer,' Mieteck replied. 'The church in the township is a satellite of the main Catholic Cathedral in Czestochowa. The people to whom we're reporting in the city, and the folk in the church ahead, must all be in the swim. We should arrive there in time for the evening service. And afterwards we'll remain behind and contact one of the officials.'

An hour and a half later we approached the lighted windows of a high and narrow church. As we passed through the iron gates chanting voices proclaimed that the service was in progress. We passed through the high doorway into the church and sank to our knees near the wall, away from the bulk of the congregation.

This was my first visit to a Catholic church and in spite of my beliefs I was deeply impressed by the beauty of the interior, the high vaulted roof of gold, the profound atmosphere, and the hushed and humble murmuring from the bowed worshippers. A gratifying sense of tranquillity swept over me.

Kneeling, we watched the church as it emptied and, feigning prayer, kept the verger in sight as he did his final rounds. Twice he walked passed us and paused, not quite certain of our prolonged and silent devotion. He came close to us for a third time and suspiciously scrutinised us. He seemed almost hypnotised by our unkempt appearances but, plucking up courage, he advanced to the end of the row of seats and uttered a few sentences in a quiet voice. Mieteck promptly replied in rapid Polish, including the words: '*Krasinski-Drohobycz.*' The verger turned white and trembled. 'Stay seated,' he told us. 'I will lock the doors. Then please tell me your story.'

He joined us a few minutes later. Mieteck told our story and the verger's manner softened.

'Our priest is in Czestochowa,' he told us, 'but you must not under any consideration call at the original address given to you. The Germans have been showing unusual alertness about the building and we do not want any disaster. Providence directed you here first.'

Mieteck was given an alternative address, a smaller church ten minutes' walk from the main edifice and much less observed by the Germans.

'So you are the two escapees that the Germans have gone to such lengths to track down these last two days,' the old verger remarked in awe. 'They have scoured all the villages and have even used an aeroplane over the plain.'

He put out the lights in the church and we resumed our conversation in a small ante-room. We were not happy to learn that every road and bridge leading into the city of Czestochowa was guarded and that to enter the city we must cross a river and a deep railway cutting, also under German observation.

When we had finished discussing our plight, the old verger took stock of our clothing sizes and told us he would get his housekeeper to prepare food for us and would scout around and procure some clean and tidy clothes.

About an hour and a half later he returned with coffee, a can of hot soup, bread and cheese. While we ate we were told of what we were to do. Before he left us, the kindly verger requested that we should kneel, and he prayed for guidance for the hazardous journey we had to undertake the next morning.

Mieteck was preparing to stretch out on the floor when it occurred to me that it would be unwise to remain in the small ante-room as it offered no escape should any hostile persons enter from the doorway. I felt it would be safer to bed down in the main body of the church with separate sleeping positions.

'We can't be too careful now that we are so near our goal,' I advised.

I selected a tombstone a few feet from the wall, half-way up the church, and stretched out beside it, well sheltered by adjacent seats. Mieteck chose a similar spot about twenty yards away. I was too acutely tired to worry much about the hard, cold flooring, or to conjure up any disturbing thoughts about the close proximity to the long-since-dead Pole. In fact, I slept as peacefully as he.

It was after daybreak when Mieteck aroused me. 'Come,' he said urgently, we have overslept. It is already late.'

We slipped out of the side door into the cold air and covered at a brisk pace the three miles to the old lady's cottage to which we had been directed by the verger. We were welcomed there as old friends and drank coffee and breakfasted on eggs and bread. While we ate she informed us that she had been a nursing sister in the city for over twenty years. She was now quite happy in her retirement, and lived only for the day when the enemy would be conquered and driven for ever from the Poland she loved.

We donned the neat and serviceable clothes our verger friend had somehow collected for us, and felt once more like respectable human beings.

The old lady handed Mieteck a letter containing instructions as to the best place to cross the river. There were no instructions for crossing the railway cutting. We were told to use our own skill and ingenuity as it was constantly patrolled.

We kissed the old lady farewell and set off along the road in the direction of the main bridge. Ahead of us, and tramping in the same direction, were a couple of ladies and an elderly man. Slackening our speed, we followed them at a safe distance. They topped a rise in the road and were obscured from view, and we were almost on the crest and preparing to follow down the other side when we heard the harsh command of '*Halt*'. We stopped dead in our tracks, and then made a bee-line for a clump of bushes.

Cautiously we advanced until we could see what was happening on the other side of the rise. Below us lay the main bridge, a yellow pole barring the crossing, guarded by two soldiers with tommy guns.

We watched the sentries examining the papers of the three civilians. Baskets were carefully searched and one of the women pulled her shawl from her head, doubtless at the request of the guards.

'Perhaps they think the two escapees might attempt to evade them in disguise,' tittered Mieteck.

We retreated a quarter of a mile up the road, and then cut obliquely towards the river, contacting it the best part of a mile from the dangerous main bridge. We were not long in spotting the partly constructed factory on the opposite bank and the important wooden bridge, improvised for workmen's use, which we had been told to look for.

'O.K.,' Mieteck said, decisively. 'Do exactly as I do, and don't utter a single word.'

Walking straight up to a stack of floor timbers piled this side of the bridge, Mieteck hoisted some to his shoulder and without hesitation strode on to the gangplanks of the bridge and headed for the opposite side. I did the same and as we stepped off the bridge a group of workmen idly looked us up and down. Mieteck dumped his planks and, turning to the onlookers, remarked crisply: 'When is this cursed snow going to disappear? Wouldn't be so bad if we could eat the stuff, eh?' Turning to me he rapped out: 'Make a note for a further supply of scaffolding poles to be delivered tomorrow.' Then without another word he turned on his heel and picked his way through the half-finished building.

On the other side a German soldier paced leisurely up and

212

down near a concrete mixer. Mieteck, without nervousness, approached him with a cheerful greeting. 'A lorry load of cement will be here in about an hour,' said Mieteck. 'Will you see that it is stored under cover as soon as it arrives? And two of your engineering officers are coming along this morning to inspect the bridge.'

'*Ja, Ja!*' answered the guard.

I followed Mieteck. Casually we made our way up the road leading into the town. In a matter of minutes we encountered the wide railway cutting. Halting, we watched two guards patrolling along the embankment.

'Guess we have to repeat the same bold performance,' Mieteck chuckled. 'Here . . . get yourself a straight stick and tie a bit of wood to the end of it.'

He showed me how to make two sticks look like rail-tapping hammers, and then we approached and dropped into the cutting at the furthermost point from the sentries. Nonchalantly wandering up the track we kept stooping to examine the rails. From our position below the level of the bank we saw that the guards had halted and were watching our movements carefully. Mieteck picked up a piece of stone and struck the rail with a loud metallic ring, at the same time pretending to swing his artificial hammer. Under his breath he whispered: 'When I swing the hammer, you strike the rail with a stone right behind me. For God's sake don't let them see the trick.'

We did this at intervals for a quarter of a mile. I was sweating like a pig as we approached and passed the guards. But Mieteck blithely yelled out in Polish: 'Good morning. Don't fancy your job this chilly weather.'

The guards merely nodded.

213

'Let's hop it now,' I beseeched Mieteck, but he merely grunted: 'A little longer. We want to win them over completely.'

We moved back along the parallel set of rails and, pausing right in front of the fat guard, Mieteck cheekily asked him what time he finished duty.

'In an hour,' was the reply, with a more friendly rejoinder: 'Couldn't care much about this lousy job. I'm going on leave in two days.'

We propped our imitation long-shafted hammers against a brick ledge, well away from the guard, crossed the rails, and clambered up the opposite bank.

'Brrr,' said Mieteck in a friendly tone as the guard walked up to us. 'Wish I had an indoor job these cold days.' He offered the German a cigarette, and added: 'We're just slipping along to get some sleeper plates and some coffee. We shan't be long. We'll bring you a bottle back with us.'

The German seemed quite bucked at this generous suggestion and without another word we walked off towards the highway near by. We soon disappeared in the close-knit pattern of buildings and crowds. We were at last safely in Czestochowa.

(11)

The streets of Czestochowa were teeming with German uniforms. As we turned into the main thoroughfare leading up to the cathedral at the top of the hill we passed a number of German military police screaming at a pathetic party of Polish Jews whom they were herding along like so many head of cattle.

'Wonder what the poor, miserable devils have done to deserve that,' I muttered.

Mieteck replied under his breath: 'Don't talk . . . just keep moving.' And he quickened his pace.

A few minutes later we turned off sharp right into a narrow, twisting street.

'There is the church,' panted Mieteck, as it appeared right on top of us. 'I pray the old verger had no difficulty in contacting the right people.'

'So do I,' I fervently replied.

We slipped into the small and empty church. In the back row of seats we bent down on our knees and cupped our hands. Mieteck was genuinely absorbed in deep prayer for about ten minutes before he stirred.

'You stay here,' he instructed me. 'I'm going to check up.'

He walked the length of the church and passed through a small door at the altar end of the building. He seemed to be away for hours. In fact, it was more than an hour, and towards the end I was really praying that everything was all right. When he returned he was accompanied by a tall, gaunt-looking priest. Silently he beckoned to me to follow, and the three of us moved out of the church into the priest's sanctum. In the warm, cosy room the priest asked me many questions in German. I shall never forget the way he looked me straight in the eye and asked: 'Are you a Jew?'

'I am an Englishman, from Yorkshire,' I replied, 'with no Semitic blood in me whatsoever.'

Then the priest told me that in Poland people with red hair were invariably Jewish.

After he had heard our story the good priest locked us in his study, telling us he was going to interview the people the old verger had already contacted on our behalf, inform them of our safe arrival, and arrange for us to be taken to a safe place of refuge.

'I will be back as soon as I can,' he added. 'Please keep your voices low and do not answer any knocks on the door. I want nobody to know that you are here. It is essential that you both move to another place before curfew.'

We were alone in the room for hours, it seemed, before the priest reappeared. Darkness was fast approaching when he quietly let himself into the sanctum.

'Everything is arranged,' he told us. 'You will be well cared for by members of the resistance movement. But we haven't a minute to spare.'

We tagged along behind the tall, stooping priest for the best part of an hour, clearing the streets of the town proper without any incidents, until we reached a large, square building, two upper windows of which revealed soft, glowing lights.

Our guide led us to a small doorway at the rear of the house. The door was open and, passing through, we found ourselves in a wide and well-lighted stone-flagged corridor. We were asked to wait and the priest moved away, presumably to announce our arrival. What happened next completely staggered me.

Instead of the priest returning with male members of the underground movement, he was accompanied by three nuns. We were greeted softly in Polish, and escorted to the presence of the Mother Superior. As we climbed a flight of stairs leading to her room, Mieteck whispered in my ear: 'We are in a nunnery. Please try not to swear.'

In all my life I never imagined that I would ever violate the holy sanctuary of a nunnery. It appeared incredible. The truth of the situation was quickly realised, however, when the kindly Mother

Superior told my friend that in the name of God, Poland and Righteousness, it was her sacred and loyal duty, and that of her establishment, to feed, protect and shelter us.

A nun was detailed to show us to our quarters in a wing at the far end of the building. It was an immense joy to enter a warm and comfortable room, boasting two neat beds with spotless linen. On a table some thoughtful person had placed three packets of cigarettes, matches and chocolate. An adjacent bathroom was pointed out to us. Before I crawled into bed that night, a satisfying meal was followed by a long and glorious immersion in steaming hot water, the most wonderful I had ever experienced.

CHAPTER 8

PLEURISY – AND CAPTURE

(I)

Despite the tragic, muddled and incredibly poverty-stricken existence of Polish people under the ruthless pressure of the German Occupation, the Sisters of Mercy treated us nobly.

But as the days trickled by a deep smouldering pain developed in one of my lungs and my temperature started to dance about the thermometer. My lungs had not resisted the hardships of our prolonged flight across the Polish plain. The long forced marches, completed when we were half-conscious from lack of sleep and almost frozen from lack of warmth, had seriously sapped my resistance, and the sodden clothing and the steaming of my heated body had struck at my lungs.

One Sunday morning the pleurisy took a turn for the worse. The pain grew to a torment, and by nightfall I was unconscious. It was thirty-six hours before I was conscious and coherent again, but my physical condition was very weak.

During my illness, a young nun called Maria was my constant companion and devoted nurse. She would whisper to me: *'Eine feste Burg ist unser Gott'* [Our God is a strong tower]. I was impressed by her charming and correct manners, her naïveté and her sensitiveness. As she sat by my bed like a ministering angel, I confided to her all my thoughts, hopes and ambitions. Quietly and whimsically she would listen, composed and beautiful, a balance of sympathy and understanding.

218

PLEURISY – AND CAPTURE

Maria, in her turn, told me about her family in Posen, and from her vivid descriptions I felt that I had known her father, mother, brothers and sisters for years.

Gradually my health improved and my strength accumulated. The prospect of my weakened lungs jeopardising further escape decreased as the tugging pain gave way to only an occasional sharp stab. But I realised that for quite a time I would not be capable of standing up to any tests of physical endurance and hardship. Yet with each day that passed our time in Czestochowa was running out. Underground organisers had made arrangements for our journey eastwards and soon we would have to go. It was planned that, in the company of a Sister of Mercy, we would leave our hiding-place, and with forged curfew papers go down to the station and take the train for Cracow. The Sister of Mercy would escort us on the first leg of the journey, and bid us farewell when we actually boarded the Trans-Polish express which would carry us to the Ukraine.

Poles of the Resistance Movement in the East would be informed of our departure, and they would meet and take us under their wing.

A forged passport was being made out for me in the name of Henryk Kowalski, a concrete labourer who, according to other papers being prepared, was being directed to the East by the German Military Directorate for duties in road construction. I was instructed to memorise the details surrounding my new name and character. First an Englishman, then a New Zealander, now a Pole. What the devil next?

A few nights later the underground people gave us a strict and final briefing. We were made to swear on oath before the Cross that if we were captured and tortured no word would pass our lips

219

about where we had stayed. If the Gestapo learned of the nunnery the loyal Sisters of Mercy would suffer torture and possibly death.

(2)

On the stroke of nine o'clock Mieteck and I, with the nun detailed to escort us, stepped outside the nunnery into the moist darkness. It was snowing. As we passed through the gate I turned to take a final look at the building which had sheltered us, and to express my heartfelt thanks to the kind women within it. The nun squeezed my arm, and said softly: 'Come . . . Brace yourself for the journey to the station.'

The streets were deserted. The houses we passed looked gaunt and browbeaten, and the big moon seemed puzzled. The swishy reflections it cast on the window appeared to suggest a sulking, downcast shame. It was not wholesome in Czestochowa after curfew, a town simmering with hate, a town suffering the most infamous treatment at the hands of its jackbooted occupiers.

We had covered half the journey to the station when out from the shadows stepped a German military policeman. 'Papers,' he barked. Quietly and with perfect composure the nun handed him the documents. In the light from a flashlamp they were closely studied. Although Mieteck and I affected nonchalance, our hearts nevertheless pounded and our muscles were tensed.

'*Gut*,' said the German as he thrust the papers back into the nun's hand.

Prickling with relief we went on.

The station was crowded with ill-clad and listless men and women, the majority of them *en route* under German orders to join labour corps behind the lines in the East. We mooched among these people, with their pathetic little bundles of belongings, for over three hours, waiting for a long-overdue train, and the freezing night air did not assist our comfort.

The station walls were splashed with big posters screaming a campaign of hate against the Jews. One registered itself vividly on my mind. It portrayed an old Jew with a beaked nose and skull cap busy dropping dead rats into a mincing machine while from the other end sausage was issuing into a bowl. The caption read: 'No more Jewish foodshops for Poland. We must exterminate Jewish poison as we would exterminate rats.'

A violent pogrom was in swing against all things Jewish in Czestochowa. The Germans had restricted all Jews to the ghettos, and Jewish property and businesses had been seized and confiscated. The nun told us that it was a common sight in the town to see former Jewish business and professional men, clad in rags, sweeping the streets with German guards, a pistol in one hand, a whip in the other, standing over them.

Public exhibitions were organised by the Gestapo in the market square and the unwilling Poles were compelled to attend. The exhibitions featured the mass shaving of female heads, a punishment meted out by the Germans for what they termed disobedience to German occupational regulations. The 'disobedience' was refusal by Polish women to consort and fraternise with the soldiers who sought to gratify themselves. The women were fastened to benches and publicly horse-sheared. Sobbing with shame and fright they were released only when they were close-cropped.

Towards the end of the three-hours' wait I felt stirrings of the burning in my lung. I became frightened when I contemplated trouble that might interfere with the second phase of our escape. By the time the train drew in I was soaking wet with perspiration in spite of the coldness of the night air. This was the first time I had ventured outside the nunnery since I had first entered it, and I endeavoured to console myself with the thought that it was purely a natural readjustment to getting about again and being active. But it was a relief when the train finally drew in, and I was able to relax on a wooden seat in the corner.

We chugged out of the station into a blinding snowstorm, and the good nun opposite took out from her bag a flask of hot coffee. Without inquiring about my condition she gave me three tablets and told me to 'try and sleep'.

The train was due to reach Cracow in the morning, and Mieteck was worried in case some delay caused us to miss the Trans-Polish express to the Ukraine.

'Don't worry,' the nun reassured him. 'This is a most important feeder train, and the Ukraine express will wait.'

The tablets put me to sleep for a while and when I awoke I was oozing perspiration. The pain in my lung was stabbing severely and a sticky heat seemed to be rising from my chest to my brain.

Snorting and slicing through a phantom world, the train breathed heavily across a desert of white towards Cracow. The high-riding moon, like an imperial spectator, washed the width of the visible world with a luminous glow. The train had acquired greater confidence as the snow had ceased to fall, and at intervals snorted a shriek of defiance.

The rhythmic optimism of the train did not stimulate my own courage to combat the sharpening pains in my shoulder, or help me to dismiss the burning behind my forehead and the prickings behind my eyes. After two-thirds of the distance had been covered I was struggling to stop myself from writhing with pain. I knew all too well that as far as further travel was concerned, I had had my chips.

222

The thick atmosphere of the carriage became unbearable. Assisted by Mieteck I was moved into the lavatory, where I was violently sick.

Facing Mieteck I told him what I had decided. 'Sorry, Mieteck . . . I can never get as far as the Ukraine in this condition,' I said. 'I'm getting worse, and I would only jeopardise your chances. In fairness to you the bond of partnership is finished. All I want to do is keep a reasonable state of mind until we get to Cracow, where I am sure to find some place to curl up and rest awhile. You carry on and get to Britain.'

Mieteck was deeply upset. He brought the nun to my side in the small space between the carriages. She told me to hold out with all the determination possible until we got beyond the barriers at Cracow. Once there she would immediately contact people who would look after me until I was fit.

'When you are fit to travel again,' she said, 'we will all return to Czestochowa, where we will get you properly well so that you can continue your escape. Mieteck refuses to leave you until you are yourself again.

I returned to my seat but during the final stage of the run a compelling voice reminded me that Mieteck's escape must go on. Since he was determined not to leave me it was up to me to leave him.

The train pulled in to the platform and thronging, bustling activity hemmed us in. The fresh, cool air was a relief, and I suggested to Mieteck that we might make a call at the lavatory. The nun waited at a coffee stall and, joining a small queue of men a little distance away inside a large lavatory, we waited our turn, Mieteck behind me.

I stepped forward to a position almost at the far end of the chamber, at least thirty compartments away from Mieteck, divided by wide and lofty slabs of slate. The instant he was out of sight behind the surface of slate, I slipped out of the narrow entrance a couple of yards away, and made straight for the waiting nun.

Hurriedly I told her not to attempt to stop me from leaving them, and that she must see that Mieteck caught the train to the Ukraine. I could not go on hindering his chances, and I preferred to leave this way. I told her to tell Mieteck that his progress would be my progress, and that she could trust me never to breathe a word about her and her loyal people.

I fell down the stairway into a busy Cracow thoroughfare. Mingling with pedestrians, I walked quickly and blindly onwards, my brain throbbing and my senses wavering. My escape was over, everything was finished, and all I wanted was a place where I could sit down and sleep. Up one street and down another I wandered at random until I came to a wide open space, a public Garden of Rest surrounded by tall, frowning buildings. I fell on a vacant bench and remembered nothing more until I came to my senses some hours later.

My mind was not functioning with any clarity. Half-dazed I looked at the intoxicated face of a public clock across the square, and in a whirl of confusion struggled to recollect its significance.

Then it came to me. Mieteck the Pole . . . He would surely have caught the express to the Ukraine by now. Good old Mieteck . . . The man I had fought in the snow . . . The man who would get through and tell my folk in Yorkshire the whole story . . . Struggling mentally with ideas of Yorkshire and Mieteck's escape I lapsed again into senselessness.

My fevered condition made me careless and stupid. Even while I honoured Mieteck's escape and the journey planned for us, I neglected to destroy the forged documents in my pocket made out in the name of Henryk Kowalski.

I awoke again. Someone was shaking my shoulder and through a hazy veil I found myself confronted by two old ladies in shawls. They chattered away in Polish, doubtless alarmed at my long state of inertia on the bench. I grappled with sanity. The sense of caution which had been developed in me consciously and subconsciously still burned. Getting to my feet I made my way back into the main thoroughfare, and wandered with pedestrians about the roads of the centre of the city.

My mind throbbed with snatches of verse from the Rubáiyát of Omar Khayyám. They hammered in my brain as in a dazed state that was almost happiness I wandered aimlessly about Cracow until dusk fell.

> But leave the Wise to wrangle and with me,
> The quarrel of the Universe let be;
> And in some corner of the hubbub court,
> Make game of that which makes as much of thee.

Of course . . . The filthy Huns, I thought, as I stood for a long time near the doorway of a German canteen and watched a procession of soldiers enter and leave the building. 'My God!' I chuckled to myself, 'Wouldn't old Omar enjoy it if I insulted the enemy?'

I slipped through the doorway into the canteen. With a sense of gleeful cunning and wild bravado at the prospect of making game of the Germans I walked the length of the hall, crammed with raucous, coffee-drinking members of the Wehrmacht, and sat down in a vacant chair opposite three uniformed Germans.

I ordered coffee and the waiter asked to see my papers.

I realised that there was no time to lose. Getting up I walked to a dais above which hung a large picture of Hitler. I stood there above the crowd. I screamed:

'*Achtung! Achtung!*'

There was silence. Faces stared.

Almost incoherently I began to shout vituperation of Hitler, of the Gestapo, of German soldiers. There was a horrified silence in the whole hall. Then suddenly it broke as the incensed Germans rose from their tables and ran at me.

Someone hit me in the face. As I staggered and fell they kicked and beat me. I lost consciousness, still shouting abuse.

When I came to life I was in a political prison on the outskirts of Cracow.

CHAPTER 9

GESTAPO TORTURE

(1)

When I recovered my senses in the hospital inside the prison, all traces of my fever had gone and my thoughts were crystal clear. Fluid had been drained from my lung, and the acute pain had ceased. My only discomfort was a dry rub when I inhaled deeply.

But if the doctors had brought me back to life for the Gestapo's benefit, the Gestapo were taking no chances. A strong circlet of steel was clamped around my ankle and connected to the wall by a strong chain. Unhappily I realised that I would have to face the sternest test of my prisoner of war adventures, and I cursed my rank stupidity in allowing my forged documents to fall into enemy hands.

How on earth was I going to explain away the possession of the name of Henryk Kowalski and all that it involved? My Polish was poor and the interrogators would break me down in no time. It was obvious, too, that by now the forged papers would have been minutely screened and examined and found to be false. It needed little imagination to realise that the Gestapo were biding their time until I was sufficiently recovered before they turned on the heat.

I had no companions in the hospital. I was guarded vigilantly and waited upon by a pallid, raw-boned male nurse with soulless eyes. He was a close-cropped German of about forty, sullen and emotionless, and from first to last he did not speak more than a few dozen words to me.

When I first took stock of the room, and noted his presence, I remarked to him in German: 'My lungs feel grand now, but where am I, please?'

I was given a long suspicious stare before he replied: 'You are under arrest in Cracow political prison. Your lung has been drained. You will remain here a little longer for treatment before you go to the cells.'

The German remained in the room most of the days that followed. He kept a strict and watchful silence. Instead of conversation he would stir the phlegm in his throat and issue a series of rattling grunts. His queer eyes stared at me. Nevertheless, he brought me four solid soups a day and potatoes and bread, and at four-hourly intervals he would thrust under my nose an upturned hand on which were two white tablets.

On the second day after I awoke, I knew beyond doubt that I was in a Gestapo murder establishment. I was awakened in the early morning by the rattle of rifle fire, followed by dull screams and more shooting. Every other morning at the same time I heard the crackle of rifle fire, and on a number of occasions terrible female screams penetrated the closed and barred windows.

After a few days the hinged circlet of steel clamped around my ankle-bone caused me considerable pain. The edges of the heavy metal band had bitten through the skin and my ankle was swelling and festering. It was only after I had entreated the German scores of times, and when I could no longer stop myself from whimpering with pain, that he brought along two other jailers to unlock the manacle which was transferred to my other leg. The silent German squeezed oozing pus from the poisoned ankle, and finished the operation by pouring iodine over the wound.

My future seemed hopeless. Reviewing everything as realistically as possible I could not but conclude, pessimistically, that I was doomed to finish my existence in this prison, once a Polish fort. No doubt the Germans would prolong life in exchange for information. Yet I had to keep my mouth shut no matter what the consequences. If I squealed it would mean imprisonment or death for the inmates of the nunnery.

I assessed myself for strength of moral fibre as honestly as I could, and I knew in my heart that I would never break faith. I looked at my escape life up to date, reflecting on all the impossible corners I had negotiated and overcome, and comforted myself with the thought that where there was life there was hope.

In this lull before the storm of Gestapo rage proper I schemed from every angle. I toyed with the idea of rushing a guard in a gamble for his gun, and using it to kill to the best advantage before they killed me. I mused continually on last-fling schemes as frail and feeble as they were fantastic. But if nothing else was accomplished, I kept despair at a distance.

My period of waiting was ended abruptly one morning when the throat-clearing German came into the room with an armed warder. Without a word I was handed a pair of old trousers, a shirt, and my own boots. I was unfettered and signalled to dress. It was good to say goodbye to the chunk of metal around my ankle and the brightly painted green chain to which it was attached; I even felt a surge of recklessness as I was pushed through the door. The sooner I got it over and done with the sooner I got my reincarnation chit, I stubbornly reassured myself.

The cell to which I was removed was sunk two-thirds below ground-level and the walls of rough stone blocks were almost four feet thick. It was nothing more than a barbaric dungeon typical of the days when the fort had been built. For centuries the place had not been washed by the honest and full light of day, and the only illumination was a trickle of light through a tiny grille ten feet above the flagged floor, level with the ground outside.

The door of the cell was five feet high, six inches thick and full of massive-headed studs. The bed consisted of three boards on a low trestle. There were no blankets or mattress. The only other article in the cell was a metal bucket for latrine purposes.

For two days I lay in the cell without interference. The door was opened at midday and a can of swede soup and three slices of black bread was thrust through the opening. The dungeon was damp. Little insects and crawlers lived in the walls, but even from these I derived some warped companionship when I detected their lightness on my face and body.

It was shudderingly cold in the cell at night and I cursed the mentality of the Gestapo in curing my sick lung in a hospital then pushing me into a damp and cold cell for convalescence.

The lack of effort by the Germans to trace my history was also unnerving. Or was this some odd kind of prelude to make their task easier? Or maybe they had decided to let me rot to death without further trouble.

Solitary confinement in virtual darkness, added to hunger, was hell. Gloom became spectral. Hunger gripped at my stomach and brain.

On the third day, soon after I had gulped down my swede soup and devoured my bread, two guards clattered into the cell. I was lolling on the edge of the bed boards when they entered and switched on a lamp in the ceiling, illuminating the place for the first time. The leading guard, a diminutive rat with a bladder-like head, walked straight over to me and hacked a blow on my shin with his jackboot. I leapt to my feet, and he delivered another blow in the small of my back which threw me on the floor. As I rose he ordered me to leave the cell and follow them.

I went up stairs and along corridors, to a room at the top of the fort where I was brought face to face with three Gestapo officers.

The two guards were dismissed and for many minutes I stood before a long table and the three men, the object of their curiosity. In turn, I studied the trio of immaculate figures as critically as my position would allow. They were smartly dressed, typical of the Hitler officer class Teuton.

The man on the left sucked at a long thin cigar as he sagged lazily in his chair. He was a broad-shouldered Punchinello whose head appeared to squat directly on his body. His face was criss-crossed with scars and two pale blue eyes, as expressionless as glass, were set in the heavy face.

The German in the centre was a complete contrast to his companions. He was tall and his face at first impression was that of a gladiator, strong, fair and handsome, without a blemish. His wide and well-spaced eyes seemed to indicate a lurking æstheticism. Here was a typical well-bred German of the Third Reich, a tall, blond, Aryan superman. Not for a moment would I have disputed his capacity for heroism in the name of the Fatherland and the Fuehrer.

The third man's face was vile. Here was a perpetrator of evil. His thick lips were pursed in a half-smile, and his features generally suggested unmodelled dough. His thick and curly eyebrows were oddly square shaped, and set deeply in a round close-cropped head were two piggy eyes.

'What an unholy trinity!' I thought. 'What a bureau of first-class bastards!'

I had carefully worked out the yarn I proposed giving them and while I anticipated the worst, I hoped for the best. But I was determined not to budge from my story in any way.

The German with the pig-like eyes was the first to speak. In throaty German he said: 'I trust we meet with your approval?'

He was cut short by the blond Adonis in the centre. It was he who commanded the situation and opened the grilling.

'What is your nationality?' he asked.

'I am a New Zealander,' I replied.

This was a surprise. My questioner leaned across the table; the man on the left straightened up; Pig Eyes on the right exclaimed 'Ah', and wrapped his teeth over his lower lip.

'When you were arrested you had in your possession unauthorised papers. You abused Herr Hitler and the German nation. Do you admit this?'

'Yes,' I replied.

Could I speak Polish? Where had I learned to speak German? How, if I was a New Zealander, had I got as far as Cracow? When, and from what place, had I started?

'I am a New Zealand soldier and a prisoner of war,' I told him. 'I was captured in Crete in June, 1940, and I was brought from the Mediterranean to Stalag VIIIb in Upper Silesia. I was sent to work in the Hohenzollern coalmine at Beuthen, along with another New Zealand soldier named George Potter. We escaped from the mine on March 17 and most of our time before reaching Poland was spent wandering about the German border in Upper Silesia.'

I was careful not to inform my examiner that I had been in Poland long. I particularly stressed the fact that we had lived from hand to mouth in Germany, and that by bad luck and bad judgment I had headed east instead of west.

'Where is your escape companion now?' inquired the German.

'He fell sick before I climbed on the train which brought me into

Poland,' I answered. 'I was compelled to leave him in a barn in Neutitschein.'

Then came the crucial and horrible questions. They were put to me slowly and carefully.

'How did you acquire a passport and documents for travel to the Ukraine as a German-controlled worker? Who took your photograph to paste inside the passport? Who stamped your papers with official Reich stamps? Who gave you Polish money and a Polish name?'

I explained that the train on which I had smuggled on the German border had carried me to Posen. 'In Posen,' I lied glibly, 'I met an old man in a café to whom I explained my difficulties. I arranged to meet him the next day to have my photograph taken and this was snapped in a side street. I lived in a disused building for a period, and the completed set of papers bearing my new name was given to me by the old gentleman who spoke German, and said he came from Breslau.'

For two hours I answered an endless barrage of questions. My questioners revealed none of the Gestapo methods I had experienced in Holland. The atmosphere of the grilling chamber possessed none of the supernormal and psychic elements surrounding interrogation at The Hague. Then suddenly the centre man, the leader of the trio, leapt to his feet and thrust out his chin with an air of *Herr des Reiches* [Lord of the German Empire], and screamed at me, his face twisted with passion and rage.

'You are a pig-dog English liar sent to spy in Poland. Your greatest offence was your insulting of the *Volksgenossenschaft* [German nation]. This is my prison and here I have full and unconditional authority over you. You are Henryk Kowalski to us and will suffer as a No. 1 political prisoner until you speak the truth about your false papers.'

He brought his hand down on the table with a thump, and then continued in a quieter voice, adopting the Gestapo tactics I knew so well.

'You are, of course, as a prisoner of war, dead. What a pity that you died a lonely death somewhere in Eastern Europe! But if you are wise you can return from the dead. You can again become a prisoner of war . . . providing the facts you have told us about Stalag VIIIb are true.'

Then came the shock.

'We know you are concealing treacherous Poles, and your papers bearing the *Arbeits Kontrolle* stamps of Czestochowa are the work of experts,' he continued. At the mention of Czestochowa my heart jumped, but I maintained my steady stare.

'We will give you time to consider voluntarily telling us the truth,' emphasised the tall blond, waggling his finger. 'Failing that we will make you tell the truth to the point of *Vernichtung* [annihilation].'

I looked at the sullen, angry faces before me, and I knew that an ultimatum had been delivered. I knew my captors would give me hell whether I squealed or not. My interrogator ordered me back against the wall and in whispered undertones addressed the other two. When they had finished Pig Eyes rose from the table and addressed me in slow, menacing tones.

'Mr New Zealander Henryk Kowalski,' he said. 'I will look after you personally.'

The guards were recalled, and I was escorted back to the dungeon. The undersized, big-headed guard kicked me down the last few steps to my cell door.

Kultur . . . *Kultur* . . . I angrily contemplated behind the locked door . . . hell and barbarism . . . concentration camps . . . political prisons and Gestapo . . . blood-stained altars of Hitler! I cursed until

I was breathless. There was nothing I could do now, nothing, nothing. I had told my story, and I would never depart from it.

(2)

I remained in solitary confinement for days – I lost count of the number for my mind became cloudy and vague. The flowing hours became as remote as the moon. Time was as a disembodied spirit floating beyond in my general mental fantasy and fatigue. Clarity of thought became impossible in the stifling darkness, and the greater part of the day and night I writhed and twisted on the three boards.

I received one bowl of swede soup and my bread ration was reduced to two thin slices. Hunger and ennui had their effects, and my brain began to whirl chaotically. I seemed to have lived in that cell a million years.

In fits of despair and weariness I may have slept for seconds or I may have slept for hours. In fitful phases of madness I became terrified of the darkness. It was only when the impression of daylight appeared in the square of the grille that the cell echoed with my chucklings, an admiring and slobbering ecstasy of realisation that I was not blind or mad. And while the light remained during the hours of daylight I would feverishly collect my scattered thoughts, marshal them into compartments of sanity and curse and scorn myself for faint-hearted weakness.

But as soon as the patch of light disappeared my heart would pound with fright; fear and madness would reassert themselves and through the silent and interminable night my imagination would be tortured. But with the coming of light again I would recharge my mental batteries with constancy and confidence, always that little extra during the day to take me through the night and keep the devil in me from making me commit suicide.

Many times during the torturing hours of pitch darkness, when hunger and cold were most intense, I was prompted to tear up my shirt and make a running noose, to turn my boards on end and hang myself from the top; or burst open the latrine bucket and use a jagged piece of tin on my throat. Twice, when my brain felt almost bursting, I defied the voice of suicide by behaving like an ostrich. I stuck my head in the bucket and laughed hysterically.

The prison was for civilians, and many men and women, including large numbers of Polish Jews, were also housed there. In 1942 it was nothing more than a ruthless extermination centre where rape and violence preceded mass murder. Once pounced on by the Gestapo and outlawed from society by the walls of the fort, recourse to truth, law and justice was for ever beyond the prisoners' grasp. They succumbed to German brutality, starvation or a firing squad. By comparison the prisoner of war, safeguarded by Geneva Conventions and the International Red Cross, lived a life of luxury.

At least twice a day, and sometimes more often, I listened to the tramp of military boots in the cobbled yard above the window grille in my cell, to the rattle of rifle fire and to the terror-stricken screams from the doomed against the wall, sometimes before and sometimes after the synchronised blaze of bullets.

I came to loathe the hoarse commanding voice, dispassionately guttural. I hated even more the stark, sepulchral silence after the heavily shod feet of the firing squad had moved away.

Every other night, sometimes for hours, I listened to debased and drunken laughter coming from the carousing soldiers at large in the women's cells across the other side of the courtyard. Hysterical screams came from the molested women as they were forcibly assaulted.

236

Raving, sobbing, cries of pain, horror and humiliation subsided into a babbling frenzy and then silence. There was no fear of any wavering in my loyalty towards the nunnery after I had heard those screams. I did not know that a woman's voice could express such horror.

Later I learned that merry-making parties of soldiers on furlough from the Russian front received special passes to visit the women's quarters. When the victims were physically and mentally ruined they were shot or gassed. Female replacements were always on tap from the Jewish ghettos so there was no difficulty in restocking the fort.

It was after one such night of female screaming that Pig Eyes came into active operation. The electric light high on the ceiling of my cell was switched on from the outside. Almost immediately the door was unlocked, bolts were drawn and Pig Eyes entered with two guards.

I jumped to my feet. The guards covered me with sub-machine-guns and slowly Pig Eyes crossed over to me. From a distance of three feet I smelt his liquor-heavy breath. He paused and from beneath his ludicrous square eyebrows scrutinised me through narrow slits.

'Who provided you with your papers to the Ukraine?' he bellowed. 'I want the truth.' He lashed me across the face with his leather gauntlet. 'Where did you get those papers?' he snarled.

I faced him with my back to the wall. 'I can only repeat what you already know,' I replied.

Without warning, Pig Eyes went mad. He rained blows into my face, and on my head and body. Falling to the floor I rolled away, cursing him in English. He drove his boot into me wherever he could and before he left my face was gashed and bleeding.

The following two days I starved. No food at all was pushed into the cell. But it made little difference. My face, particularly my mouth, was too swollen and painful to allow me to chew or swallow.

237

On the fourth day the electric light was again switched on. This time Pig Eyes was in company with the Punchinello with the scarred face.

'Do you still refuse to answer my questions?' Pig Eyes snarled. 'Or do you prefer to die from natural causes?'

I refused to answer. My battered face seemed to add spice to the amusement of my tormentors.

'You certainly need a shave, Mr Henryk Kowalski,' sneered the scarred-faced thug. 'You have a nice red growth which mustn't get into those cuts.'

I maintained a strict silence but my heart was pounding and my nerves were jumping.

Suddenly Pig Eyes bawled out: 'Bring in the food.'

A guard entered with a metal tray stacked with steaming sausages and cooked vegetables, bread, cheese, butter and two bottles of beer.

'Sit down,' I was ordered. 'Here is good food to keep you from dying . . . from natural causes, of course,' he smirked. 'Now, like a sensible man, tell me all about the underground people who helped you in Czestochowa . . . Tell me, and all this food is yours and as much more as you desire.'

Delicately he lifted one of the sausages and started to nibble. 'A nice bottle of good German wine, too, and a new cell with bed and blankets and books to read. Now come . . . One truthful conversation, and all your troubles are ended.'

'I got the papers in Posen,' I answered quickly. 'I got them from an old man in a café. I have already told you everything.'

With a bellow of rage Pig Eyes lifted the tray of food and slammed it into my face. Again I found myself rolling about the floor trying to shield my face from a merciless barrage of blows. Food was all over me and all over the floor. Pig Eyes, like a raving lunatic, pranced and danced, mashing sausage, vegetables, bread and cheese into the muck and grit of the flagged floor. Then with a parting kick, the two Gestapo officers and guards left me in peace.

As I lay on the boards that night smarting with physical pain and distracted with hunger, I realised that I had no chance of ever returning to civilisation. I resolved to thwart them by cutting my throat with a jagged piece of the bucket. I wanted badly to die. I, too, went berserk. I hurled the bucket about the stone walls and jumped on it in a blind fury, trying to open up a seam.

But I was beaten by lack of speed and the fearful noise I made. Two guards opened the cell door, after switching on the light to investigate the din, and while one covered me, the other raced off, and quickly returned with Pig Eyes. For this midnight act of vandalism I got my kidneys bruised by the jackboot, my bucket was taken away and I was too weak and sick after I was left alone even to worry about suicide.

The following two days I received three strong soups, half a loaf of bread and a jug of coffee daily, in addition to a wooden bucket of hot water with which to bathe my face. I ate all the food, and bathed my face, but I couldn't understand the motive behind this unexpected generosity.

Eventually I was collected by the guards and taken to a room on the next floor where I was brought before the blond gladiator and Pig Eyes. I was told that I was to be punished for creating a disturbance, for not observing prison discipline, for not respecting German property and for behaving like a pig in that I had deliberately thrown food all over the cell. If, however, I cared to reveal certain required information, the whole matter would be dropped and I would be given better food and quarters.

I refused to depart from my original story, and forthwith was led to the next room. The walls were covered with red splashes, as if someone had been cascading blood. Standing by a table, my hand was fastened to the wood by a metal clamp about my wrist. Under the watchful scrutiny of Pig Eyes, a German in a white smock drew out a knife, and pressed the point into the knuckle of my first finger, and then stopped.

'Are you going to tell us the truth?' snapped Pig Eyes. Again I refused to reply.

'Carry on,' Pig Eyes told the man in the smock.

Slowly, as if scoring pork, the knife opened up the flesh of my finger for at least an inch. Carefully selecting the next finger the operation was repeated.

'Now the next finger,' hissed Pig Eyes. 'Unless our friend wants to talk. But this time we will work from the nail.'

I did not answer, nor did I feel faint. The cutting of the flesh had not been painful. My intense hatred and anger protected me from fright or, for that matter, any other feeling. The knife was forced under my nail, and the blade cut through the flesh for almost an inch, a fraction at a time. Pig Eyes chuckled with perverted glee as my wrist was unshackled and my hand pulsed out a flow of blood on the floor.

'Let that teach you that in future your hands must respect German property,' he gloated. 'And now you will learn cleanliness.'

Back in the cell I was given a bucket of hot water and a brush, and the water was rich with soda. Without complaint I washed out the cell and removed the dried food smears. When I had finished I ripped away parts of my shirt and used the pieces as bandages.

But Pig Eyes was as determined to unseal my lips as I was that he should not. After a brief period free from molestation, I was marched into the prison courtyard, where I was strapped by my wrists to a ring in the wall. Other poor devils of prisoners were brought from their cells to witness my flogging, intended probably to instil fear in their hearts, or perhaps degradation in mine.

Twice I was taken outside and flogged before an audience. After the lash had done its work I was further reminded of the punishment by being forcibly immersed in brine baths.

But I managed to hold out, and after that I received no more physical torture. Pig Eyes had failed to extract any information from me that way, so he worked on a new angle. He started threatening me with a firing squad.

Shortly after I had recovered from the last flogging, Pig Eyes stamped into my cell one day, gesticulating with his cigar, and in almost solemn tones asked if I had decided to rescind the false information I had originally tendered and kept stubbornly repeating.

'I have told you where I obtained those papers,' I replied. 'Aren't you convinced by now that I am not lying? Is it honourable of the German Gestapo to treat a prisoner of war so lawlessly?'

Pig Eyes allowed me to continue. This was the first time he had attempted to be conciliatory, so I put forward my case as strongly and sincerely as I could.

'It is laid down,' I said, 'by international law that any legitimate prisoner of war has the right to escape and negotiate his freedom. You must know that German prisoners in British hands possess that privilege.'

He was obviously ruffled by my challenge, but sharply he rapped out: 'You came into our hands as one Henryk Kowalski. You carried no scrap of p.o.w. identification. You wore civilian clothes and carried civilian documents. You publicly reviled the German people and their leader. An escaping prisoner is not allowed to discard his uniform or prison disc. It is forbidden that he should use civilian attire or acquire

241

false identity. He must not join up with combative forces or indulge in espionage. You have forfeited all rights accorded to prisoners of war. Until you are ready to prove otherwise you are still Henryk Kowalski in our eyes . . .'

I laughed inwardly at his logic. My God . . . what a heart attack he would have if he knew that I was a British airman and not a New Zealand soldier, and that on many occasions I had bombed and blasted his beloved Fatherland.

Pig Eyes glared at me, slowly nodding his ugly head up and down. 'Tomorrow,' he almost spat, 'tomorrow, unless you decide to tell us everything, you will be shot by a firing squad.'

Suddenly taking a flying kick at my bucket, Pig Eyes left the cell. That night, as I gazed into the darkness, I felt happier than for a long time. Death would be a release. It represented the only solution to this hideous and unnamable existence – the only way to leave a revolting political prison where cruelty in the name of the Fatherland was equal to the sordidness of the Inquisition. With perhaps only a slight tightening of the heart, I actually experienced a most gratifying night's sleep.

(3)

Early the next morning a mug of black coffee was pushed into the cell and soon afterwards, dressed only in pants and boots, I was escorted by two guards to the courtyard. The firing squad was already there, lounging at ease, laughing and smoking, their rifles propped against the wall. I was positioned a few yards away and my guards covered me closely with their tommy guns.

But first I was compelled to watch callous and hideous murder.

As I stood there eight women were led into the fort's arena,

242

accompanied by two male guards and two female jailers. The women guards were trimly dressed in black uniforms and carried pistols in a most professional style. Surprisingly, they were quite young, and their fair prettiness seemed incongruous.

The average age of the condemned women I assessed at about twenty-five. They huddled together in rags and tatters, three of them with shaved heads. The entire party was sobbing pathetically with the exception of one tall and slender girl. Her raven black hair fell over her shoulders, and her head was magnificently erect; her grey countenance showed a fearless, almost arrogant, expression.

The other women were ashen but, apart from their racking sobs, not one gave way to uncontrollable hysteria. They were led to a position facing the wall, and eight pairs of wrists were fastened to steel rings attached to the stone. The women's backs faced the rifles, and the men who comprised the firing party had already taken up their positions.

The big fair German who had given me the impression of a gladiator, was a professional gladiator all right. The courtyard of the political prison was his arena, and his combatants represented eight defenceless Polish-Jewish women. He strode through the guarded doorway, casually surveyed the scene, and as he made towards the firing squad, called out: 'Fire'.

It would be impossible to record my feelings at the moment when ten firing pins released ten bullets. My legs almost gave way and my head felt as if someone had poked a stick into it and was waving it in circles. As the bullets hit home, the women's bodies bucked upwards. For a second they remained rigid before they flopped and sagged grotesquely from suspended wrists. Sixteen taut white arms raised to Heaven against the darkness of the wall . . . pleading . . . as if beseeching Heaven . . .

The bodies were unleashed. Even in death the Germans had no respect. They stacked the bodies, like carcases of dead animals, against the wall. The dead girl with the raven black hair whose face had shone so fearlessly a few minutes before, was the last to be slung on the mound.

The big blond Gestapo murderer spoke quietly for a few minutes to the firing squad before he turned and walked across to where I stood with my guards against the wall. Confronting me, he looked me up and down with almost friendly grace before he spoke.

'You still have time to reveal to me where, and with whom, you lived in Poland, and how you came into possession of a forged passport and papers,' he said.

I found it difficult to articulate. When I spoke I did not look at the man before me but at the dead girl. I thought of Maria the nun lying like that, with perhaps all the other kind creatures of the nunnery underneath her. What mercy would the Gestapo afford them if they were told the truth?

'It is no good my repeating where I got those papers,' I replied. 'No good whatsoever. You refuse to believe me. I am not a political prisoner, and you know it. I am as truly a prisoner of war and a soldier as you are a German soldier.'

Without another word I was fastened to a circlet of steel.

Facing the wall, I looked for what seemed an interminable period at a confusion of compact markings in the stone just below me where bullets had flattened themselves after ripping through bodies. I heard laughing behind me. Then I heard the screaming order to fire, and the voices seemed to come from another planet as the shattering burst of noise rent open the universe.

An appalling confusion of sensations burst within me. I was alive . . . I was dead . . . I was ascending . . . I was descending. I burned with a volcanic heat. I froze with cold. I was floating with delicious and bewildering ease . . . I was plunging through roaring water . . . And then, as it all receded, I saw the stone wall, and I was pressed against it, erect and trembling.

The voice of the Gestapo officer purred gently in my ear: 'Where did you get those forged papers? Come, you still have an opportunity to tell me.'

'I got them in a café in Posen,' I sobbed, and rubbed my face against the wall.

It had all been a scheme to frighten me. Momentarily it had succeeded. But the fear fell away, just as the lead of the bullets had fallen to the ground.

I was taken back to my cell. For hours I clung to my bedboards, hardly daring to breathe, cringing at times when I believed that I was not breathing.

Three times more I was informed that I would face a firing squad the next morning. Three times I was prodded into the courtyard by armed guards. But it was only to witness the murder of Polish patriots. I merely watched. It was terrible to see the Poles die, but nothing like the same revulsion overtook me as when I watched the Polish women shot.

(4)

As the days passed I regained some of my composure, and with it some remote sense of optimism. Inwardly, I sensed that the Gestapo had tried everything to make me talk and were now beginning to believe that I was telling the truth.

A few days later the electric light in my cell was switched on and three young German soldiers came in. Three camp beds were also pushed into the cell by the guards outside, and the light was not extinguished.

The three soldiers, all privates, were totally unlike the hard Gestapo inhabitants of the prison, and they informed me that they were on leave from the Russian Front, and had fallen foul of a military policeman. Placed under arrest, they had been handed in at the nearest detention prison, which happened to be the fort.

'The officer in command of this disgusting dump,' said one of them, a small fellow in spectacles with thick lenses difficult to associate with the Russian Front, 'informs us that we will be taken to military barracks tomorrow.'

I could not fully grasp the hang of things, but I realised the need for caution. Intentionally I displayed no hostility, but I weighed every word spoken to me, and by me.

We talked into the early hours. From my German cell-mates I received cigarettes, a piece of soap, liver *Wurst* and two apples. This convinced me that a Gestapo scheme was being tried out. Since when were delinquent soldiers, jailed for the night, allowed to retain their knapsacks?

The men were casually inquisitive. They wanted to know about me, my escape adventures and New Zealand. They applauded my efforts at escape, and were lavish with their compliments. They felt that as a loyal soldier I possessed a true sense of duty to try to escape.

I elaborated on my train trip to Posen and fluently, with all the sincerity to fit the situation, I worked on the phoney café and the imaginary old man from whom I had received my papers.

Another of the soldiers, an ex-bank clerk from Leipzig, rakish and with blunt features but not strained and weather-beaten as they should have been from the stories he related about his sojourn at the Russian

Front, spanked his knee and assured me that the Gestapo would undoubtedly return me to the prison camp.

'This frightful war is none of our doing,' I was soberly informed by the bespectacled German. 'We are mere pawns, and must suffer and obey orders blindly.'

At last, after the fashion of long-standing barrack companions, pleasant good nights were exchanged. Feigning slumber, I did a lot of conscious talking in my sleep that night.

Late the following morning the guards threw open the cell door and with forced curtness told the three Germans to prepare to leave. The soldiers said goodbye and wished me luck, but their departing smiles and politeness were just a little too touching to be sincere.

Next day I was visited by Pig Eyes. I was staggered when he gave me a packet of cigarettes and a bar of Norwegian chocolate. I was told that my prisoner of war name and number had been verified and that, in view of my sickness when arrested, no charge would be brought against me for publicly insulting the Reich and its Fuehrer.

'We have received orders from Berlin,' said Pig Eyes, 'to return you to your Stalag. This will be arranged when you are in a better state of health.'

I was flabbergasted. It was wonderful news. A prisoner of war camp after Cracow political prison would be a Paradise. To mix again with my own countrymen, to leave behind the black, damp dungeon, were prospects too glorious to contemplate. My heart pounded with joy at the thought that I was not altogether lost.

I listened quietly as Pig Eyes gave me a pep-talk on the necessity for force against rebels and the plague of the Jewish race in the interests of mankind. Then he affected decorum, and stressed 'the hope of Hitler and the Germans' that some day they would get together with the British Commonwealth of Nations for the lasting benefit and security of mankind.

'Germany,' he said, 'although Britain does not yet appreciate it, is forcing evolution towards the construction of a higher human plane by relegating the Slavonic menace . . .'

I was removed to the hospital and met again the bovine, raw-boned German orderly. The orderly even broke his silence and, after rattling phlegm in his throat, passed the time of day and growled other odd pleasantries. My wounds were given attention and I received extra rations to rebuild my strength. I had lost a lot of weight in the dungeon. I could not have weighed more than seven stone when I returned to the hospital.

I received hot baths and violet ray treatment to help the disfigurement of my face. I was even permitted to take exercise with a guard, in a separate courtyard to the killing arena. I took everything and said virtually nothing.

The sudden change of attitude could not easily dismiss from my mind the outrageous punishment and maniacal hatred and blood lust which the Gestapo had shown me. And the scars on my face, hand and back remained as ready reminders of the psychological climate in which Hitler and his infamous S.S. and Gestapo thrived.

BOOK 3

SOUTH TO HUNGARY

CHAPTER 10

A PRISONER OF WAR AGAIN

(1)

From the moment I was told that I was to be returned to a prisoner of war camp, the passing time was an agony of suspense. During my convalescence my imagination conjured up dreaded possibilities of things which could reasonably occur to re-awaken Gestapo suspicions and renew interrogation. My hopes and my life were finely balanced on the promises of maniacal and scheming Gestapo officers.

But the promise held. One morning, in the dim and streaky light of dawn, I was aroused and told I had twenty minutes to get ready before guards collected me for the return journey to Stalag VIIIb. Hardly daring to believe my good fortune, and in a welter of emotions, I struggled into a suit of old clothes which Pig Eyes had slung across the bottom of my bed. Two burly guards, snugly topcoated, one tugging on the strap of a tommy gun, clattered into the room.

Unceremoniously I was handcuffed to the other soldier, who produced a vicious pistol, and waggled it menacingly in front of my face. Between the two black steel helmets, via a series of passages, I was brought to the main door of the political prison. The sentries wound back the doors and in joy and bewilderment I crossed into a new realm, suffused and flecked with advancing daylight. In spite of the clinking chain which still joined me to Germany, I felt as free and alive as the fresh cold breeze which rustled across my face.

As the train carried me closer to the German border and the p.o.w. camp, my excitement grew at the prospect of reuniting with my fellow countrymen, of speaking my own language and of meeting the real Yeatman and Potter again and gaining news of home.

The evening was well advanced when I was signed over to camp guardianship and freed of the handcuff. My anticipation of cheery voices and familiar faces, however, was quickly dispelled. Instead of being shown to a communal barrack, I was prodded into a solitary cell in the camp jail. But my immeasurable thankfulness at being safe inside the camp, and my satisfaction at realising how narrowly I had cheated the Gestapo, offset the disappointment.

I reviewed my new quarters almost affectionately.

What luxurious improvements! There was a large grille, low set, which gave a broad view of the camp; there were spacious bedboards and two blankets; there was a dixie of drinking water; and there was reading material in the form of a Red Cross Bible fastened to the end of the bed.

Next morning, shortly after the camp had awakened to activity, I was led before the camp security police. I still preserved my masquerade of Private Winston Yeatman, New Zealand soldier, but the non-return to base of my Polish companion, known to the enemy as Private George Potter, involved me in a three-hours' session of sticky cross-examination. I recited in the finest detail the story which I had given to the Gestapo in Cracow.

Eventually satisfied, my interrogater, a heavy-jowled and excitable major, closed the interview. 'You have already undergone severe punishment in Cracow,' he reminded me. 'Therefore, your camp imprisonment will be reduced to twenty-one days' solitary detention on bread and water.'

He glowered at me for half a minute before informing me that if Private George Potter had not already died from starvation, he would certainly be captured sooner or later.

'You pig-dog English fools are wasting your time in trying to flee German Occupied Europe,' he barked. 'We always win. And don't try any more escapes otherwise you will not be dealt with so humanely.'

On my return to the prison I was photographed with the real Yeatman's p.o.w. number in bold figures across my chest, and I was also fingerprinted as Yeatman.

During the first four days in the cell, to discount the monotony, I applied myself to a close study of the Bible. I had not realised that it was the greatest thriller and sanity-revealing work of philosophy ever compiled.

Then I received a welcome visitor. He was a British Army medical officer of the Royal Army Medical Corps, a bright and breezy captain named Spencer. His job was to examine all inmates of the prison who were undergoing solitary confinement. The Germans could not obstruct this twice-weekly check-up as it was laid down in International p.o.w. regulations.

In spite of my cell door being left ajar, and a suspicious raw-boned guard standing outside shuffling his big feet, I told Captain Spencer the origin of my scars, my emaciation and what had happened to me at the hands of the Gestapo.

'Swine,' he muttered. 'I'm going to try and convince the German *Lager* doctor that you're pretty low, and see if we can get this sentence quashed. I'll be back. Chin up.'

Captain Spencer was the first man of my own side with whom I had spoken since re-entering the camp – or for that matter, for many a long week. The meeting had the same effect on me as a good stiff whisky on a cold night.

Two hours later Spencer returned with the German horse doctor, as he was commonly called, and after an assault with a stethoscope he exclaimed with an explosive number of '*Ja's*' that I was virtually dead. Then I was laid on a blanket on the bedboards and pummelled and prodded from neck to ankles by podgy fingers. During this I became aware of something being pushed under the blanket between the boards and my chest by Dr Spencer as he pressed against me and pretended to examine a scar on my neck.

I lifted myself slightly to allow whatever it was to reach the centre of the boards. 'Thanks,' I grunted.

The German and British doctors confronted each other as I got into my pants. 'He is fit enough to serve out his sentence,' croaked the rotund horse-doctor. 'He is thin, yes, and I will order him to have every third day two soups, 500 grammes of bread, cheese and hot coffee. His cuts are healed over and are not infectious. That is all, Herr Spencer. Come.'

Before the steel door closed Captain Spencer winked at me. As the footsteps moved away I dived to discover the hidden something under the blanket. It was a cellophane packet of twenty cigarettes and fifteen matches split in half to give me thirty lights. A brief note said: 'Tear cello into small bits and do not throw matches below window. Hide all carefully. Frequent searches.'

Before I lit up I studied the cell for a safe hiding-place. A foolproof place of concealment struck me as I observed the interlocked bedboards. Each board had a quarter-inch flange which fitted into a similar groove in the next board. I prised up the bottom two boards and broke away the extending flange, leaving only a little at each end. The boards were four feet wide and into the recessed grooves I carefully squeezed the cigarettes. Then I forced the boards back into position with the light retaining nails.

I stretched out on the bed and smoked two cigarettes. Life was good!

(2)

With a knowledge of the Bible from Genesis to Revelation, and twenty-one days of 'solitary' behind me, I left the *Straflager* at the height of a thunderstorm. The short distance through the barricades of wire around the 'God-Gut building, as the jail was termed, and turning into the camp at large, was sufficient to drench me to the skin. But the torrential rain was cleansing, morally refreshing and inspiring. All the mental and physical scars I had incurred flowed away like the rain along the gutter. My mind swam with a buoyant happiness as I strode towards my friends in the soldiers' compound. Lightning, thunder and torrential rain combined to give me a mental wash and brush-up. The newness and horrors of my Polish escape, plus a cowardly fear which prompted me not to risk any further breaks for freedom, had vanished completely. The cloudburst somehow retempered my moral fibre, and before I joined my buddies inside the noisy barrack room I was prickling with enthusiasm and determination to have another crack at escape just as soon as my house was in order.

My first shock came a few minutes after re-uniting with the barrack sergeant-major. He told me that all the R.A.F. personnel in the camp, including the Poles, had been removed to a special Luftwaffe camp near Berlin.

'They wheeled 'em out all of a sudden a month ago,' he explained. 'We managed to snatch a few words with your swops, Yeatman and Potter, and they told me they would play their parts as long as humanly possible. They said your old lady was well, but that your sister-in-law had passed away.'

'Was there any trouble?' I inquired, 'after we'd left the camp?'

'Plenty,' he chuckled. 'After you and the ruddy Pole made the successful swop-over, other R.A.F. chaps tried it on. The German security police got a whiff that something queer was afoot and a photo and fingerprint check-up was called at the card-index office.'

'How the hell did you get around it?' I asked.

'Well,' he said, with a grin, 'we knew it would upset the whole apple cart for you and the Pole, so we acted quick. The snappiest bit of fire-raising this side of hell!'

'Go on,' I exclaimed impatiently.

'Well, it so happened that three Palestinian Jews were detailed to clean out the German office which housed all the prisoner of war records. We got 'em together and threatened 'em with sudden death, no Red Cross parcels and what-have-you if they didn't hood-wink the sentry and start a 100 per cent. bonfire. Twenty minutes after they returned to their barrack the entire building was a ruddy inferno and 25,000 photographs and fingerprints went up in smoke. Guess you ought to pray regularly for those three Jewish boys. They're doing a two-year stretch apiece for sabotage in a civilian prison at Hanover.'

Gradually I got all the news. The camp and its food was no different but the Russians had been moved to quarters some distance over the plain, and were completely segregated from British and Allied prisoners. Nobody was permitted to know what went on in the Soviet *Lager*, and voluntary medical assistance and excursions by British prisoner doctors had been stopped.

Since my departure, eight chaps had been shot for attempting to breach the wire.

The cabbage soup still contained as many slugs and caterpillars; the bread was slightly blacker than before; and the guards were more obscene and cocky in view of their successive victories in Russia.

Captain Spencer was a staunch friend to me, and he arranged that I should receive special vitamin foods and milk beverages from Red Cross medical supplies. As I gained in strength and put on weight my resolve to attempt my third break grew stronger.

I had a heart-to-heart talk with my understanding army friend, the sergeant-major.

'Bill, it's no good,' I said. 'I've got hot feet again. I'll go stark staring mad if I don't get on the escape trail soon.' I asked him to get me on another working commando as soon as possible. 'There are working gangs being sent to Sudetenland,' I reminded him. 'Working on the land will suit me fine. I don't want any more coal-mines.'

Bill Charters studied me carefully before replying. 'You are a private soldier under my discipline even in this ruddy land called Germany,' he said. 'I am obliged to look after the interests of my men and to keep them ticking over for the eventual return to Blighty. How's the lung?'

'It's O.K.' I assured him.

'Right,' he replied. 'I'll get Captain Spencer to examine you. If he thinks you're in condition to have another bash at it I'll get you attached to a working party.'

CHAPTER II

SABOTAGE ON THE FARM

(I)

Ten days later I was waiting at the little station of Annahof for a train along with three guards and nineteen other private soldiers. We were on our way to Troppau, in Czechoslovakia, to the German Land Directorate for Labour Control. From this headquarters we would be detailed to different German-controlled State farms within a hundred-mile radius.

The weather was now glorious, the hours of daylight long and the hot and strengthening sun was as kind and friendly as the frost had been cruel and destructive. Conditions for escape were perfect. One could sleep without the dread of frostbite, and walk on clear, solid earth instead of ploughing through deep snow and being constantly soaked to the skin. This was the time of the year when fruits, corn and vegetables were ripening and maturing. This was the ripest period of all for my bid.

Already I had vainly sought freedom in the west, via Holland. My strength and ingenuity had been pitted against the east – Poland – and again I had failed. But now I was all set for the south – Czechoslovakia – and, God willing, still farther south to Yugoslavia. My previous escapades had taught me a great deal in the technique of escape, and the strength of my optimism and resolve reached new heights.

During the train journey to Troppau I sat next to a man called Rifleman Godden. The train chugged by a number of aerodromes

258

and we watched with great interest the movements of scores of low-flying aircraft. I was impressed by Godden's comments which suggested a well-balanced knowledge of aircraft and flying. I listened and studied him. Here was a man of obvious character and breeding, and his crisp authoritative way of speaking placed him above the ordinary soldier. His strong face mirrored a well-developed intelligence.

Off-handedly I plied him with questions about his Army career. He was unruffled, and sure of his facts from A to Z. But I knew instinctively that he was lying, and that he was no more a private soldier than the man in the moon.

At the same time – we had been travelling for a couple of hours by this time – I knew that Godden was suspicious of me, and that he was adroitly angling for clues.

'Is this man Godden an R.A.F. swop-over like myself?' I mused. 'Or is he a German stooge?'

I treated him with polite caution up to the moment when he unexpectedly demonstrated beyond all shadow of doubt his loyalty and bravery. But at no time did he tell me his true rank, the nature of the work on which he was engaged, or any of his personal history.

At Troppau the party was split up. Godden, four others and I moved on to Partschendorf, an idyllic village, with a background of magnificent blue mountains. It was a picturesque community of quaint white-washed cottages, and it boasted a dignified manor house. The Germans shot its Jewish owner and commandeered his property to house thugs of the S.S., after carrying off all its treasures and antique furnishings.

A deep river ran beside the village. It was typical of a traditional peaceful, pretty, yet industrious pivot of general and dairy farming, as it had been throughout the centuries. The tall wooden cross on the mountain-side still inspired the oppressed Czechs with courage, as did their little religious shrine with holy pictures on the road-side, to which they paid their respects with bowed heads and closed eyes, and mumbled prayers whenever they passed it.

With the annexation of Slovakia, the village had passed completely under German control and domination. German land workers and their families had been moved in among the Czechs, and they never failed to express their arrogance and belief in their super-race.

A German-appointed controller, a harsh, unscrupulous man, together with his band of uniformed henchmen, cowed, threat-ened and intimidated all civilian workers, both Czech and German. His aim was food production: greater wheat and potato crops and more cattle and eggs for Germany, and every minute of daylight was a working minute for all and sundry. Inaccessible, deeply sloping patches on the mountains were made accessible by stren-uous p.o.w. labour and human Russian oxen, and ruthless demands on workers carried out the ploughing and planting. Every possible square yard of arable land was put under cultivation.

My party of six happily augmented a British team, and the fifty men in all were given as their quarters the village schoolroom. A single wall of interlaced wire surrounded the building on the edge of the main road through the village. The windows were guarded with steel strips, but neither the windows nor the encircling wire dismayed me. Both were comparatively easy to overcome if necessary.

At the back of the school there was a room which housed the officer in charge of the party and his six guards, all fat, sluggish, lazy Germans over fifty years of age. I soon weighed them up and concluded that they presented no formidable deterrent.

No escapes had previously taken place, the prisoners worked well, and the nature of their manifold tasks scattered them all over a wide area. Frequently individual prisoners and small parties

260

performed their duties without any German military surveillance at all. The six obese guards apparently imagined that the prisoners were too well treated, and appeared too happy and contented, ever to be so stupid as to contemplate escape. Such a belief fitted in beautifully with my plans and movements. I felt that escaping from Partschendorf, when it suited me to do so, was going to be a piece of cake. First, however, I had to study the topography of the area, and survey and utilise any outside sources of likely assistance. I resolved not to be pig-headed and do anything to annoy soldiers or civilians; to obey all orders 'on the turn', and to work enthusiastically and industriously to win the fullest measure of trust.

My first job was as navvy. In the grounds of the manor house a number of buildings, quite new, which had housed servants, were ordered to be pulled down by the controller. The new bricks were required for building purposes somewhere up the line.

During my fourth day of pick wielding, and after dislodging the last roof beam, I saw a small leather wallet in the recess which had held the timber. Shoving it into my pocket I waited for a safe chance to examine its contents. I found inside three precious rings, two containing magnificent diamonds, superbly cut. The third was exquisitely set with rubies and sapphires.

I returned to the *Lager* full of satisfaction with my reward for navvying, and contemplated with amusement the consternation of the thief if ever he returned to Partschendorf to find the servants' quarters demolished.

(2)

It was not long before I was promoted from the pick and shovel, and there followed a series of jobs from trimming sugar beet to the exalted and coveted job of driving a tractor and ploughing the land. After the tractor I was given a more refreshing job with the Slovakian peasant girls in the cow byres, and scores of pints of milk ran down my throat instead of into the churns.

As I got to know my way about the seven farms in the area, and made the acquaintance of the locals, I worked up plenty of rackets, and extra bread, eggs and cheese came my way.

I also worked hard and got fit for the strenuous escape trek ahead. The stolen and secretly-acquired food added greatly to my physical well-being.

The Germans expressed their pleasure at such a model prisoner, but it hurt sometimes when I realised that I was incurring the displeasure of my own countrymen. I could not explain to them that it was a means to an end.

Godden came to me one night as I was sewing up my second pair of boots, cracked, tattered and torn.

'Why waste your time doing that, Yeatman?' he remarked: 'Your other pair of boots are in first-class fettle. Or are you keeping them for the homeward march, when that day arrives?'

I stood up and looked him straight in the eye.

'What are you getting at?' I replied. 'Perhaps that army shirt you're wearing would look cleaner if you washed it in black dye.'

His face tightened. Gripping my shirt about the base of my neck he pushed me up against the wall between the dark, two-tiered bed recess. Nobody saw the move and, relinquishing his grip, he quietly said: 'I'm no bloody black-shirted S.S., and you know it. Come on . . . Let's play a game of cards . . . you and me.'

We sat down. I opened the conversation. 'What's your game, Godden?' I asked.

'I play any and every game,' he replied, without looking up. 'Just

262

so long as the pack has a King and Queen in it, and it's made in Britain.' He shuffled the cards. 'Rummy? Everything's rummy among the boys in wartime.'

We played in silence for ten minutes. He was dealing when quietly he asked: 'R.A.F. or M.I. something or other?'

I knew what the M.I. reference meant. 'R.A.F.,' I whispered.

'That's fine,' he said as we played on. 'Now we know where we are. I came into Europe from an aeroplane, too.'

'Going to do a disappearing act from Partschendorf?' I challenged him.

'Yes . . . But I can't do it with you, unfortunately,' he replied. 'I've got to stick around here for some time, and something tells me you'll be on your bike next month. You're Yeatman to me, and I'm Godden to you, and now we trust each other. That's all that really matters. I'll help you all I can for the push-off, but take my tip . . . Mix in with the boys more . . . They don't like your industrious allegiance to the German *Arbeits* machine.'

I was surprised when he explained what the boys had done, and were doing, to dislocate German efforts at food production.

'But I never knew that!' I exclaimed. 'They all seem such a placid, harmless, easy-going bunch, and they've never discussed their sabotage activities.'

'Of course not,' Godden interrupted. 'They couldn't make you out . . . Couldn't understand why you always played the lone wolf. As a matter of fact, I had to speak to you tonight because plans are afoot to do you in . . . Accidentally on purpose.'

'Christ!' I snapped. 'Tell me what you want me to do, and I'll bloody well do it.'

'Instead of milking cows with a lot of tittering women, get on to the party of twenty due to start work tomorrow in the sheds housing all the agricultural machinery,' Godden told me. 'We're getting it ready for taking in the harvest. Most of it is manufactured by the International Harvester Company, and I imagine it's difficult to get spares now, unless they have 'em made.' He laughed. 'By the way, all the machinery they've used recently for broadcasting seeds is coming into the sheds for oiling and greasing before it is put away for next year.'

I looked up and saw that most of the men were watching us from beds, and around the tables. I got to my feet and, without raising my voice too high, addressed them. 'You ruddy bunch of bone-headed fools', I said. 'I'm with you! And I'm with you in the machine sheds as soon as I can quit being a dairymaid.'

Next day I spoke to the German officer and told him I was tired of working with women, and asked if I could do other work. He laughed, and remarked: 'I don't suppose pulling cows' tits is much fun. Sorry you and one girl can't do the lot, then you wouldn't have to worry about safety in numbers and lack of opportunity.'

Later in the morning I joined the British party of twenty in the agricultural machine sheds.

'Good show,' Godden said, thumping me on the back.

The six long, low, wooden sheds accommodated all the agricultural equipment which served the demands of seven German State Farms with a total of thousands of acres. Machines of all descriptions were loaned out from this central pool. In the case of the seed-sowing machines – broadcasters as they were called – they had now finished their seasonal duties and were assembled outside the sheds for cleaning, adjusting, oiling and packing away for the following year.

Under the supervision of two German civilian labourers and the eyes of two German guards, the party of prisoners with oil, grease

264

and rags, set about cleaning and smearing the many rods and scores of cog-wheels. The two civilians made all necessary adjustments and tightened up the nuts and bolts. As each machine was passed and completed, a few men hauled it next door into the storage shed.

Half a dozen had been neatly packed away when Godden, who was working alongside me, whispered as he passed me a monkey wrench and a pair of pliers: 'You help to trundle the next machine into the shed. Don't return with the others. Take out this cotter-pin and slide off these three bevelled pinion wheels on all seven machines. Replace the metal covering plates and tighten into position. The boys who bring in the eighth machine will help to carry the cogs out and hide them behind the stack of bricks to the left of the door. There is no need to hammer. Work quick and don't panic.'

I helped to push the next machine into the stowage shed.

'Don't come back on your own,' repeated Sunnly, an Australian. 'You've got about twenty-five minutes to complete the job before we reappear. Good luck.'

I crouched low and worked rapidly, keeping an eye on the open doors twenty feet away. I had removed the pins and bolts and the twenty-one bevelled cog-wheels by the time the next machine was dragged into the shed.

'Fine,' said the Aussie. 'Come on, boys, carry 'em out behind the brick pile.'

At midday we all marched back to the *Lager* for our soup. Ten agricultural machines had been rendered useless and thirty vital cog-wheels, washers and pins were concealed about the persons of some twenty prisoners.

'Where do we dump the ruddy iron?' I asked Godden.

'Everything's planned to a nicety,' he grinned. 'We spread it about the river tonight. Care for a midnight leg stretch?'

'Sure,' I said, and I realised that Godden was a most remarkable organiser.

In the *Lager* the party dispersed, some going to the trench lavatories, others for a wash and clean up at the rear of the schoolhouse. In five minutes all the cog-wheels and other pieces were carefully hidden.

We returned to the sheds in the afternoon and while the guards were sitting outside sunning themselves, completely disinterested in our labours, Godden and I sneaked off to the largest of the stowage sheds fifty yards away.

A few days before, while mixing concrete near the sheds, he had managed to prise loose four boards. Inside the shed there were five large, caravan-like combine harvesters.

'Amazing contraptions,' whispered my companion. 'They do about fifteen major harvesting jobs all in one. The corn is fed in, threshed, packed, sacked, tied up and the chaff and stalks are chucked out.'

We worked furiously for well over half an hour, removing as many small-and medium-sized cog-wheels as we dared.

'O.K.,' Godden panted, a glistening mass of sweat. 'We've done enough to muck the bloody things up quite seriously. Unless they have blue-prints, the Germans will have to redesign and machine-cut every part.'

We placed the detached components behind the boards near our point of exit and joined the others. The two civilian Germans were still inside the cottage 100 yards away. Godden gave instructions to three of the party to carry the pieces to safe hiding behind the brick pile. At six o'clock twenty weary men returned to the *Lager* and about their untidy garb were hidden irreplaceable odds and ends of small and medium cog-wheels.

'A good day's work,' I commented to a tired-looking Godden.

'Unfortunately it's not finished yet,' was his sober reply.

The clock at the top of the village church had just struck twelve when Godden came over to my bed and whispered: 'Five of us are going. Ready?'

Every night at nine the officer of the *Lager* came in and counted us, and after bidding us good night securely locked the schoolroom door. It was opened again at six the next morning, when another count was made. The guards were absolutely certain that with strongly barred windows and a solid, padlocked door their charges were safely secured for the night, and off they would go to the beer garden and get drunk.

I watched Godden push a double-storey bed aside and with no effort lift up four short pieces of wide floor boarding. I felt ashamed to think that while I had slept so much activity had taken place, and that I had egotistically imagined that my wits and personal inge-nuity and cunning were a match for all my fellow prisoners, even Godden.

One by one, without the slightest noise, we dropped ten feet into the cellar below and into the door's well-oiled lock Godden slipped his own key. Every move had been most carefully planned. The pieces of agricultural machinery had been restacked before roll-call into two well-hidden groups, ready for easy collection. Godden had a list of every single part stolen, and as each man loaded his quota into a sack he checked his list by the light from his torch.

The wire had been cleverly doctored, and we all passed through an easy gap into the deep shadows along the side of the road. Slowly we moved to the river and we distributed the contents of the sacks over a quarter of a mile of its length. The pieces of metal sinking with dull flops into deep water.

We regained the *Lager* wire without any interference. Placing a restraining hand on my shoulder, Godden allowed the others to creep through.

'Well, boys,' he whispered. 'Quite satisfied that brother Yeatman is the goods?'

'Sure,' replied the Aussie. 'He's just our cup of tea.'

'O.K., boys. Get back inside.'

In the inky darkness Godden and I cut across the village and, following a half-circular route across the potato field, dropped down behind the church.

Here Godden paused, and faced me in the darkness. He spoke softly but authoritatively.

'Nobody knows what you are soon going to learn, so keep your mouth shut until you get back to Britain,' he said, adding: 'If that is what Fate decrees.'

I followed on his heels through the gate of a semi-isolated neat and largish two-storey cottage. I had frequently paused to admire its old-fashioned timbered frontage.

The house door was open, but as soon as we had crossed the threshold Godden closed it with three slight bangs, and slipped home the bolts. Touching his shoulder I followed him into a darkened room. When he struck a match to light the lamp I quickly blew it out, and crisply reminded him to make sure that the windows were covered. He chuckled softly and told me that the curtains were always drawn before his arrival.

Our coming was anticipated by the occupants and less than a minute after we entered we were joined by two neatly dressed women of thirtyish and a man of medium height, aged about forty.

Mr and Mrs Karel Cech fell into animated conversation with Godden as soon as introductions had been made, and I listened with the greatest interest, and no small amount of surprise, to a most detailed account of the bombing of Hamburg the night before.

Mrs Karlstadt, the other woman, excused herself, saying that she was going to make some hot coffee and buttered toast.

It was not long before I learned that Karel Cech was employed in an administrative capacity at a Schnapps distillery in Troppau, and that for seven years before the Germans had annexed his country he had been a Slovakian Army Officer. He was discharged from the army owing to diabetes.

Gretel Karlstadt, a somewhat pallid and anæmic woman, was his wife's sister, and both were of true Slovakian stock. Unfortunately, while on holiday in 1939, she had met Manfred Karlstadt, a German army officer. She bitterly regretted the day that she consented to become his wife. He was on the Russian Front, and apparently as true and fanatical an adherent of Hitler and Nazism as any man in the German army.

Mrs and Mr Karel Cech and Gretel loathed the Nazi régime, and all their sympathies and prayers were for the success of the Allied struggle. Their faith in an ultimate Allied victory seemed to be unshakable.

I was, not unnaturally, most curious to know how Godden had become so closely associated with these people, and when we left I asked him, only to be rebuffed with the polite answer: 'Sorry . . . Military secret,' followed by a long pause, and then: 'A secret for all time.'

It appeared that each night Karel's powerful radio receiver, secreted in the cellar, was tuned in to the B.B.C., and by this means a faithful account of war news came to Godden. In Troppau, too,

Karel elicited a remarkable amount of information about troop movements and secret military matters for Godden's particular benefit. I thought it vastly amusing to learn that the detestable Manfred Karlstadt had recently been on leave, and that all his stories and secrets about life and happenings on the Russian Front had been carefully noted and passed on. It was Gretel's secret longing that her husband, after returning to the Russian Front, might stay there.

The village clock had chimed three when we left the cottage for our cautious return to the schoolhouse prison.

'What a set-up!' I exclaimed. 'And so stimulating to know that such people exist in Hitler's Europe!'

'Britain has such true helpers in every fair-sized community,' Godden replied. 'But they have to be unearthed.'

We paused in the shadows before we left the potato field to cross the road. Godden helped me by the arm and whispered: Anyway, Yeatman, your escape stands more likelihood of success after their promises tonight. Karel will certainly get you travelling papers, and they will give you sufficient money to get you south. Unfortunately they are folk of very modest means.'

Before we crossed the road I told Godden that if Karel could dispose of some fine diamond rings for me I could furnish myself with sufficient capital to meet all escape requirements, and at the same time leave them a cash gift for services rendered.

'Really, Mr Barney Barnato from Kimberley,' said Godden, meditatively. 'Tell me more.' I told him.

270

CHAPTER 12

THE OLD LADY OF TROPPAU

(I)

It was arranged that I should escape in ten days' time, and only
Godden was to be aware of the details surrounding my disappearance. When I had gone he would explain to the other prisoners my
regret at not taking them into my confidence, and seek their understanding. It was decided that, to avoid inquiries, I should not leave
from the school but make the break from Number 5 Farm, four
miles from the *Lager*. I had no trouble in getting a job there, and
as I was considered to be one of the best and most reliable men
no guard was detailed to watch me.

During the mornings I performed various tasks in the cowsheds
and pig-sties, and in the afternoons I journeyed across the fields
with two horses and a cart full of manure. At various selected points
I unloaded the wagon and built up reserves of cow dung to simplify
the process of manure scattering at a later date.

The German civilian employees took a liking to me, mainly
because I intended that they should. I told them I was captured on
Crete, and they gloated over my cooked-up stories about the
German aerial armada which darkened the skies over the island,
and how thousands of their brave parachutists descended and smothered all resistance.

'Yes,' I would solemnly tell them. 'Your soldiers are wonderfully brave fighters, and when we were captured we were treated
by them with courtesy and extreme decency. Isn't it a pity,' I added,

271

pretending regret, 'that the British and the Germans are not brothers in arms against the Russians.'

'*Ja, ja!*' they would reply with friendliness. 'What you say is true.'

Rewarding me with cigarettes as tokens of their gratitude for my generous praise of the German soldiers, they would tell me my duties, but not bother about checking up on me.

The first two days on the farm I removed such a quantity of cow dung from the central deposit that the civilian overseer specially contacted the officer at the *Lager* and praised me to the skies. On the third day I intentionally approached him at 5.30 in the afternoon, my body naked except for shorts and boots, covered with smears of cow dung and dripping with sweat. I requested that I might be allowed to take a dip in the river before returning to the *Lager*.

'It is *verboten*,' he replied. 'It is a deep and dangerous river, and I am charged to look after you.'

'Please,' I begged. 'I'm an expert swimmer. I've worked hard all day, and if you let me swim I will work still harder tomorrow. Come with me to the river and see for yourself how well I can swim.'

We crossed the fields together, and at my selected spot I took off my boots and plunged into the fast-flowing water. I swam easily and with showmanship, and when I scrambled up the bank the overseer appeared quite satisfied that I would not drown. From then on I made a point of taking a dip every morning before I finished work, and it soon came to be regarded without suspicion.

In the *Lager* schoolroom, Godden and I planned every move. When I made my break, I would as usual place my boots on the same spot and enter the water. In mid-stream I would discard my shorts so that they would be discovered later, and swim down-river for a quarter of a mile. I would leave the water directly opposite a fair-sized wood; get out of sight, and get into overalls previously hidden there. From there I would make a half-circular detour to another wood six miles away, and remain closely concealed until darkness fell. Under cover of night I would make straight for the cottage where Karel Cech would be awaiting my arrival.

Godden laughed cheerfully at the idea of the German overseer reporting that I had drowned myself.

On the morning of the day I was to escape Godden whispered to me as I left for the stables: 'See you at Karel's this evening. Don't panic. If anything interferes remember there is always another day.'

Near the cow byre there was a small cottage occupied by a Czech labourer and his wife and two little girls. They were delightful little girls, and very friendly. Often they would ride on my horse and cart after school hours, and invariably I was given a packet of home-made cookies specially sent along to me from their mother. It was, therefore, with no small measure of concern that I saw them advancing across the fields towards me just before I was about to take my last swim. All smiles, they handed me a packet of cherry tart, and the younger of the two cheerfully informed me that they would wait and ride back to the barn with me.

'You must go back to your mother at once,' I snapped. 'At once . . . I have still lots of work to do.'

'But you've emptied the wagon,' remarked the older girl.

'Please go back . . . Now . . . Scram!' I commanded harshly. 'I do not want you waiting here . . . Go!'

The unaccustomed severity of my voice caused hurt and puzzled expressions on the little Slovakian girls' faces. 'Get off that cart and go,' I yelled. 'Otherwise I shall tell your mother how rude you both have been.'

273

Like two cowed and frightened puppies, with looks of dumb surprise, they slunk away. The dark-haired little girl, whom I had nicknamed Jeannie, gave me a parting glance, and I knew that she was close to tears. Just before they topped the rise that would hide them from sight, they stopped, turned and looked back at me.

'Good girls,' I yelled. 'I've left some chocolate for you both with your mother.'

They waved and slowly dropped out of sight over the crest.

I rubbed my head against my horses' necks, walked to the bank and took off my boots. I dived headlong into the clean, cool water. Rolling on my back I shed my working shorts, and struck off downstream.

After I had rounded the river bend I felt safer, and slackened my pace between the two high banks. Finally I clambered from the water at the spot I knew to be opposite the wood. As I raced for the cover of the trees, I almost collapsed in my tracks as a voice broke the silence from the opposite bank. Once in the wood I turned and anxiously scanned the landscape, and saw about 500 yards away simple old Sudermann, an eccentric recluse of over eighty, with his sheep. Like a fool, I had forgotten that of all cultivated land around here, the few acres boasting grass for grazing were bang opposite the wood!

Slipping into the overalls I had hidden the previous day, I wasted no time in picking my way across country to the second wood, where I hid until darkness. Then, cautiously doubling back to the village, I reached Karel Cech's door without scare or incident.

I listened carefully before raising the latch, but all appeared serene and quiet. I entered, locked the door behind me and coughed. A door immediately opened and Karel's broad figure was silhouetted against the background of lamplight.

274

'Nice work, my boy,' he exclaimed. 'Come in and have something to eat. Gretel has excelled herself tonight in your honour. Was everything all right? . . . Any incidents? . . . Did your departure from the farm go according to plan?'

Solemnly I told him of my unavoidable harshness towards the two little girls, and of simple Sudermann calling out as I raced in the nude for the cover of the wood.

Karel's eyes narrowed. He lapsed into deep thought.

'Most unfortunate, my friend . . . Most unfortunate,' he said. 'The whole point is . . . will Sudermann squawk? That old man is certainly not as stupid as most people imagine. I pray that he is not cross-questioned.'

We were expecting Godden, but he did not arrive. Next morning Karel returned from Troppau, agitated.

'The military and police for miles around are on the lookout for you!' he said. 'The German members of our community, and the local boys of the Hitler Youth Movement, were out in force last night scouring the countryside. You will certainly not be able to leave here until the panic has died down.'

It was after three in the morning before we retired to bed after a disappointing wait for Godden. All sorts of unpleasant speculations passed through my mind as we drank endless cups of coffee, but no disquieting thoughts were spoken aloud.

It was soon after midnight on the third night when a series of light coughs in the passage brought us all to our feet. It was Godden.

'Sorry, everyone,' he chuckled, quite unconcernedly. 'But the *Lager* officer was in such a state of infuriated jitters at your breach of trust that he dragged out all his six guards and has made 'em do two hours on and four hours off throughout the whole of the

275

last two nights. Now they're so shagged out that they can't keep it up! What happened, Yeatman?'

I told him.

'The general story is that you collided with Sudermann on the bank and threatened to bash his brains out,' Godden told us. 'He raced off as fast as his creaking legs would carry him and told the foreman on Farm Five. Then, of course, things started humming.'

Like the fine chap he was, Godden attempted to make light of the trouble. 'No use crying over spilt milk,' he said. 'And the man who never makes a mistake never makes anything.'

Ten days later I started my adventure proper. The German military had generally assumed that I had successfully fled the district, vigilance had relaxed and it was considered safe for me to be on my way.

(2)

Gretel and Mrs Cech put the finishing touches to my neat old lady's attire while Karel brought the pony and trap round to the door. I wore a black taffeta dress which fell into a full long skirt from a gathered waist. My bust and all the necessary upholstery to achieve a correct female figure had been thoughtfully considered, as well as my silver-grey coiffure: a first-class wig which fitted snugly beneath a close-fitting black hat complete with draped veil. My button boots pinched a little.

As we trotted through the village in the early morning we overtook a party of my old *Lager* pals moving up the road accompanied by two armed guards. If they had only known who the old woman really was!

We cleared the village and bowled along the highway to Troppau.

Outside a neat, detached house in a quiet and isolated locality Karel helped me from the trap and, escorting me by the arm with an air of gentlemanly consideration, led me indoors to met Mr Maurus.

Before Karel Cech left he handed me a wallet containing the equivalent of £200 – the proceeds from the rings. As he left I shook him firmly by the hand, and there was no need for me to say again that if my luck went awry, and the Gestapo collared me for a third time, no squealing on my part would implicate him or the members of his family.

Mr Maurus was a man of few words. In his parlour I discarded my female attire and donned a well-darned but tidy suit. Under my cap there showed enough blond hair to give me some of the appearance of a German. The transformation had been achieved at the Cech's, where frequent application of peroxide had cleared away all signs of my natural red hair.

'Here are your zonal movement papers, made out in the name of Schmidt,' Mr Maurus said, 'and here is your railway ticket to Vienna. Your seat is in coach C, specially secured for you because this carriage is reserved for the most part for foreign workers, Poles and Frenchmen *en* route to Vienna through the direction of the German Labour Directorate. The fact that you are presumably a German, because you understand German best, should discourage any conversation. Foreign workers speak bad German, and most of them avoid talking with real sons of the Fatherland. When you leave Troppau you will completely forget all the people who have helped you.'

He gave me an address in Stockerau, thirty kilometres north of Vienna, and the vitally necessary password.

'Remember the words *Reichenberg-Szekula*, and respect them,' he said. He gave me clear instructions regarding my route to

Troppau station, and a detailed sketch to guide me out of Vienna and place me on the road to Stockerau. I had to commit to memory the name of the house to which I was being sent – *Katuana* – and its precise location near the railway just short of the built-up area.

At Troppau I passed through the ticket barrier with aplomb, and expressed a polite 'Thank you' and 'Good day' to the uniformed collector.

On entering coach C I saw half a dozen Frenchmen busy jabbering away in voluble French.

'*Heil Hitler!*' I rapped out tartly as they looked up.

'*Heil Hitler!*' replied a couple of them meekly. Automatically the jabbering ceased and six faces noticeably stiffened.

The next block of seats past the party of Frenchmen seemed my safest bet and, leaving the section that seated four, I chose the two single ones on the right. Here I slumped down with a grunt and put my small attaché-case on the opposite seat.

The carriage filled rapidly, mostly with Poles. Four of them, lads of about eighteen, spread themselves out in the four seats in the entire gangway. When the train pulled out only three seats in the whole coach were vacant, and my attaché-case reposed on one of them. Things were working out well.

Arrogantly turning on one of the young Poles I said in a rough and uncompromising voice: 'Give me a light.'

From then on the youngsters regarded me furtively, and made no attempt at conversation. When I realised that I was the object of scrutiny from the Poles opposite, I turned my head quickly in their direction and gave them a look which I hoped expressed hate and loathing. Quickly they raised their eyes, and one slender and pasty fellow blushed pathetically.

But it guaranteed silence for me on the journey south, a journey which was not particularly speedy. It was 5.30 in the afternoon when I alighted at Vienna, and so far the trip had proved successful. Only twice did I have cause to experience a flutter of nerves and a tightening of muscles, and that was when the inspector examined our travelling vouchers. But nothing strange or suspicious prompted him to hang about or start any cross-questioning.

(3)

Outside the station I took my bearings and followed the route which Mr Maurus had given me, picking my way out of the crowded city into the neat suburbs. I covered a few miles on the Stockerau road before I dared to relax my pace and breathe with ease.

I had to foot-slog the best part of fifteen miles before I arrived at the house of *Katuana*, and I calculated that, all being well, I should be safely indoors and among friends by 11 o'clock. I constantly repeated to myself the words *Reichenberg-Szekula*, and wondered about the people I was going to meet, and what I should receive.

At the outset the roads I followed were by no means deserted, but everybody I passed, and those who passed me in vehicles and on bicycles, were intent on their own business. As the shadows lengthened the highway became empty and my spirits climbed. But I was ravenously hungry and horribly parched.

'God!' I murmured as I topped a rise. 'If only the blasted river Danube had wound its course in this vicinity instead of through the city!'

But my luck was in, and about five miles from Stockerau I heard the gentle tinkle of running water near the roadside. I drank my fill from the brook, washed and set off on the last leg of my journey like a giant refreshed.

As instructed, I closed with the railway tracks, and as I advanced I studied the terrain and checked on the disposition of guiding features explained by Mr Maurus. It was not difficult to calculate that I had approximately a quarter of a mile to go.

Gingerly I edged into the trees and trod as silently as I could. A wan moon flecked the night with just sufficient light and when at last the house to which I had been directed appeared, I knew that there was no doubt that it was labelled *Katuana*.

Isolated, and surrounded by a well-constructed hedge, the building was double-storied and with a steep roof. Four windows along the length of the upper floor, long, narrow and equidistant, were identical with the description given me. But positive proof that this was my rendezvous lay in the fact that the top half of the house was white-washed down to a line a few inches above the top of the entrance.

I moved low along the dirt path which brought me up to the gate, and it was with no small thrill that I picked out the name *Katuana* in bold black letters. No sign of life came from any of the windows but, knowing the nature of the work going on behind the walls facing me, I was in no way perturbed at the total blackout.

I knocked softly. There was no reply, not a stirring of any sound. I knocked longer and a little louder, but still no movement came. After half an hour of knocking at the door and encircling the house, softly calling close to each window the words, *Reichenberg-Szekula*, my heart weighed as heavy as lead and I began to experience the bitterest disappointment.

'What could have happened?' I asked myself in a panic. 'Have they left? . . . Have they been arrested? . . . Are they in Vienna on a visit?'

Hiding in the bushes at the bottom of the garden I prayed for the sound of returning feet and voices. No one came. I stayed there until three o'clock in the morning, and then I advanced again to the front door and knocked and rapped at the windows; but the house was dead.

I explored the sheds at the top of the garden and, after a further half-hour, the window in what appeared to be a large garage yielded to the probings of my knife. I carefully propped the pane of glass I had removed against the shed and, wriggling through the opening, dropped inside. My lighted matches revealed lots of junk, picture-frames, old pans, scores of empty bottles, gardening equipment and, most encouraging and pleasing of all, a healthy pile of old sacks in the corner.

Within a few minutes of spreading out a bed of sacks for myself, I was out, dead tired. Even hunger pains could not stop my eyes from closing instantly.

My watch showed it was 9.30 when I awoke in the morning. A bright shaft of sunlight came diagonally through the glassless window opening, and fell on a large oil painting propped against the wall. Bending to examine the work, I was surprised to see that the caption read: 'Moving Up the Mississippi'. It was an excellent painting of a large paddle steamer with the wide and mysterious river and an undulating landscape on either side.

Lacing up my boots, and still contemplating the painting, I was suddenly aroused by the sound of footsteps and throat clearing from outside. Whipping over to the window opening I looked out into the garden. Not more than ten yards away an old and bowed man in shirt sleeves had his eyes rigidly focussed on the aperture in front of me. Our gazes met and, for a matter of seconds, neither side flinched. Then I politely called out a good morning and, allowing a few seconds interval to lapse, followed it up with a carefully enunciated: '*Reichenberg-Szekula.*'

'What are you doing in that shed, friend?' came the immediate response.

'I was specially directed here by loyal friends in the north,' I answered.

The man came forward, unlocked the door and sat down opposite me in the shed. We remained in conversation for over an hour.

His name was Heinrich and he was the gardener. His news was shattering. Mr and Mrs W— and their two sons, whom I had travelled to meet, had been arrested by the Security Police in Vienna only four days earlier. They were in on a charge of complicity in secretly distributing printed news-bulletins among the anti-Hitler Viennese whose activities in the Allied cause had created consternation among the Gestapo.

The police had visited the house six times since the actual arrest and had carried off the radio and all the private documents, letters and papers they could lay their hands on.

'They still haven't found a lot of personal property hidden in the garden,' he said, and smiled wanly. 'And I am seeing that they don't. It is all being hidden in a safe place in Stockerau.'

I realised full well that I had had my chips so far as assistance from *Katuana* was concerned. Heinrich was all that was left and I got to work on him immediately to secure what help I could. I explained my troubles, my plan to escape to Yugoslavia and what I needed to continue the journey on my own. His sympathy, understanding and desire to help were genuine enough, and he listened gravely as I ate the sandwiches and gulped the beer which he had brought for his own lunch. Giving him fifty marks, I asked him to get for me all the provisions he could obtain in Stockerau, with a further eighty marks to buy his brother's bicycle. I had had enough of foot-slogging.

Before he left I was suddenly prompted to ask the serious-faced little Viennese gardener if Mr and Mrs W— had any American relations.

'No,' he replied, 'my employers have roots deep in Austria, but they both lived for many years in Tennessee, U.S.A. In fact, both the boys were born there.'

CHAPTER 13

THE FIGHT IN THE NIGHT

(I)

In the late afternoon I swung into the saddle of the bicycle and pedalled in the direction of Vienna, *en route* to Hungary and still farther south, to Yugoslavia.

The basket strapped on the handlebars and the container behind me on the carrier contained a good supply of food. Heinrich had got for me two loaves of bread, two pots of dripping, five good-sized lengths of meat *Wurst*, two tins of meat paste, four tins of herrings and two packets of Italian biscuits. Two beer bottles filled with coffee, a pair of socks, a dixie, a bar of soap and a towel, a razor and a flashlight completed my travelling kit.

The only maps he had been able to obtain, unfortunately, were a large scale. Nevertheless, I could follow well enough the road directions from one large centre to another. Heinrich's compass, too, was quite effective, even if it was a little on the large size.

Cautiously, I threaded my way through Vienna, got out on to the Baden road and steadily pedalled on all through the night.

The light of early morning found me a few miles from Sopron, a large town just inside the Hungarian border. The night ride had been gruelling, and my legs were stiff after the sixty-odd miles. A good meal added to my desire for sleep and, nestling down, I slept solidly in a wood until three in the afternoon.

I resumed my journey in a warm and friendly sunshine. The road was bounded by a wonderfully green landscape and I felt as free as a bird. I prayed that when I came to the Hungarian border Fate would continue to act as generously towards me as she had done since I left the prison camp in Germany. Instinctively I felt that once I was safely across the Hungarian border zone, the 160 miles separating me from the mountains of Croatia and Tito's strongholds would present no formidable undertaking.

I still had my railway papers, naming me Schmidt. They would be useful at the frontier post. I could say that I did not have to start work in Vienna for a fortnight, and was using the time to visit my brother on military duty at Veszprem, and that unfortunately I had left behind my movement papers and passport.

Sopron was not far ahead of me when I caught sight of the usual red and white barrier pole across the road ahead, with the white sentry box and two guards.

Instantly I slackened my speed to allow a party of six cyclists, girls and youths, which I had just passed to get ahead of me. As soon as they were in front I followed close behind. The pole was raised, but as we drew level the cyclists halted. The girls laughed and joked with the Germans and one of the young fellows threw a parcel across to the nearest sentry. Without any requests for papers, and without the slightest trace of suspicion, the leading cyclists moved forward, past the grinning Germans. A few yards beyond the post one of the Germans yelled out: 'Don't forget the eggs tomorrow!' A few heads turned, and two or three arms waved confirmation . . . including mine!

It was a phenomenal stroke of luck. My not being one of the party had never occurred to the guards, and the cyclists themselves had not bothered about my being attached to them.

A short distance up the road the six young people turned off on to a dirt path to the right in the direction of a cluster of farm buildings. I acknowledged their cordial good-nights, and pressed down on my pedals with renewed energy.

Casually I rode through the streets of Sopron, and only when I had to jerk into the kerb to get out of the way of four German military caterpillar vehicles did my heart start to pound. For a few minutes the jitters got the best of me, and I toyed with the idea of retreating and hiding in the woods until darkness. It struck me that it might be wiser to cross the frontier zone away from the road, carrying my bicycle across my back. But as quickly as the idea occurred to me I discarded it as being quite impracticable. To labour over rough country with my bicycle was stupid, so I steeled my courage to forge ahead and bluff my way past any opposition.

I must have cycled ten miles after passing the frontier post before the blow fell. Merrily I bowled around a blind corner on a down-hill grade and, directly in front of me not more than twenty yards away, there was a second red and white sectioned pole, horizon-tally across the road.

The pole ended on a raised concrete slab. Between that and the sentry box on the extreme edge of the road there was a four-foot space with a white gate affixed. The gate was open and, without a second's hesitation, I accelerated and shot through, just beating the appearance of a yelling German by a fraction of a second.

Immediately I was aware that I had made a gross blunder, but I had no intention of dismounting and entering into a phoney conver-sation with the guardian of the gate. The road in front of me was dead straight, and I worked frantically on the pedals, leaving screams of rage behind me.

The German was quick-witted, and a good shot. His first bullet whined low over my head; his second must have pierced the carrier because it smacked with a high metallic ring just below my seat.

I should immediately have zigzagged from one side of the road to the other, but the suddenness and fearful reality of what was happening quite robbed my mind of any cunning, and like a fool I maintained a straight course!

The third bullet proved that the German was a first-class shot. I do not really know exactly what happened except that the lead hit the machine and seemed to keep on striking parts of the metal in rapid and thudding succession, and I went slithering over the gravel of the road, all mixed up in the framework of the bicycle. Before I could disengage myself a fourth shot snarled between my arm and body, and exploded one of the coffee bottles in the front carrier.

I had had quite enough of being a live target and before the marksman could aim and pull his trigger a fifth time I hurtled off through the trees. I raced blindly forward until I was forced to sink to the ground to steady my pounding heart and regain my breath.

What filthy luck . . . What a lousy trick Fate had played when all seemed to be going so well! I had lost my precious bicycle and all my food. But I consoled myself with the thought that I had not lost my life or my money, maps and compass.

I studied my maps and decided to work away due east from the frontier region to gain the hinterland of Hungary. Then, when the air had cleared, I would alter course due south and continue towards the border mountains of Croatia.

For two days I struggled across rough terrain, dragging myself through heavily wooded areas, thick and retarding. My clothes were in tatters and my face and hands were criss-crossed with innumerable scratches. I swam two rivers – and ruined my cigarettes. The lack of an occasional smoke did not improve my temper or my morale.

I covered thirty miles of the forty to Csorna, subsisting on berries, ears of corn and odd turnips and potatoes scrounged from the fields. But forty-eight hours of such a diet was not adequate to cope with the physical exertions of a cross-country trek, and I became ravenously hungry. As the hunger pains grew and tormented me like a raw and throbbing wound, so my caution lessened. The maddening and impatient voice of hunger whispered to me to stand for no restraint or interference.

On the third day I swung south by east, resolving to strike the railway line running into Papa. Still I had not eaten proper food. The relentless voice of hunger could no longer be ignored, and I decided on drastic measures before I reached the railway tracks. I intended to try to hide away on a south-bound train, or ride the roads . . . or do any damned thing but walk.

But food first.

(2)

It was the fourth night of foot-slogging, as evening was falling, that I marked the house which was to give me food and clothes . . . food at any price!

It was a largish, double-storey, old-fashioned type of dwelling, standing in large grounds. An old lady and gentleman were moving about the garden picking pears from the trees, and I watched them until darkness compelled them to go indoors.

I had not seen any full-bodied and capable younger people about the house, and this was comforting. I would not have to fight against strength and formidable opposition. As I crouched below the trees in the darkness, waiting, I fashioned a dummy pistol with my knife out of a piece of wood.

It was close to two in the morning when I eventually left my place of hiding, forded the deep stream which marked the garden boundary and scaled the low railings. Before I set about breaking into the house, I had a meal of pears from the trees.

In soft moonlight, I carefully circled the house, keeping close to the wall, and carefully tested the windows and doors. It was with no small surprise and relief that I discovered that the smallish side window overlooking the kitchen-garden offered easy access. The top section opened outwards on a metal strip and, hoisting myself up on an old cistern, I reached inside and downwards to the catch which secured the main window.

Once across the window-ledge it was obvious that I was in a lavatory, and it was not the wooden seat alone which told me so: it was the rustic, non-flush type.

Picking my way out into a stone-floored passage, I turned through a doorway on the right. This led into a large room, heavily furnished, with a grandfather clock ticking away with a disconcerting and threatening loudness. In the moonlight I saw a formidable stone fireplace, and from the hearth I picked up a long and massive-headed poker.

I passed through a curtained doorway at the end of the long living-room into what I assumed was the owner's study, or library. There were several well-filled bookcases in the room, and a strong smell of tobacco hung in the air.

Searching a number of drawers in a corner writing-desk, I joyfully transferred to my pocket three packets of cigars each holding six good solid smokes, in addition to four boxes of matches. So far so good.

I left the room and went back to the paved passage. The last door on the left turned out to be the pantry, and proved that the occupiers of the house did not endure any shortages of food. From a healthy joint of pork I hacked off several pieces and washed down the meat with a drink of fresh milk. I ate a dish of potatoes, and then started in on a fine piece of ham. But I quickly decided not to make serious inroads in this as it was just the stuff to take along as cross-country rations. If the old lady I had watched in the garden was responsible for the baking of the apple pie which I more than sampled, then my mother had a rival in cookery of no mean capability. I had a go at everything, and finished by breaking four eggs into a bowl of milk and drinking the mixture off.

From behind the door I unhooked a canvas bag and filled it with meat, bread, butter, cheese and two solid apple pies which I carefully packed in a tin. I found four cans of something (they had no labels) on the top shelf, and stuffed them, too, into the bag.

The food bolstered my courage but instead of being satisfied with my bag of supplies, I thought I might as well make a quick search for some clothing. The garments I wore were in tatters. Anybody seeing me would instantly have their suspicions aroused.

I retraced my steps through the rooms on the ground floor, but found nothing until, behind the door in the hall where the staircase led upstairs, I pulled out from a recessed cupboard two overcoats and a corduroy jacket which fitted me perfectly. In one of the pockets I found a flat cap which was exactly right. I donned my new-found garb and stuffed my own pathetic coat on top of my bag of food against the wall.

Now I needed only a pair of trousers. The things I was wearing were finished, and another day's cross-country rough and tumble would result in my being completely nude about my nether region. My backside and a good section of my left leg were already visible in the moonlight.

I mounted the stairs, and at the top found a corridor running the length of the house. As I tiptoed forward my outstretched fingers contacted a door knob. In my left hand I gripped the heavy poker. I held the knob lightly and for the first time that night I experienced qualms of nervousness and panic. I decided to abandon the search and had actually descended two of the stairs in retreat, when the natural desire for a whole pair of trousers overcame my timidity. Trousers were absolutely vital to my success. If I left the house without them, I would only have to break into somewhere else to steal them.

The door creaked as I gingerly pushed it open. Quickly I was in the room and flat up against the wall, the poker still tightly gripped in my left hand. I remained motionless for a few minutes, listening to the strong and rhythmic breathing of the occupant of the bed over by the window. Sweat dripped from my face and my body was sticky under my corduroy jacket. Fortunately, there was not too much moonlight coming through the window, owing to a large tree immediately outside.

When my eyes became accustomed to the dim outlines of the room, I moved silently towards what I assumed was the wardrobe. I had left my boots alongside my bag of food near the door. The wardrobe door opened the first few inches without the slightest sound, but suddenly it emitted a high-pitched croak. I started and dropped the heavy poker on the floor with a loud thud.

The events that followed happened quickly. As I stooped to retrieve my poker the occupant of the bed leaped into startling and horrifying life with a blood-curdling yell and bounded to wards the door. It was a man's voice.

I jerked to my feet and on the turn brought my bar of iron down with a powerful crack on the spectral-looking white-shirted apparition at the door. It crunched into his shoulder which I had misjudged

291

for the skull, and screams of rage and pain rent the night air. The man immediately sprang forward and grappled with me. By his power and weight I could tell that he was no mean size and the grip of steel he locked about my throat would have spelt my end in a matter of seconds had I not reacted instantly.

I used – and thank Heaven I had learned it – a ju-jitsu countering move which I had practised in the R.A.F. gym. Stiffening my throat muscles I brought up my hands to the encircling fingers at the back of my neck. I grasped and levered on the first finger of each of the man's hands, and with a strong backward jerk let him have it. As if the fingers had been sticks firmly locked in a vice they bent to the limit, and then snapped with crisp cracks.

The man immediately released me, screaming with sheer agony. From the other side of the door came more wails and yells. Fortunately our struggling bodies prevented it being opened. I fought savagely, but at the same time tried to keep myself anchored to cold cunning. This was a fight for life.

As his fingers snapped I followed through with my doubled-up knee to the groin and then to the pit of his stomach. I put every ounce of strength behind the drives. The hot hulk of flesh whined and gasped, and then slumped to the floor emitting fast sobbing hiccoughs. I picked up the poker and let him have two good lashes over the skull.

The person pushing at the door could not open it more than a few inches because the heavy body was acting as a stop. I rolled the body away and jumped backwards, gripping the poker. In the opening stood the old man and woman, the man holding a lamp in a trembling hand. Before he had time to do anything I jerked forward and seized the lamp, at the same time striking him across the shoulders.

'Get into the room,' I yelled in German, driving them both forward with swings of the poker.

The old woman was so terrified that she fell headlong over the outstretched legs of the unconscious man on the floor, and began screaming a blaze of hysteria.

By the light of the lamp I checked on the inside of the wardrobe, and yanked out three pairs of trousers. With these in a bundle I dashed from the room. I slipped into my boots, stuffed the slacks across the top of my food sack, undid the door bolts and, gripping my stolen possessions, streaked down the garden and over the road beyond the gate.

The old couple in the house were screaming and raving worse than an air-raid siren. Up the hillside which sheltered the village I rushed, not pausing until I could watch from a high vantage point the fluttering lanterns all about the house.

As I remembered what I had done, I felt sick. I turned my back on the scene and marched away. It was not until I lit a cigar that the throttling sense of fright left me.

'Hell!' I consoled myself. 'There's no justice, sportsmanship or decency in war or escape! What choice did Fate leave me?'

(3)

I cleared the area of the village by a wide circuit, and readjusted my course 15 degrees east of south. I forced a five-miles-an-hour pace all through the night and as the first streaks of dawn spread across the sky and the trees lost some of their sinister appearance I looked about for a hiding-place.

The comfort and security that a bush had provided in Holland — was it a million years ago? — prompted me to find something similar. My Hungarian selection was just as screening and hospitable, and beneath a mass of close-knit covering I curled up and slept.

It was two o'clock when I opened my eyes, awakened by the roar of a low-flying aircraft. Twice it screamed across the tops of the trees.

'Now you've really got to watch things, my boy,' I told myself. 'Maybe you're a murderer. Maybe, in addition to breaking his fingers, you killed that man.'

For two days I dared not leave my protection. To attempt any further advance was to invite disaster. The whole area for miles around would be most carefully watched. The Hungarians would be suspicious of all strangers. The police would be trigger-happy, and any lone prowling figure would be shot first and given the benefit of the doubt only when he was a corpse.

But on the third day, at dusk, the monotony of the dark wood became overpowering. I could stand it no longer and, shouldering my possessions, I started off. For forty-eight hours I made satisfactory progress. Then I ran into tortuous and mountainous terrain.

I knew that I was not far from the town of Veszprem but, after seeing from a concealed vantage point three miles from the town a considerable volume of heavy military traffic, I resolved to give it a clear berth. I decided to trek south until I came to the northern shore of Lake Balaton, Hungary's inland sea, and the railway lines which skirted it. Here I would try my hand at sneaking a free ride on a train and, if luck smiled, I would possibly get to a spot not more than fifty or so miles from the Croatian border of Yugoslavia. If luck treated me indifferently and I jumped the wrong train, I would find myself at least 100 miles north of the Yugoslav frontier.

All the rations I had stolen were now exhausted, except for the unknown contents of the tins. These I planned to keep intact as extreme emergency rations. My will-power was in fine fettle, but my endeavours to maintain almost a superhuman caution lost their efficiency when bodily fatigue overtook me and started to play tricks with my mind. My mental weariness found a reaction in ridiculing and scorning all dangers.

It was during such a spell of mental fogginess at the close of the day that I wandered into a turnip field to get something for supper, not realising that in less than thirty minutes darkness would have descended. I had barely put a turnip under my arm when a voice screamed at me from the opposite side of the field. I dropped my supper and bolted, galvanised into alertness and action. I kept moving, fast, and the yells from the person I had not even seen faded into silence.

But my emergency rations, my precious tins, lay somewhere on the edge of the turnip field.

I did not attempt to find a sleeping-place, in spite of the fact that my legs were weak and wavering and my head was throbbing painfully. At first I imagined that the flashes in front of my eyes were due to lightning. I felt full of panic and fear, and had the disconcerting premonition that I was in for trouble.

Sitting on a pile of rocks, I looked out over a flat mountain plateau with the moon washing everything in a soft glow. But discomfort prompted me to start thinking and to go through my pockets. I still had sufficient control of my senses to remember that once before when I was feeling all in – in Cracow – I had neglected to destroy forged papers. So the railway documents and zonal movement papers given to me by Mr Maurus in Troppau I stuffed into a crevice and burned.

Then I started off. But as I plodded on through the night things grew worse. I passed farmsteads and the dogs bayed. I began to believe that the Germans were after me with blood-hounds. I plucked up strength from somewhere and put on a burst of speed, floundering and pitching forward over the rough ground, picking myself up and crashing headlong until I was finally compelled by exhaustion to rest and try to subdue my panic-stricken breathing.

When I had steadied myself I attempted to ridicule my weakness . . . until I passed the next farmstead with a barking dog. I felt in my pocket for my compass. It was not there! In one of my falls I must have lost it. I looked to the stars for guidance as I had done once before in Holland.

I had only just pulled myself together after a further panic caused by shrieking dogs from a farmstead in a narrow valley, when I saw him. I fell flat on my face, scarcely daring even to breath. Twenty yards in front was the perfect silhouette of a German steel helmet on slightly raised shoulders with, a few inches to the right of it, the gentlest swaying of a rifle.

Flat on my belly, absolutely motionless, I kept my eyes glued on the outline. I watched him till my eyes bleared.

'The swine's waiting for me to get up,' I thought. 'As soon as I move he'll let me have it.'

The steel-clad head never moved a fraction for the first hour; only the rifle barrel, pointing upwards, swayed at intervals. But after the second hour I could have sworn that the head frequently turned to the left and then to the right. I was soaking with sweat over the agonising suspense, but I tried to pull myself together and work the whole thing out as logically as possible.

If I stayed there until daybreak, I concluded, he would spot me for a certainty and give me a bullet. But with darkness on my side I at least stood a sporting chance of rushing and attacking. And if I could overcome him I could use his clothing and rifle.

I noiselessly loosened a handy stone to use as a weapon, watching all the time the occasionally moving rifle. He was drowsing, I assured myself. I sprang to my feet, hurtled across the intervening ground and delivered a gigantic kick at the German's face, at the same time gripping with both hands the vertical barrel of the rifle. My boot shot straight through a clump of gorse, and the rifle barrel pricked my hands and collapsed under the weight of my body. I lay and sobbed, and felt as if my brain was going to explode. What in hell's name was wrong with me?

When I recovered my composure, I moved on. Dawn was breaking, and the morning air was noticeably cool and heavy with moisture. I felt that I must be very close to Lake Balaton. The ground became easier and more thickly covered with trees, and as I strode from a small wood I stepped smack on to a concrete roadway.

As I casually clattered across to the opposite side of the road, a voice suddenly caused me to rear as if I had been hit. It was a harsh, yelling Slavonic voice, and although I did not understand what was being said, I knew that it was a command to halt, and that I had not the slightest chance of bolting into the trees only a few yards ahead. As I raised my arm, I turned. Not more than ten feet behind and to the right of me there stood a heavy man in a black uniform and a peaked cap. He had me covered with a sub-machine-gun. A few yards to the left of him was a green hut, built into the fringe of the wood. I had walked straight into a police road guard.

Prodding me savagely until my face was against the wood of the hut, my Hungarian captor yelled questions at me. I replied in German, telling him that I was a New Zealand prisoner of war, and that I was escaping. I could do nothing more; I did not even care about anything any more.

The Hungarian policeman was not running any risks and he took the law into his own hands. I did not see him raise the sub-machine-gun, and I did not feel anything when it crashed down on my skull.

I came to my senses, my head pulsating, my skull swathed in bandages, in a cell in Veszprem, guarded by a young German.

The Germans had taken me from the hands of the Hungarian police – which was a lucky break for me. The Hungarians would have jailed, and perhaps executed me, for the attack on the house-holders. As it was, I was treated with the utmost courtesy and consideration – a startling change from my experiences in Cracow at the hands of the Gestapo – and two weeks after my capture was returned to Stalag VIIIb.

BOOK 4

NORTH THROUGH SWEDEN

CHAPTER 14

BLINDNESS BEARS NO HATE

(I)

Within fifteen minutes of my re-entry into Stalag VIIIb the camp security police had me in solitary. But I cheated them. During the first night I was suddenly overtaken with a brain fever and the initial stages of blindness. The first symptoms of meningitis manifested themselves in acute bouts of dizziness, retching and a thickening mist before my eyes. Before dawn I was raving and shouting, half delirious, from violent pains at the nape of my neck and a panic-sticken, if bemused, realisation that my eyes could define nothing clearly. I could not rise from my back, and my knees seemed to be slowly stiffening towards my chest.

The noise I made and my appearance convinced the guard that I was genuinely ill. He notified the main guard-room. Both German and English camp doctors were summoned, and I was taken from the cell to the camp hospital. For days my mind was a blank. During unconsciousness I was given lumbar punctures, cerebral spinal fluid being drawn off to lessen the pressure on the brain.

When I finally regained some sort of reasonable control of my senses, it was a hideous shock to realise that although my eyes were fully open, all I could see was an impenetrable wall of mottled darkness.

The medical orderlies and doctors endeavoured to pacify my tortured state of mind and I kept my mouth shut; but their kind and optimistic words that all would eventually right itself and my sight would return fell on empty ears. I made up my mind during the first two weeks of blindness that I would not return to England in such a condition. I would rather take my own life. But one day, as I lay in bed, a strong and cheerful voice broke the silence, the voice of none other than Captain Spencer, the medical officer, who had just returned to Stalag VIIIb after a spell of medical duty on a large working party.

Spencer was the finest tonic and inspiration I could have had. It was he who talked sense and instilled patience into me; who sat by my bedside for hours on end reassuring me and encouraging me to take a firm grip on myself. Daily he would make a special point of coming along to my bedside and giving me a pep talk, in addition to cigarettes.

'Take it easy . . . and slowly,' he said. 'Your sight will return. I tell you it will return if you control your nerves and keep calm. A lot of pressure has to subside before the papilloedema of your eye nerves clears.'

I owe it to Captain Spencer that I got back on my feet again. He was the only man of whom I never wearied while in hospital. His words were the only ones that I instinctively trusted and hung on to while I gradually built up a determination not to despair or quit – sight or no sight.

And as I learned fortitude, so, too, I learned tolerance. In blindness there is no hate or rancour. My loathing of the Germans for all they had done to me and my country and to the girl I had loved, gradually fell away. I began to realise that individuals mirror their leaders; that minds warped by false doctrines could be straightened again by teaching right instead of wrong. Never again did I see the Germans as beasts and maniacs to be exterminated ruthlessly, but as men and women, albeit deluded.

(2)

It took three months for the papilloedema of the eyes to lessen sufficiently to allow me to define objects blearily, and a further three months before I could see things with anything like normal clarity. And meanwhile, during my fifth month in hospital, I was overtaken by a second reaction to my Hungarian escape, this time another bout of pleurisy, more severe than the first breakdown in Poland.

It was eleven months after I first entered the hospital before I was discharged from the sick bay and returned to the main barracks in the camp. But for months before my discharge I had suffered from violent headaches, and every second day or so the Germans injected intravenously 20 cc. of *Traubenzucker* into my arm. This, I learned, was some kind of glucose to lessen blood-pressure.

Upon return to the main camp I was given a medical pass to receive a *Traubenzucker* injection whenever my head troubled me, but I resolved that I would cure myself. Gradually, I managed to beat the headaches just as I had beaten everything else, and six months later they were a thing of the past.

A great deal had taken place on the war fronts during my eleven months in hospital and life was lived to a much happier and more optimistic tune. The combined American and British air forces were pasting the German as he had never been pasted before, and as the enemy had never thought possible. The Russian forces had ceased to retreat so alarmingly, and were reversing the tide of attack. The Germans had been kicked out of North Africa, and the Americans were slowly and remorselessly sealing off the Japanese.

During my stay in hospital the Dieppe raid had taken place, and for a while the whole camp was in a tumult of excitement believing that the Second Front had actually opened up. Later, 500 badly wounded Canadians were brought into the hospital. Many were horribly smashed up from the onslaught they had faced on the Dieppe beaches, but they proved a magnificent tonic to the old lags of Stalag VIIIb who had endured the rigours of soul-stifling captivity for two years or more.

The Canadians revitalised flagging spirits with their firsthand accounts of happenings on the home front. They told us about the old country being one huge camp with millions of fighting men rampaging to go. We learned of the American legions and the colossal strength of armament which they had brought across the Atlantic. Invasion was inevitable at an early date. Just around the corner, they told us.

I found the German camp guards, too, were considerably more docile and conciliatory, less brutal and trigger-happy. Food had not improved or increased. The rations were still disgustingly lean, and Red Cross supplies erratic. Nevertheless, the gladdening war news bolstered up our spirits.

I was still known as Winston Yeatman, and my mail from Britain still came to me cleverly constructed, giving me all the news and instructions without incurring the slightest suspicion from German Intelligence. I learned that the real Yeatman was in a camp at a place called Heyderkrug, Luft VI, on the East Prussian-Lithuanian border, north-east of Königsberg. I had become so accustomed to being Winston Yeatman that my real name of Dick Pape seemed strange to me. My masquerade had weathered all the storms, and now seemed securely established until the end of the war, and I resigned myself to returning eventually to England as a New Zealand private soldier.

(3)

After a time, my health restored, I once again joined up with a working commando. On this occasion I did not live permanently apart from the parent camp but travelled to and from the village of my daily employment with some twenty men. At this town, fifteen miles away on the river Oder, I worked in the carpenter's shop, and it was from the old German joiner who was in charge of me that I secured by bribery, threat and blackmail a seven-valve radio receiver in first-class condition.

Herr Schmidt was a man over sixty years of age, bullet headed and a hard task-master, whose bite was not as bad as his bark. Day in and day out I planed timber and drilled holes with a brace and bit and gradually, when he came to realise that I was a consistent and reliable worker, his stern disciplinarian manner relaxed and he behaved more like a workmate, even to the extent of giving me a pipe of tobacco occasionally.

I assisted this change of attitude by presenting Schmidt with a bar of Red Cross soap. Skilfully I played him day after day, a means to an end, with offerings from Red Cross parcels. First soap, then chocolate, followed by other gifts of Red Cross tea and coffee. The coffee was almost magical in its effects of taming him.

In Stalag VIIIb there was a special panel of men known as the Escape Committee. It was all secret, and numbered not more than two dozen trusted men. The aim of this organisation was to obtain from the German captors, by graft or any other means, articles and materials urgently necessary for the well-being and success of escapees, and for the general good of the camp. By such methods the committee worked on certain guards to secure a camera, with films and the necessary chemicals. The committee then set about

305

photographing all those Germans who committed crimes against prisoners and international law. Unobtrusively, German offenders were snapped and records prepared to facilitate arrests when the post-war days of reckoning arrived. Special Red Cross supplies were diverted for the exclusive use of the Escape Committee, to facilitate bartering, graft and corruption.

I told the committee that Schmidt had a powerful radio receiver in his cottage at the rear of the workshop. I was provided with a liberal supply of Red Cross goods and instructed to get to work on blackmail, and by hook or by crook to get the radio into the camp.

Decent soap and edible chocolate were luxuries almost impossible for the common German folk, while Red Cross coffee invariably persuaded them to discard all warnings not to fraternise with British p.o.w.s.

Schmidt was a glutton for Canadian Maxwell House coffee, and after the first packet his craving for it became insane. Schmidt's wife fell for the rich, fatty, sweet-smelling Red Cross soap, and his daughter pestered her father to persuade me to bring along more chocolate.

For three weeks carpenter Schmidt imagined that he was on a good wicket. I lied, telling him that the camp was stuffed with Red Cross supplies, sufficient to last the Stalag for many months, and that he need never go without soap, chocolate or his precious coffee.

They were not unappreciative, and Schmidt's wife frequently sent into the workshop hot meals and tasty cookies, and my pipe was well supplied with fuel.

Then one morning I gave him the gun. Casually I informed him over the work bench that I had stolen the twelve bags of Red Cross coffee which I had given him, as well as the twenty tablets of soap and ten blocks of chocolate. I gave him to understand that I had purloined them from the barrack store especially to oblige him, and that unfortunately I had been found out by the Sergeant-Major, and had been compelled to confess to whom I had given the supplies.

'I hope the Gestapo are not severe with you,' I commented. 'The Sergeant-Major says he'll have to report you to the Military Intelligence for fraternising with a British p.o.w.'

Herr Schmidt became violently angry and promptly threw his box of nails at me. 'You pig-dog,' he exclaimed. 'What proof has anyone that you gave articles to me? Do you think the Gestapo will take your word against mine?'

'I have very serious proof,' I said. 'I have a letter written and signed by your daughter which is now in the camp. In it she requests soap and chocolate. Ask her if that is not true?'

With a bellow of rage old man Schmidt tore out of the workshop and into his cottage to find out the truth. It was perfectly correct. I had played up to his daughter whenever I had met her. I had won her confidence, and often paused for a brief talk. She never failed to ask me when I would bring her more chocolate in my weekly parcel. I told her: 'It is possible that I might be able to get extra supplies from my two companions. But you can hardly expect them to believe me. If you wrote a note, and told them you would secure in exchange drawing-paper and water-colour paints, and perhaps provide them with an occasional egg or two and a few onions, you would get two packets of chocolate and two bars of soap each week without fail. But they must have proof that I am not stealing their goods.'

She dropped for it, hook, line and sinker. She even told me not to mention anything about the note to her father, but to give the soap and chocolate direct to her. In return for my silence she would get me cigarettes.

The letter I handed to the Escape Committee. In it she praised the generosity of Herr Yeatman, who worked for her father, and praised highly the wondrous excellence of Red Cross soap and chocolate. She promised to supply without fail a nice amount of drawing-paper and paints; and whenever she could get eggs and onions, these she would send back to them with Herr Yeatman.

Schmidt returned to the workshop white about the gills. His hands trembled as he addressed me in a tone now meek and mild.

'What is your game?' he inquired. 'What do you want in return for that letter?'

'Your radio receiver,' I informed him. 'Unless you let me have it within three days, the whole matter will be placed in the hands of the Gestapo.'

Each day for three days I left the workshop laden with pieces of the radio receiver. When I joined the other members of the party for the return ride back to camp I carefully distributed among them the various items. There was no search at the camp gates after the first two weeks of the working commando's existence; the nightly return to the camp of dirty and tired men soon ceased to be a novelty to the security police and invariably we were allowed to wander straight back to our barracks once we were all safely counted and behind the wire for the night.

By the fourth evening the committee had all the parts assembled, and the B.B.C. news report was clearly picked up. A shorthand writer recorded the broadcast, and two days later it was carefully passed around the entire camp.

It meant that the set had to be most carefully concealed. A deep shaft was sunk into the ground in the church hut, and four wooden runners permitted the radio to be swiftly and gently raised or lowered on greased bobbin spools. A close-fitting cover plate in the floor completely hid all traces of an opening.

When the letter which Schmidt's daughter had written was handed back to the old carpenter, I purposely went sick and so ended my duties as a labourer-carpenter.

It was about this time that the Canadian p.o.w. engineers completed their magnificent eighty-feet-long tunnel, which led from a barrack to a point twelve feet beyond the wire. It was the most skilful piece of work. Throughout its length it was reinforced with stolen bedboards set in concrete stolen in pocketfuls by gangs of Canadian soldiers employed by the Germans on building large cement-lined water reservoirs. By a wondrous Heath-Robinson set of pulleys, gears and fans, the simple winding of a large handle at the tunnel's entrance set the fans whirling and the entire tunnel was efficiently ventilated. At the exit the winding of another handle raised four posts, and the platform on top of these carried eighteen inches of earth, the topmost and visible layer being of unsuspicious grass sods and twigs.

A mass escape was planned, but two nights before it could take place a squad of German Security Police, armed with tommy guns, entered the barrack and without hesitation walked straight to the concealing square of perfectly fitting concrete. Prising it up, they blazed away with their weapons down the twelve-feet-deep well leading to the tunnel proper. Two of the Germans then descended the well and, pointing their sub-machine guns along the passage, blazed off a couple of pans of ammunition. Fortunately, no prisoners were working there.

Somebody had squealed to the enemy at the eleventh hour. As in most barracks, a traitor existed, and months of painstaking and backbreaking work had come to nothing.

(4)

Early one morning I was picked up at my barrack by two armed guards and taken off to the German Intelligence office.

For three hours I was grilled with merciless precision. Scores of questions were asked about my home in New Zealand, about the work I pursued before the war, about my army career and all details of my military activities in Crete right up to the time of my being captured by German parachutists.

My photograph and finger-prints were checked, and these tallied. Fortunately, the original sets of evidence had been destroyed in the fire in the card-recording office, and the ones which the Germans now held were those which had been renewed after my return to the Stalag from Poland.

Finally, the major in charge of interrogation fired his last question:

'Are you rightfully Richard Bernard Pape, a navigator of the Royal Air Force, No. 937484, shot down on September 7th, 1941?' he asked. 'Did you not exchange your identity with Private Winston Yeatman, a New Zealander, two years ago?'

I looked at the officer with a calm and puzzled stare. 'Never heard of Richard Pape,' I answered, 'nor have I ever been in the Royal Air Force. I am Winston Mearil Yeatman.'

I felt he was giving me the benefit of the doubt, but this did not persuade him to allow me to return to my barrack. Instead I was taken to the camp prison and placed in solitary confinement.

The demoralising spell of solitary confinement and maddening speculation came to an end at last. I was prodded from the cell by a burly guard and again taken in front of the intelligence officer. Within seconds of my arrival, the major bawled: 'Bring him in.'

Under escort they brought in Winston Mearil Yeatman.

He was thin, dreadfully thin, and his face was pale and taut. One glance was sufficient for me to realise that the Germans had been working on him. When Yeatman saw me he grinned and quietly remarked, 'Sorry, Ginger, they know . . .'

The German thundered: 'Quiet, you lying pig-dogs . . .'

Gradually – and it must have given them some man-size headaches – the Germans unravelled the masquerade.

In the camp of Luft VI on the Prussian-Lithuanian border, the two New Zealanders with whom the swops had been first enacted – George Potter as the Pole, and Winston Yeatman as Dick Pape – had complicated themselves by making a second change of identities. It was done principally to save the real George Potter from the dire consequences of being removed by the Germans to a special Slav concentration camp.

The camp *Kommandant* had notified all the Polish personnel that they would be removed from the British camp in a week's time. Not unnaturally, Potter, who had been faithfully representing Mieteck, became dreadfully alarmed. He knew only too well, as did every other inmate of the *Lager*, that the Germans detested the Poles as much as they loathed the Russians, and that once the Polish fliers were segregated and the Germans had them exclusively in their power, they would be in for a thin time. It was quite reasonable for Potter to conclude that once he moved out of the gates with the Polish party the chances that he would ever again see New Zealand were pretty remote.

An Australian named Foxley considered this news of the Polish move a wonderful opportunity to make a break. Foxley was tremendously keen to join the Polish party so that he could jump from the train which was to carry them to some unknown destination.

311

He was fanatical. He cared little about acquiring a Polish name and his anxiety to make a break completely blinded him to the inextricable tangle he would get himself into if he failed and finished up, lost, in a Polish camp.

On the other hand, Potter was certainly not keen to be 'lost'. A deal was made. The big snag was that the Australian was not at all like the New Zealander, Potter, neither facially nor in stature. But Winston Yeatman, posing in my name, was a fairly good approximation. A three-cornered swop therefore took place: Yeatman became Foxley the Australian. The Australian became Mieteck and Mieteck, alias George Potter, became me, Dick Pape.

The Poles left two days later with Foxley as a member of the party. As the train moved up the Baltic coast, he jumped and got away. Unfortunately, he was captured a short time later.

Foxley was taken to the Gestapo, and his claim to be Mieteck was soon exploded. He could neither speak nor write a word of Polish. They worked on him ruthlessly and discovered that he had done a swop-over with Mieteck, who, he said, was still in the camp of Luft VI posing as an Australian.

Into the camp the Gestapo hurried. They pounced on Winston Yeatman believing they had collared the Pole. But, to their anger and consternation, after giving Yeatman the third degree, they were compelled to realise that he was no more a Pole than the man in the moon. Then the balloon really went up. Two phoney prisoners were hiding a Pole. Where was the real Mieteck?

Yeatman had to talk to save his neck. He told the Germans that his real name was George Potter and that he had engineered a change of name with Mieteck in Stalag VIIIb two years before. Down to Stalag VIIIb came the Gestapo to get hold of the real Pole living as George Potter. Apparently they threw seven kinds of fits

312

when they learned that the prisoner of that name had escaped with Winston Yeatman and had never been recaptured! Nothing was said to me about this at the time.

The Gestapo then switched back to East Prussia, to Luft VI, and again tackled the man they knew as George Potter, but who was the real Yeatman. The real George Potter, who was living as Dick Pape, was keeping dead quiet, hardly daring to breathe. The Germans informed George Potter – the real Yeatman – that the Pole carrying his name had been shot dead while escaping with another prisoner, also a New Zealander, by the name of Winston Yeatman. They told him that they had grilled this Winston Yeatman in Stalag VIIIb, and that I had confessed to being a phoney. They also told him that I was in serious trouble, and that only he could clear me by confessing all he knew.

Yeatman was in pretty bad shape by this time and did not know what the hell the Gestapo had up their sleeve. He told them that he was not George Potter at all; that Potter was masquerading as Dick Pape, and that his name was honestly and truly Winston Mearil Yeatman.

This sent the Gestapo almost around the bend. Here was a man who was at first an Australian, then a New Zealander, and now claiming to be a New Zealander with a totally different name, which admission brought in another man, a Royal Air Force flier named Dick Pape. It completely upset their sense of balance, their sense of humour and everything else. It also hurt their pride to think that prisoners had made monkeys out of them. And so 'Dick Pape', the real George Potter, was roped in. At the same time I was also roped in and jailed in Upper Silesia.

For three days Winston Yeatman and I appeared before the German Intelligence. Eventually we managed to convince them that all that we had said was the truth, and that all persons concerned in the business were now in possession of their correct names.

Sentences were passed. I got five weeks' solitary, but poor old Yeatman got the biggest scare of his life. The major leaned on his elbows and looked at the New Zealander.

'You are no longer Winston Mearil Yeatman,' he declared. 'Henceforward you will be registered and known as Mieteck, a Pole, born in 1917.'

Two of the other officers present laughed, and the major, his face creased in smiles, lit a cigar before continuing.

'It is not our desire to have any depletion in the number of our Polish prisoners,' he continued. 'Not even one. You will, therefore, be a substitute for the man who escaped, the man who should still be here. You were given a p.o.w. number; you possessed a correct name and rank; these you did not treat with respect. You will be re-photographed and re-fingerprinted as the missing Pole, and you will be despatched to a Polish *Lager*.'

I saw Yeatman's face twitch, and his lips compress. Fate had acted like a boomerang. For generously taking risks to help me and then to prevent George Potter from being removed to a Slav camp, he was going to be swallowed up in just such a concentration prison himself.

It was time for me to speak.

'You can't do that,' I told the beaming major. 'It is a contravention of Geneva p.o.w. ruling. Yeatman is a true New Zealander with a definite p.o.w. number, and I request that we see the Camp Leader, also the New Zealand senior officer . . .'

'You lousy R.A.F. murderer!' screamed the enraged major. 'Quiet!' He spat at me from a distance of four feet, and such was his temper that some of the saliva ran down his chin.

Yeatman and I were both lodged in solitary cells. On the third day I was visited by the British padre, and I prayed that this call was not too late. Briefly I explained what had happened and the predicament which Yeatman was in. I beseeched him to act with all haste, to see the Camp Leader and the senior New Zealand officer, and for them to approach the camp *Kommandant* immediately.

The padre did his stuff and the *Kommandant* was cornered by the two British officers. Yeatman, apparently, was due to leave Stalag VIIIb for the Slav camp within two days of my telling his story to the padre, but his departure was postponed.

But the Germans were not going to be thwarted. They worked on the story that Yeatman was the Pole and that he was refusing to speak Polish in order to misguide them for all manner of reasons. They were adamant for five days and even refused permission for the senior British officers to visit either me or Yeatman in the cells.

Then good fortune came to our aid. The camp was visited by some people from the Swiss Red Cross. The senior British officers gave them all the details of our cases, and the Germans found their hands forced. We were interviewed by the Swiss, and they in turn insisted that we should not be removed from Stalag VIIIb until Geneva was informed of what had occurred. The whole business, before it was reluctantly dropped by the Germans, because of International Red Cross pressure, bubbled for some weeks.

At one stage, when the Germans proved to be particularly difficult, Yeatman was asked if he had ever been fingerprinted in New Zealand. It so happened that he had, when he was working on the Lewis Pass before the war. A New Zealand murder case brought about a great deal of fingerprinting and Yeatman, although he was not implicated, had his fingerprints recorded. He may have cursed the matter at the time, but now, in Germany, with the enemy attempting forcibly to turn him into a Pole, he was truly thankful that the New Zealand police had his identification. The senior New Zealand officer requested that Geneva should contact Christchurch and get duplicates of the fingerprints rushed to Upper Silesia to convince the German Intelligence beyond all doubt that they were barking up the wrong tree.

In the meantime, I was serving my sentence. A few days before it was due to end the padre visited me and joyfully imparted the news that Yeatman had been released and was back in the New Zealand barrack. He had at last been officially recognised as a genuine Kiwi.

(5)

When my sentence ended I was moved to another cell and, instead of bread and water, I received coffee, bread and soup. I was visited by the German Intelligence Officer, and told that as I was not a soldier any longer, and as I was a dangerous character, I could never again be permitted to mix with other soldiers in case I attempted further subterfuge, deceit and trouble. I was told that I was to be moved to the R.A.F. camp, Luft VI, on the Lithuanian border.

Fourteen days later, at 5.30 in the morning, I was awakened in my cell and told to get ready to leave. It was dawn when I passed through the *Grossen Tor* [the great gate] of the prison camp in Upper Silesia for the last time. Between two rigid guards I walked the intervening miles to Annaberg railway station, and at no period of my captivity did I feel so utterly sad and close to weeping.

For four days, *en route* to the Baltic, I was chained to a guard, except for the period at night when I was housed in a jail. And so

I came to Luft VI as Sergeant Richard B. Pape of the Royal Air Force. For months that name seemed odd and unreal.

In my new camp there was an organisation known as 'Tally Ho', similar to the Escape Committee in Stalag VIIIb, which facilitated escape, and bribed, corrupted and blackmailed prison guards.

Shortly after my arrival one of the guards was arrested by the Gestapo for fraternising and conniving with R.A.F. captives. He was the camp photographer, responsible for photographing and recording all prisoners as they arrived, and he had been receiving from 'Tally Ho' a great deal of Red Cross food and cigarettes in return for chemicals and other special requirements for forgery, and a liberal supply of photographic equipment. He also took letters for 'Tally Ho', stamped them with the official Reich postage stamps and placed them in the outside mail box for despatch to guards in other camps.

A splendid system of exchange of intelligence existed between all the R.A.F. and big British Army camps in Germany. In each of them, separated by hundreds of miles, certain German guards had been blackmailed. Thus a letter would go from East Prussia to Upper Silesia from one German guard to another. In one case two radio valves were sent 1,000 kilometres across Germany.

It was while I was in Stalag Luft VI that I began work on a new method of smuggling messages out from Germany to England – openly, in rings worn by repatriated prisoners. It was a crazy idea, but it worked. There was no attempt to conceal the rings. If there had been the whole scheme would have failed. But because the prisoners wore them even while they were being stripped naked and searched by the Germans none were ever detected.

I made the rings from the stems of old toothbrushes, collected from dust-bins or bought for ten cigarettes each. First I boiled the stems and then bent them round ring-sticks of various sizes. Next came the cutting and polishing. It was essential to make them as small as possible and I tried to keep them to much the same size as the ordinary signet ring.

In the head (where in a normal ring the jewels are set) I hollowed out a tiny aperture into which I coiled a strip of paper containing the message. Above the message I laid a minute snapshot of the person who was to carry the ring, or of someone close to him – sister or wife or mother – and sealed the whole affair with a strip of celluloid. Once the celluloid was removed, the snapshot and coiled paper popped out.

The job was not easy. The various parts of the ring had to be cemented with acetone. At first I had great difficulty in obtaining supplies but eventually I got a German guard under graft and black-mailed him. He had a brother who was a laboratory chemist in a Breslau Military Hospital and once I had the guard properly under my thumb I got as much of the stuff as I needed.

The first ring was taken out by 'Wingy' Woodhead, a Yorkshireman who had lost his right hand while doing forced labour for the Germans in a Polish mine. The ring contained my photograph, and I urged him to deliver it to Ernest Osborn, of the *Yorkshire Post*. 'Give it to nobody else,' I told him. 'And guard it with your life. When you hand it over tell him to take a sharp knife and lever just below my picture.'

Afterwards 'Wingy' told Osborn that his only anxious moment was during the final searching by the Germans for concealed messages. He was stripped naked and his clothes and body searched minutely. All the time the ring lay on his finger in full view – yet the Germans ignored it.

The first success was followed by many more. One by one the

repatriates went out with my rings, some of them to Canada, some to Australia and some to New Zealand as well as Britain.

The rings proved useful for other things, too. On one occasion it was vital that a diamond, needed for special cutting purposes, be sent from our camp, through the secret chain of bribed guards, to a Russian watchmaker in hospital in Breslau. On another occasion I sent a tiny phial of deadly poison half-way across Germany to Slovakia. It began its journey in the custody of pro-British German guards, was later put in the post and finally delivered to its recipient buried inside a potato.

Each ring took from ten to twenty hours to make, and a South African, H. J. Boking, helped me with the carving and polishing. He never knew that I was slipping messages inside them; he really thought they were genuine mementoes.

When the little photographer was arrested and his damning hoard of Red Cross tinned goods and cigarettes unearthed by the Gestapo, 'Tally Ho' was worried. It was feared that under torture he would name all the captives with whom he had done business and squeal on the guards who operated the chain across Germany. He did not. Next morning he was found dead in his cell, poisoned.

Three hours later the camp swarmed with uniformed and civilian-attired Gestapo. The prisoners were herded into a compact square in the open and covered with machine-guns, while the invading Germans went through each barrack with a toothcomb. Beds were pulled apart, straw sleeping bags ripped open, floor boards prised up and personal possessions torn or smashed. When they finally departed it looked as though a hurricane had passed through. But they had not found anything, and that evening we tuned in as usual to the B.B.C.

The lurid record which had accompanied me from Stalag VIIIb

resulted in strict scrutiny of all my moves. I was frequently hauled up in front of the German Intelligence and my photograph and fingerprints carefully checked. I was reviled and warned of my fate if I engaged in any subversive activities. Particular attention was paid to all my mail, incoming and outgoing.

To spike their guns I wrote in code a brief résumé of what had been happening to me, and two Americans transcribed the message in their own handwriting in their letter-cards sent to England. My friends in Britain stopped writing and my family also wrote only occasionally. From time to time my American friends generously used their precious letter-cards to tell London that 'Ginger' was well and happy.

But in spite of the acute vigilance of the camp security men, I still managed to defy and cheat them. I organised the writing of a book of 30,000 hand-drawn words and lots of humorous and topical drawings of camp existence which was smuggled out of East Prussia by a pro-British member of a Swedish Y.M.C.A.* delegation and was in the hands of the Air Ministry within three months of being written.

There lived in Luft VI more than 300 Yorkshire airmen whom we organised into a society called 'The White Rose Club'. We formed our own concert party; organised a fine debating and sports club and, quite unknown to the Germans, produced every three weeks our own newspaper. I was the editor, layout artist and printing press.

The paper usually contained not less than 10,000 words, and every letter had to be hand drawn. We called it the *Yorkshire Post*, in acknowledgement to Yorkshire's influential morning newspaper.

---

* It has now been established that the man referred to was not a member of the Swedish Y.M.C.A.

The book was a combined effort of literary and artistic talent drawn exclusively from the membership of 'The White Rose Club'. Drawings and articles were submitted to me and included if they proved of sufficiently high standard. 'Tally Ho' procured the necessary paper and ink for its construction, whilst my pen nibs were fashioned from the steel tape which bound Red Cross crates.

We called the book *The Kriegie Edition*. It was completely hand lettered throughout, and possessed a most impressive hand-carved cover in Red Cross plywood. The original of *The Kriegie Edition* excited considerable interest in the Press in Britain, and the *Yorkshire Post* reproduced and printed the volume in facsimile. Copies were presented to all the next-of-kin of the 300 Yorkshiremen in Luft VI. The Prime Minister, Mr Winston Churchill, the Air Minister and the Minister of Information publicly acclaimed our enterprise and ingenuity.

The book took three weeks to produce. I would begin work on it at seven o'clock in the morning and continue until darkness. Barrack friends took it in turn to remain seated at either end of the barrack block and at the approach of a guard they would yell 'Goons up'. At the warning I would cork my ink, pack my sheets together, remove three floor boards and conceal the manuscript below the floor under my bed. The entire *Kriegie Edition* was penned stretched out on the floor under the bottom bunk of a set of three-tier beds. By the time the investigating German patrol had reached my bed I was stretched out on the straw and snoring in a most healthy and harmless manner. As soon as the guard on the door yelled: 'Goons gone!' I was back at work under the bed.

CHAPTER 15

SICK MAN OF LUFT VI

(I)

It was now April, 1944. The Russian legions were relentlessly rolling back the German armies across the plains and it began to appear that soon Estonia, Latvia, Lithuania and East Prussia – including Luft VI – would be overrun by the Soviet forces. I had no particular desire to be liberated by them and so I decided to make my last escape bid: this time through the International Red Cross medical mission, which visited the prison camps and nominated sick men for repatriation.

My problem was to convince them that I was a very sick man.

A chap named Jimmmy N—, occupied the bunk next to me, was suffering from acute nephritis, a disease of the kidneys. His face was a horrible yellow, and his ankles were always badly swollen. The German doctor told him that he was already classified as a certainty for repatriation.

I made a careful study of Jimmy's case and then outlined my plan of campaign. He promised to co-operate. The idea was that I should visit the German medical officer and complain of swollen ankles, dizziness and other symptoms of kidney disease. Jimmy explained to me exactly what took place when he was examined.

The medical orderly in the doctor's office, who did all the blood counts, was under 'Tally Ho's' thumb, especially since the sudden death of the camp photographer. It was arranged that he should engineer it so that the contamination of my specimen

322

should tie in with the evidence of the other tests usually carried out.

Certain items of equipment were required before I could safely carry out the performance required at the examinations. I got hold of a piece of rubber hose-pipe from the camp kitchen of approximately the same thickness, but longer, than a normal male organ. One of the ends I plugged with wood and Taffy, the best carver in the camp, minutely fashioned a faithful reproduction. The hollow rubber held a reasonable supply of fluid, and the duct at the end, part of Taffy's skilful carving, was plugged by the insertion of a matchstick. Our best camp artist, Freddie, excelled himself and finished the job off with the most realistic flesh colouring.

The contraption was then provided with two tape straps to hold it securely in position. A cork blocked the other open end and safely retained the fluid in the hollow rubber. The whole contraption was concealed inside my pants.

The night before my first visit to the Medical Officer a full dress rehearsal took place in the barrack. Jimmy, who acted the part of the German doctor, doubled up in fits of laughter.

'Oh, boy . . . oh, boy!' he tittered, 'I've never seen anything so damned natural in all my life. Feel quite ashamed!'

Mac, pre-war physiotherapist, then played his part. For three and a half hours he methodically flicked my ankles with wet towels until they ballooned out without the slightest trace of bruising. I did, however, soil them slightly, which indicated the neglect of soap and water.

At seven-thirty next morning Jimmy filled the artificial organ with his nephritis-laden urine, it was corked and I strapped the contraption on. Off I toddled. Fifteen minutes later I was standing before the German doctor. The four pieces of soap I had swallowed had reacted magnificently upon my complexion and had produced a superb greenish hue which gave complete reality to Jimmy's specially concocted 'jaundice' solution. He had scalded some yellow crêpe paper and procured a perfect skin discoloration dye. The German doctor examined my ankles, pressing here and there with his thumb. He spoke to his orderly and I was taken into the doctor's office where I was told to undress except for my pants.

'Pass water in this,' he snapped and handed me the beaker. I managed things quite naturally, even though the doctor was looking on. A certain amount of concealment was necessary but I took my time and filled the beaker satisfactorily for test purposes.

Next day I was called before the doctor again and told the result of the examination. I was suffering from an advanced disease of the kidneys, and I was to visit the sick bay every other day for further tests. From then on, with each successive visit, I acquired greater proficiency at camouflage, as well as confidence.

For safety's sake I decided to have a further string to my bow in the way of illness. As a result of my bouts of pleurisy my lungs still continued to give me rather sharp stabs at times. For three days I smoked dried sun-flower seeds. It was positively amazing what those seeds did to my bronchial tubes! When the doctor applied the stethoscope to my chest I was wheezing and croaking like an old man of ninety-five. The doctor looked at me askance and managed to remark: 'Sick . . . very sick man!'

I shot the old soldier patter that I was getting thinner and thinner, and that I suffered from the most horrific night sweats, and all the other angles indicative of T.B.

Next day, with four other prisoners, I was taken by the medical orderly, under guard, to have X-rays taken. The orderly had been primed and did his stuff. When the plates were submitted to the doctor they revealed that I was just as seriously afflicted with T.B. as I was with nephritis. The plates submitted in my name were those of a sick Pole. All the usual markings on the plates were altered to suit my particular case. As the markings were photographically a part of the plates I wondered how it was done, but 'Tally Ho' merely told me that the medical orderly had studied radiology, and had supplied the radiologist at the hospital with Red Cross cigarettes.

Only three weeks now remained before the arrival of the medical commission. I ate nothing more than one slice of bread a day, and before long I naturally started losing weight and by the time I faced the medical board from Geneva I was positively haggard.

The doctors examined my X-ray plates, scrutinised me closely and conversed with each other in undertones. They carefully examined the records showing the many tests I had been through. Again they put their heads together and held a short whispered pow-wow. I was instructed by a big, uniformed Swedish doctor to take off my shirt. He placed the stethoscope cap at various points back and front. The sun-flower seeds promoted a wheezing that should have tickled the doctor's eardrums.

A Swiss doctor walked round the table and pulled up my trousers to take a squint at my ankles. Their appearance of puffiness was not attractive. Mac had put his best into towel flicking for hours the previous evening.

The two doctors returned to the other side of the table, and together with the other members of the visiting team I was silently reviewed for a few seconds. A soap-swallowing feat had taken the colour from my face; three weeks of almost solid starvation had worked wonders in giving me the appearance of having one foot in the grave; and fighting off sleep for two nights before confronting the board convinced them that I was dying on my feet.

'Thank you,' said the spokesman of the board. 'You will go home.'

The examination had taken six minutes.

Scarcely daring to believe my good fortune I returned to the barrack in a state bordering bewilderment. Jimmy greeted me enthusiastically as I came through the door. He, too, had passed for repatriation.

'Boy . . . oh, boy!' he chanted as he danced about the barrack. 'We're really going home at last!'

'And a specimen of your urine ought to be kept in a golden vessel in the British War Museum!' I laughed.

(2)

Thirty men in all had passed the repatriation board which visited Luft VI in May, 1944. But it was not until a month later that we were removed from the camp – and then at twelve hours' notice – and taken to Leipzig.

For two monotonous months we remained in Leipzig with other repatriated British and Allied prisoners from camps throughout Germany. As the weeks passed the hammering of Germany grew more intense from both east and west; but we gradually lost hope of despatch home.

But our luck held. Twelve hours after a heavy Flying Fortress raid had blasted hell out of Leipzig, we were hurriedly put on a train for Sassnitz, the German Baltic naval base. There we boarded the German vessel *Deutschland*, and eight hours later, on September 7th, 1944, we stepped ashore to freedom at Trelleborg in Sweden.

It was exactly three years to the day after I had been shot down.

For a week we remained in hospitable Sweden and we were fed and fêted magnificently. Overnight life had become glorious, ecstatic.

We left Sweden aboard the *Gripsholm*, arriving six days later in Liverpool.

At long last it was all over.

EPILOGUE

HOME IS THE HUNTED

I was glad to get away from the cheering mobs and the blaring brass bands assembled on the quayside at Liverpool to welcome us home. I should have felt elated, excited. For three years I had devoted all my energies to getting out of Occupied Europe, and now I had succeeded. Yet everything suddenly appeared unreal, artificial and fantastically out of focus. I realised that I was genuinely scared at the prospect of taking up the threads and renewing a safe and orthodox life. I even felt scared at the prospect of reuniting with my own family and friends.

It was a natural reaction. Most prisoners of war went through the same experience. Ex-prisoners had to fight desperately to overcome the legacy of the cage – a state of suspended animation.

After rest and recuperation I was passed fit to return to flying duties. I had almost finished my refresher course when fate again gave me a hefty kick in the pants. I crashed, and when I regained consciousness in a small Manx hospital, I found that I was disfigured with scars and far from a pretty sight.

One thing was certain; my flying days were over for as long as it would take the eminent plastic surgeon, Sir Archibald McIndoe, to restore my face.

So instead of going to the Far East, I headed south-east to the home of the Guinea Pigs at the Queen Victoria Hospital in East Grinstead, in Sussex, for plastic repairs. It turned out that, in addition, I also received the best cures for my mental condition. I met at East Grinstead the finest bunch of Royal Air Force men I had ever encountered, the grandest body of men that I am ever likely to know or live among.

Man is capable of many expressions of courage, but none, to my mind, compares with the magnificent spirit which emanated from East Grinstead. The Guinea Pig Club was formed in 1941 after the Battle of Britain. Its membership is made up of those whose wounds have been treated at the Queen Victoria Hospital. Many airmen received ghastly facial injuries and disfigurement. German cannon shells and blazing aircraft wrought havoc with skin and flesh and bones. But hospital beds did not rob these men of their superb spirit.

I found at East Grinstead that sanity of happiness and calmness which I had imagined would for ever elude me. It was there that I experienced such humane, constructive decency that, in three months, it offset all the inhuman destructive indecency I saw and experienced during my three years in German Occupied Europe.

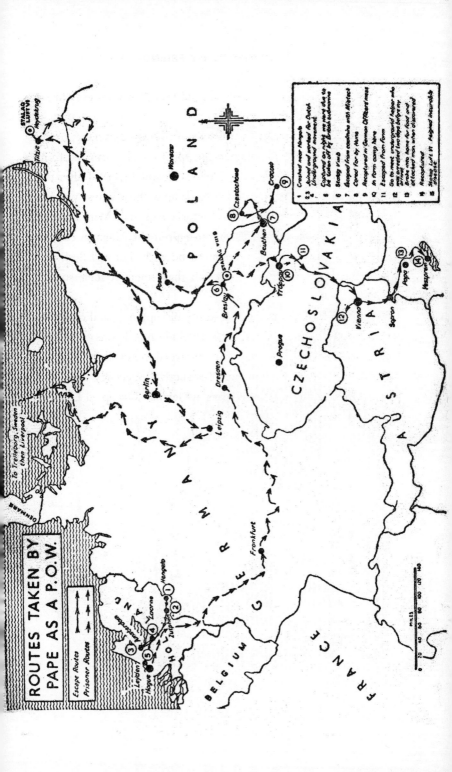

ROUTES TAKEN BY PAPE AS A P.O.W.

Escape Routes →
Prisoner Routes →

POLAND

CZECHOSLOVAKIA

AUSTRIA

GERMANY

BELGIUM

FRANCE

HOLLAND

DENMARK

To Trelleborg, Sweden then Liverpool

STALAG LUFT VI
Heydekrug

Tilsit

Warsaw

Posen

Czestochowa
Beuthen
Cracow ⑨

STALAG VIII B
Breslau ⑥
⑧

Berlin

Leipzig

Dresden

Prague

Troppau ⑩ ⑪
⑫
Vienna
Sopron

Pápa ⑬
Hegyshalom ⑭

Frankfurt

Hengelo ①
Lochem ②
Zutphen ④
Leyden ③ ⑤
Hague

1. Crashed near Norgelo
2,3. Joined and cared for Dutch Underground movement
4. Captured on night escape due to be taken off by British submarine
5. Stalag VIII B
6. Escaped from confines with Market
7. Cared for by Nuns
8. Recaptured in German Officers mess
9. In farm camp here
10. Escaped from farm
11. Go to meet underground helper—who were arrested two days before on arrival
12. Gave his home for food and sat locked in barn then discovered
13. Recaptured
14. Staying Luft in Hospital incurable disease

MILES
0 20 40 60 80 100 120 140

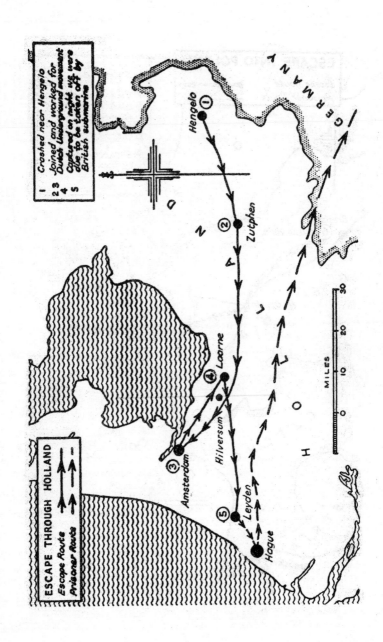

ESCAPE THROUGH HOLLAND

Escape Route →→→
Prisoner Route ---→

1 Crashed near Hengelo
2 3 Joined and worked for Dutch Underground movement
4 Captured on night trip
5 were due to be taken off by British submarine

GERMANY

Hengelo ①

Zutphen ②

Laarne ④

Amsterdam ③

Hilversum

Leyden

Hague

⑤

MILES
0   10   20   30

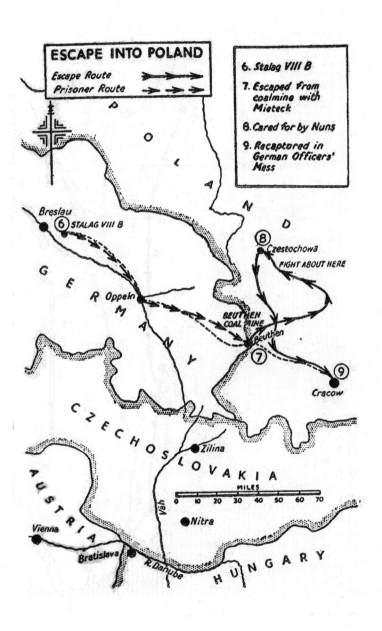

ESCAPE INTO POLAND

Escape Route
Prisoner Route

6. Stalag VIII B
7. Escaped from coalmine with Mieteck
8. Cared for by Nuns
9. Recaptured in German Officers' Mess

P O L A N D

Breslau
⑥ STALAG VIII B

⑧ Czestochowa
FIGHT ABOUT HERE

G E R M A N Y

Oppeln

BEUTHEN COAL MINE
Beuthen
⑦

⑨ Cracow

C Z E C H O S L O V A K I A

Zilina

MILES
0 10 20 30 40 50 60 70

A U S T R I A

Vienna

Váh

Nitra

Bratislava

R. Danube

H U N G A R Y

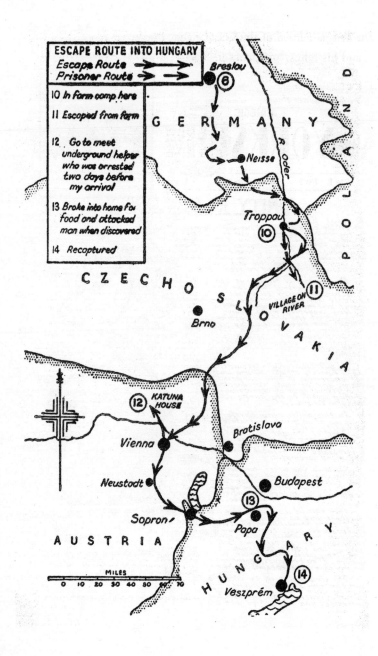

ESCAPE ROUTE INTO HUNGARY
Escape Route ➔
Prisoner Route ➔

10 In farm camp here
11 Escaped from farm
12 Go to meet underground helper who was arrested two days before my arrival
13 Broke into home for food and attacked man when discovered
14 Recaptured

The Kriegie Edition of the *Yorkshire Post*, produced secretly by Pape and his fellow prisoners in Stalag Luft VI (*see* pp. 320–321)

Cartoons from *The Kriegie Edition*

'Tornado' R B Pape
Editor

THE NEW P.O.W. WHO, AFTER BEING GIVEN SOUP, ASKED WHEN THE SWEET WAS TO BE SERVED

Some years after writing *Boldness Be My Friend*, Richard Pape set out to discover what had happened to the various people who had helped him in his efforts to elude capture. He was to find out that 'Tiny Peter', the member of the Dutch Resistance who had conducted Pape to Amsterdam, and co-ordinated his initial escape attempt, had been captured, and, under torture, had disclosed everyone else who had assisted Pape. Bernard Besselink, the farmer who had concealed Pape immediately after his crash-landing, and 'John the journalist' – Jan Agterkam – who had procured the aid of the Resistance, had been executed by the Germans.

'Tiny Peter' survived the war. Pape tracked him down and confronted him.

He was sitting at a small table, awaiting my arrival; nobody else was near. I almost touched him before he stirred from gazing into space.

'Hallo.'

He raised his eyes and I saw a grim, thin and desperate face. He was fingering something nervously and his hands trembled. I shuddered.

Jerkily, he rose to his feet, staring at me. There was a hang-dog look about him; poorly and untidily dressed, he also looked grubby. His big eyes never left my face; for a time he stared transfixed at the airman he had once known in the Dutch Resistance Movement thirteen years before.

'Sit down.' I tried to keep my voice calm. He was still staring at my face across the table. 'Have some beer,' I suggested.

He gave a vague shake of his head and just sat and stared. I might have been an avenging apparition from beyond the grave. He looked at me as though he was expecting anything. My sense of understanding told me that the man's morale was broken, his self-confidence smashed. My whole body trembled. The man was his own greatest torturer, more so than all the Nazis who had violated the Netherlands and persecuted. Suddenly, his lips trembled with an agitation he could not disguise.

'I never thought I would see you again, what do you want with me?'

His voice was low and shaky. I contemplated the ex-agent who had done his best for Moir and me until the Gestapo had done their worst for him. I could almost feel my heart beating in my mind. There was no trace of hate left in me at all, only a deep surge of pity, a kind I had never before known. 'So this is the man,' I thought, 'who aroused my animosity, whom I had dreamed of getting even with.' I looked at him and turned my eyes away. It would have been as cowardly and as unfair as if he had been armed with a bow and arrow and I had been charging him inside a tank. I seemed somehow to understand that no matter what rules or laws a human being may violate or break, in the realm of human dignity, from every moral and religious viewpoint, a person with the disease of reason is to be pitied, not attacked.

The man before me was once big and powerful, keen faced, with challenging eyes. Now he was a doubting, despairing, heartrending figure. His strange eyes turned on me again, and I found I wanted to think more than I wanted to talk. Without concentrating, things flowed through my mind. Before returning to Holland I had pursued my own relentless way of life, obeying my own will. After a lapse of thirteen years I had come to the country where so much had begun in human destiny. But, unexpectedly, the visit had given me a profound awareness that to take the spiritual out of life is to endanger its real meaning and purpose. There can be no human happiness for a man anywhere who was not free within himself.

'Why do you want me?' exclaimed the former Underground man, suddenly, and his face winced. I decided at once that there would be no pecking, sparring or scathing inferences, that I would try and avoid all personal reminiscence.

Quietly I remarked: 'Nice to see you again. I hope everything is well for you after that damned irrational war.' I attempted to throttle any outward show of feelings.

He waved a hand. 'It was a hideous, horrible nightmare; it always will be a nightmare.'

He looked at me meditatively and I realized that he knew I was no adversary.

Excerpt taken from Sequel to Boldness *by Richard Pape*

Richard Pape sums up his life in 1978, in a letter to Charles McConnell, Secretary of the 609 Squadron Association.

Now about myself. Age 62, still have some of my beautiful red hair left, but not much. I inform my wife that when it finally loses its ginger colour and turns grey, then and only then can it be said that Richard Pape has lost his temper and is pacified and peaceful. Blimme, Charles!

Suffer from nine pensionable war disabilities, full of arthritis, eyesight getting worse, but hope that I'll have finished the autobiography before the surgeon removes the cataracts. One has to be just about blind before they'll skin one's eyeballs. Otherwise keep plodding away at home. Now retired so to speak, not able to work at a job. Quit working for the Department of Aboriginal Affairs 18 months ago. They asked me to write a book on the Australian Aboriginals when I came to live in Canberra after 9 years in that hot and primitive land, Papua New Guinea.

I guess you'll know all about my wartime career in the R.A.F. Being shot down after bombing Berlin (night of Sept 7, 1941) crashing in the Stirling bomber, escaping, escaping, and escaping. I finally got clear of Hitler's bloody Europe in 1944, and was back in the U.K. a year before the war ended. Crashed again and had my beauty spoiled somewhat. Should never have flown again after getting home in one piece. But as Lord Lincoln wrote: 'Mad Englishmen (Yorkshiremen)'. Spent the best part of two years in East Grinstead R.A.F. plastic surgery hospital – Sir Archibald McIndoe, famous R.A.F. plastic surgeon, did a pretty good repair job on my face. That was the end of my flying career.

Went to South Africa in 1946 and returned to Britain 1953 for the publication of *Boldness Be My Friend* . . . Couldn't settle down so took up test-endurance driving for Austin Motors (B.M.C.). A book followed, *Cape Cold to Cape Hot* . . . From Arctic North Cape to African South Cape. Nearly bought it in the stinking Sahara. Returned to U.K. Tried to settle down. Impossible. Fell in love with a ballerina and fell out of love quickly when she wanted her mother to live with us upon marriage. Joined Rootes motors and did test driving for them in America, Canada, Yukon, etc. Nearly bought it again in Alaska at 90 m.p.h. Decided I'd had enough of car racing and all that. Fell in love with a female co-driver, got married. Settled in New Zealand. (She may have been a wonderful co-driver around the 48 states of the U.S.A. but she drove me up the ruddy wall otherwise.) Four months after marriage decided to join the U.S.A. 'Deep Freeze' Operation (after Geophysical International Year) 1956–7. The elapsed, elongated honeymoon was causing me to have moods and itchy feet. Left the bride for the penguins and roamed around the Great White Continent. Fell in the sea at McMurdo Sound and nearly froze to death. Returned to the neglected bride but she found me permanently cold. She nicknamed me 'Sealskin Pape' . . . That was that, divorced her, or maybe she really wanted her freedom. Back to dear old U.K. and I visited Yorkshire, Yeadon, etc. and the 'Yorkshire Post' wanted me to return if I felt inclined. Didn't …!!!

Started drinking too much as a resident of the 'Pathfinder Club' in Berkeley Square, London and met Group Captain Leonard Cheshire, V.C., D.S.O., D.F.C. He asked me to do something useful with my life instead of trying to kill myself by taking risk after risk. I joined Cheshire V.C. and left London for Australia en route to Papua New Guinea to start up a home for mentally handicapped native children. That was in 1964. I remained in that savage land for 9 years rather than the intended two years. But it was for the best. On the plane to New Guinea, an old DC3, I sat next to Helen, my future wife. She was a lawyer and visiting New Guinea for a stint on legal work for the Australian Government. After a few weeks in that 'Hot Land' I was put in jail for dangerous, or squiffy driving. I remembered the lovely female lawyer and got her to get someone to bail me out. So started a romance and we married in 1966. Helen is a grand person, 8 years my junior and we are very happy. No children, of course, but we have a glorious 'Golden Retriever called 'Pumpkin'

When we left Papua New Guinea the Leonard Cheshire Home was an established reality . . . caring for a dozen mentally defective and spastic native children. So at least I did something useful and worthwhile in the long run. Cheshire came to see us twice and is a grand, reliable fellow. We are very good friends.

Douglas Bader is visiting Darwin in the Northern Territory in May, and I may see him. We were in the same prison camp together (Dulag Luft, near Frankfurt) Luftwaffe Interrogation Centre. We had a tunnel going there and I was told I had to carry Douglas Bader up the mountainside when we broke free outside the wire. I always had a good strong, Yorkshire rugger back. It didn't come about, however, for a big German decided to stamp just above the tunnel to warm his feet (it was winter) and the big bastard came straight through the topsoil and into the tunnel. Fortunately he broke a leg. That was that! Bader was despatched to the Baltic and I was taken to the Polish border, Stalag VIIIB, and one hell of a place. I met up with Bader again in Breslau two years later, after I had changed my identity. He was a bit of a nuisance to the Germans, to say the least, and was sent to finish his term in Colditz. I was sent to one hell of a place on the Lithuanian border. The Russians pounded the place when they advanced in 1944 from Witebsk. Actually heard the big guns booming. It was from Luft VI that I found my freedom. But the happiest part of the final chapter was seeing Berlin three years after I had bombed the place. I was on my way from Lithuania via Berlin to Leipzig and had to spend a night in a Berlin railway siding. Damnation, the Mosquitoes came over and dropped 4,000 pounder cookies. 'Cripes', I muttered as everything shook, 'Hope those Mossy boys don't come any closer...' Berlin was a glorious sight . . . Flattened, a massive landscape of rubble. It was good to see the Germans running, shrieking and moaning. And once clear of Berlin and on my way to Leipzig I silently thanked the R.A.F. for wreaking vengeance on my behalf and all other R.A.F. aircrew p.o.ws. I got away from Lithuania just in time, but unfortunately some 30 R.A.F. aircrew were shot down by machine-gun fire from attacking planes.

And the first thing I did when I finally got back to Leeds was to get drunk on Tetley's Special . . . A glorious pub-crawl including Yeadon haunts (but the barmaids had changed, and one lovely little Yorkshire lass I used to wink at and take out from that top Yeadon pub had gone and married a bloody G.I.)

Helen and I were in Britain four years ago and I took my wife all over the Yorkshire Dales, and proudly showed the county that bred the best males in the Sacred Isles...

Regards to any members of the old 609 Squadron, and again I say that the story of 609 Squadron under the White Rose is indeed a inspiration to anyone anywhere in the old country, and to Yorkshiremen, born and bred . . . Well, it just engenders a terrific glow of pride, which I find difficult to put into words.

Now you can buy any of these other World War II stories from your bookshop or direct from the publisher

Odette   *Jerrard Tickell*   £12.99

In the darkest days of the Second World War, a young Frenchwoman, a wife and mother, became a secret agent. Leaving England to aid the French Resistance, she was betrayed, tortured, consigned to a concentration camp and sentenced to death. Yet her spiritedness mystified her captors; and she kept, in the abyss, her trust in goodness. *Odette* tells the story of an ordinary woman who, when tested, displayed an extraordinary courage and compassion.

The Honour and the Shame   *John Kenneally*   £12.99

John Kenneally won the VC in 1943 for attacking a whole company of Panzer Grenadiers on his own. Years later, he confessed that he had joined the Irish Guards under an assumed name after deserting his original regiment. *The Honour and the Shame* - a tale of riotous living and incredible courage - brings vividly to life the adventures of a free-wheeling youth and the horror and exhilaration of the battlefield.

REMARKABLE TRUE STORIES FROM WORLD WAR II
Action-packed stories of real courage by real heroes.

To order, simply call 01235 400 414
visit our website: www.madaboutbooks.com
or email orders@bookpoint.co.uk

Prices and availability are subject to change without notice.